Reading for Academic Success,

Grades 2–6

Reading for Academic Success, Grades 2–6

Differentiated
Strategies
for Struggling,
Average,
and
Advanced
Readers

Richard W. Strong   Harvey F. Silver
Matthew J. Perini

CORWIN PRESS
A SAGE Publications Company
Thousand Oaks, CA 91320

For information:

Corwin Press
A Sage Publications Company
2455 Teller Road
Thousand Oaks, California 91320
www.corwinpress.com

Sage Publications Ltd.
1 Oliver's Yard
55 City Road
London, EC1Y 1SP
United Kingdom

Sage Publications India Pvt. Ltd.
B 1/I 1 Mohan Cooperative
   Industrial Area
Mathura Road, New Delhi 110 044
India

Sage Publications Asia-Pacific Pte. Ltd.
33 Pekin Street #02–01
Far East Square
Singapore 048763

Printed in the United States of America.

Library of Congress Cataloging-in-Publication Data

Strong, Richard W., 1946-
Reading for academic success, grades 2–6: Differentiated strategies for struggling, average, and advanced readers / Richard W. Strong, Harvey F. Silver, Matthew J. Perini.
    p. cm.
Includes bibliographical references and index.
ISBN 978-1-4129-4175-4 (cloth)
ISBN 978-1-4129-4176-1 (pbk.)
    1. Reading (Elementary) 2. Reading comprehension. 3. Study skills. I. Silver, Harvey F. II. Perini, Matthew J., 1973- III. Title.

LB1573.S895 2008
372.4—dc22

2007004787

This book is printed on acid-free paper.

07 08 09 10 11 10 9 8 7 6 5 4 3 2 1

Acquisitions Editor:	Rachel Livsey
Editorial Assistants:	Phyllis Cappello and Megan Bedell
Production Editor:	Diane Foster
Copy Editor:	Barbara Ray
Typesetter:	C&M Digitals (P) Ltd.
Proofreader:	Caryne Brown
Indexer:	Kay M. Dusheck
Cover Designer:	Michael Dubowe

Contents

List of Figures and Organizers

Acknowledgments

Any book about teaching will always have many authors. There are the authors in the traditional sense—the writers, if you will—and then there are all those other authors, who are no less important but rarely receive proper credit. These authors are the true artists. They author ideas. They author moments of wonder and excitement every day in hundreds of thousands of classrooms across the country, across the globe. It is to our teachers, the authors of learning, that we express our deepest appreciation, for they have done much more than make the words and ideas in this book possible; they make our children better learners, better citizens, better people.

If authors are not really authors, then it is also true that they are not really much of anything without good people supporting them. In fact, it would be impossible to imagine this book without the help of Daniel Strong and his refreshing take on the connections between reading and learning styles, Dean Auriemma and his insights into how vocabulary instruction plays out at the building level, Meredith Lee and her exhaustive and systematic approach to research, and Justin Gilbert, who held everything together for all of us and (unlike Richard, Harvey, and Matt) without breaking a sweat. We would also like to acknowledge Eva Benevento and Joyce Jackson for their wonderful curriculum units (which they let us steal from) and Peta Feiner, whose uncanny ability to decipher scribble allowed us to indulge our nostalgia for pen and paper. And a special thanks to Heidi Hayes Jacobs, whose friendship and ideas continue to inspire us.

Finally, we would like to thank Rachel Livsey and the staff at Corwin Press for their support, their confidence in us, and most of all, their endless supply of patience.

About the Authors

 **Richard W. Strong**, Vice President of Silver Strong & Associates and Thoughtful Education Press, is an author, a program developer, and a trainer/consultant to school districts around the world. As cofounder of the Institute for Community and Difference, Richard has been studying democratic teaching and leadership practices in public and private schools for more than 25 years.

 **Dr. Harvey F. Silver**, President of Silver Strong & Associates and Thoughtful Education Press, was named one of the 100 most influential teachers in the country. He has conducted numerous workshops for school districts and state education departments throughout the United States. He was the principal consultant for the Georgia Critical Thinking Skills Program and the Kentucky Thoughtful Education Teacher Leadership Program.

 **Matthew J. Perini** serves as Director of Publishing for Silver Strong & Associates and Thoughtful Education Press. Over the past 10 years, Matthew has authored more than 20 books, curriculum guides, articles, and research studies covering a wide range of educational topics, including learning styles, multiple intelligences, reading instruction, and effective teaching practices.

Richard Strong, Harvey Silver, and Matthew Perini have collaborated on a number of recent bestsellers in education, including *So Each May Learn: Integrating Learning Styles and Multiple Intelligences* and *Teaching What Matters Most: Standards and Strategies for Raising Student Achievement*, both published by ASCD; *Reading for Academic Success: Powerful Strategies for Struggling, Average, and Advanced Readers, Grades 7–12* for Corwin Press; and Thoughtful Education Press's *Tools for Promoting Active, In-Depth Learning*, which won a Teachers' Choice Award in 2004.

Introduction

The A+ Reader

Take a minute and step back from the fury and adventure of life in your classroom. Take a look at your students. Try to imagine their futures—as readers.

Stefanie loves to argue—perhaps she'll be a lawyer, burning the midnight oil as she pores through stacks of legal briefs. Jared is a real nature lover, always a frog in his pocket or a wounded bird under his arm; maybe he'll be a veterinarian, and a good one too, with all the new veterinary journals on the nightstand next to his bed. Sarah and Larry have been making eyes at each other for three months now. Imagine them married, cruising the Internet looking for a good buy on their first home. And Zachary. Chances are he might already be researching stock options or 401(k)s. And what about Daryl? I haven't seen him this excited about anything until we started our mystery unit in Language Arts. I can just see him waiting impatiently for his local bookstore to open so he can devour the newest release from the hot mystery writer of the day. Then there's Zoe—the latent politician, the do-gooder. Just try to imagine her not surfing a dozen online newspapers, talking back to the editorials under her breath.

No matter how we imagine our students' futures, it is nearly impossible not to see a world in which reading is critical. Here's how the Commission on Adolescent Literacy of the International Reading Association puts it:

> Adolescents entering the adult world in the 21st century will read and write more than at any other time in human history. They will need advanced levels of literacy to perform their jobs, run their households, act as citizens, and conduct their personal lives. They will need literacy to cope with the flood of information they will find everywhere they turn. They will need literacy to feed their imaginations so they can create the world of the future. In a complex and sometimes even dangerous world, their ability to read will be crucial. (Moore, Bean, Birdyshaw, & Rycik, 1999, p. 3)

And yet, as clear and as pressing as this future may be, we do not need to look quite so many years ahead to see that advanced reading skills are prerequisite to success. As students progress through the grades, their lives in middle school, high school, and college will be dominated by reading: primary documents in history; lab directions in science; French and Spanish newspapers in foreign language class; word problems in mathematics; magazine articles and editorials on nutrition in health; novels, poems, plays, short stories, and literary criticism in English; and, of course, all those textbooks. We can't help but notice that the elementary students we teach every day depend on us to make them ready for the reading challenges they will face immediately as students, and eventually as workers and citizens of the twenty-first century.

Here's something else you may have noticed in imagining your students' futures as readers: (We bet) you imagined most of your students as *successful* readers. There are a couple of reasons we're willing to take this bet. First of all, chances are very good that if you purchased this book, you're an educator. And as an educator, you want the best for your students; you work hard to help students become powerful learners and to prepare them for lifelong success. Plus, we have some data to support this bet. You see, we've asked quite a few elementary teachers over the years to conduct this little thinking experiment and imagine their students' reading futures. We have found that the overwhelming majority envision successful futures for their students. Whatever kind of reading elementary teachers imagine their students doing, they tend to see them doing it easily, navigating through texts with proficiency, digesting big ideas, and making inferences without too much struggle.

The second reason we're willing to take this bet is this: While chances are good that if you purchased this book you're an educator, chances are even better that you're a reader. Nonreaders buy few books, rarely visit libraries, and are much more likely to go online to play video games or download music than they are to check out the latest research on alternative energy automobiles, scan the daily blogs and online periodicals for the day's most important news stories, or participate in an online discussion on the achievements of Satchel Paige. So, in imagining your students' futures, you probably relied on the closest and most personally meaningful model of a successful reader you could imagine—yourself.

This is a book about how you can turn average or below-average readers in elementary school into thoughtful, high-achieving readers—readers like yourself, who can find and remember the information they need, reason their way through challenging texts, and feel at home in libraries and bookstores, both virtual and real. We call these readers A+ readers.

WHAT DOES AN A+ READER LOOK LIKE?

For almost four decades, reading research was traveling down a dark road, focusing almost exclusively on the difficulties readers faced. You might say this research was more concerned with what readers could not do than with what they could do—with readers' disabilities rather than their abilities. Then, in the late 1970s and early 1980s, reading research took a sharp turn in a different direction. Under the leadership of researchers such as Robert Tierney, P. David Pearson, Ruth Garner, James Cunningham, Annemarie Palincsar, Ann Brown, and others, reading research began to focus on the mental activity of proficient readers. What these and other researchers realized was that as students moved through the elementary grades, teachers relied more and more on students' ability to read well. No amount of direct instruction, inquiry, videos, or lectures could cover all of the essential material. Articles, literature, biographies, primary documents—all of these and many other resources served as a foundation for powerful teaching and robust learning. Thus, students who weren't reading at a high level of proficiency were missing a vital piece in the learning puzzle. In response to this situation, these researchers began asking a simple but revolutionary question: What do good and great readers do with their minds while reading that makes them more successful than their peers? What they found was that good and great readers shared common characteristics that made them A+ rather than C+ readers:

- A+ readers know how to organize ideas and information to fit the task at hand.
- A+ readers know how to use questions to filter out the most important information and to clarify points of confusion.
- A+ readers know how to use their imaginations to make predictions, draw inferences, and create pictures that mirror important concepts in the text.
- A+ readers know how to use conversation, dialogue, and retelling to deepen their understanding of the texts they read.
- A+ readers think actively while reading; they recognize when their understanding of texts is confused or mistaken and use strategies to repair their comprehension.

Armed with this new vision of the talents and skills employed by successful readers, researchers such as Michael Pressley (2006) and Robert Marzano, Diane Paynter, John Kendall, Debra Pickering, and Lorraine Marzano (1995), teacher-researchers such as Ellin Keene and Susan Zimmermann (1997), and thousands of teachers across the country began to craft instruction in these skills into strategies teachers could use to improve reading while continuing to teach their specific content. And, because of the new research base behind them—because the focus was on ability rather than disability—the strategies worked. Weaker readers grew stronger. C+ students earned more A's.

HOW THIS BOOK IS ORGANIZED

The proficient-reader research, then, gives us our map for this book, which is a collection of strategies that have emerged from this important research base. But the map is not the same as the terrain and, to be sure, there will be a few detours along the way. We'll take a tour through the most current fluency research and strategies at the end of Chapter 1. We'll explore a new model for direct vocabulary instruction in Chapter 3. And in Chapter 7, we'll take a close look at how to use reading styles to differentiate reading instruction so that all students can experience the joys of success. Regardless of the research base behind it, each chapter focuses on a specific reading challenge students face in elementary school and the strategies that will help them meet that challenge.

- *Chapter 1* focuses on helping students get the *big picture, the main idea, the gist* of what they read. It also highlights the relationship between main-idea comprehension and reading fluency.
- *Chapter 2* turns our attention to the importance of *notemaking* as a tool for focusing attention and building reading comprehension.
- *Chapter 3* is designed to help students learn how to manage and master the wealth and variety of *vocabulary* that they confront in all content areas.
- *Chapter 4* contains strategies that develop students' abilities to read beyond the information given, to move from the gist to deeper, more *inferential reading*.
- *Chapter 5* asks, How can students become better and more thoughtful readers by tapping into the power of *questions?*
- *Chapter 6* demonstrates how to use *informal writing and journals* to keep readers active, reflective, and connected to their own interests and experiences.
- *Chapter 7* looks at students' *reading styles* and helps teachers to differentiate and individualize teaching and learning so that all students receive the reading instruction they need and deserve.

In addition to the strategies that populate each chapter, this book contains two other special features: The first is a repeating section called *Helping Struggling Readers.* In these sections, you will find tips and tools for working with our weakest readers in heterogeneous classrooms or special-needs settings. Wherever possible, we have also included in this *Helping Struggling Readers* section specific tools for adapting particular strategies to the needs of English language learners. In most of the chapters in this book, each individual strategy comes with its own *Helping Struggling Readers* section. In Chapters 3, 6, and 7 (which, by nature of their content, follow a slightly different structure from the other chapters), the *Helping Struggling Readers* section appears once, at the end of the chapter.

The second special feature of this book is its wealth of classroom reproducibles. Many of the strategies in this book come with full-page reproducible organizers designed to make classroom implementation easier on the teacher. We encourage you to copy, use, and modify these reproducible organizers to best suit your needs.

BEFORE YOU BEGIN . . . FOUR QUICK TIPS FOR NURTURING A+ READERS

Tip #1—Remember the Three S's

In deciding which Strategies to use, keep one eye on the relevant Standards you want to meet. Keep the other eye on the reading Situation by asking:

- What are students reading?
- What makes the text difficult or challenging to read?
- Which strategy will best help students wrestle meaning from the text and become more independent, A+ readers?

Tip #2—Try It a Few Different Ways

This book is designed to help students overcome seven common reading challenges. Each chapter highlights one challenge and presents several strategies for helping students develop the skills needed to address each challenge. What this structure affords the reading teacher is flexibility. For example, if you're working with students to develop their ability to separate essential information from nonessential information, the different strategies in Chapter 1 will allow you to build this skill through:

- Systematic, step-by-step training in developing ideas (Main Idea strategy)
- The use of Graphic Organizers
- Reading partnerships in which student pairs use questions to filter information (Peer Reading)
- The development of retellings (Read and Retell)
- Icons and visual representations (Split Screen)

Each of these strategies will speak to different students in your classroom. Certain styles of learners will be drawn to step-by-step instruction while others may do better with visual representation or by working in partnerships. What's more, all students will need to develop a repertoire of reading strategies if we expect them to become A+ readers. Therefore, you should strive to keep a moderate number of strategies in play in your classroom. The best way to ensure that students have a manageable variety of strategies at their disposal is for you to have a manageable variety of strategies at yours.

Tip #3—Strategies: They're Not Just for Teachers Anymore

Reading strategies are more than vehicles for delivering instruction. In fact, reading strategies are for learners every bit as much as they are for teachers. When you use a particular strategy in your classroom, tell students its name. Explain how it works and why it is important. Teach students the individual steps within the strategy and clearly define the roles they will be playing during each step. Why? Because when students are given explicit instruction in how to use reading strategies, they learn how to apply those strategies on their own. Better yet, students who are taught how to use reading strategies outperform academically those students who are kept in the dark when new reading strategies are used by their teachers (Brown, Pressley, Van Meter, & Schuder, 1996).

One highly effective way to keep young readers "in the loop" and to help them master new reading strategies is to display strategy posters prominently in your room. A strategy poster outlines the steps that *the students* will follow in working through a strategy. Often, teachers look for ways to make the steps easy to remember and internalize. Figure I.1, for example, shows one teacher's poster for the Main Idea strategy. Notice how she designed her poster around the acronym IDEAS to make the steps memorable for students.

How to Use the Main Idea Strategy

Identify 10–12 key words.

Determine the topic of the reading.

Establish a main idea in one sentence.

Ask yourself, What details support my idea?

Share how you found your idea with the class.

Figure I.1   Main Idea Poster

Tip #4—Moving Forward
Always Involves Looking Backward

After using a strategy, encourage students to look back on what happened and what their minds were doing. Help them access the quality and depth of their learning by asking questions like, "What actions did you take in using the strategy? What challenges did you face? How did you overcome these challenges?" Then, help students turn their reflections into learning goals with questions like, "What advice would you give yourself next time you use this strategy?"

* * * *

We all want our students to learn. And we all know the importance of reading to both academic and lifelong learning. The strategies and tools within these pages (along with the tips above for getting the most out of these strategies) will help you nurture the skills your students will need to become confident, thoughtful, A+ readers.

What's the Big Idea?

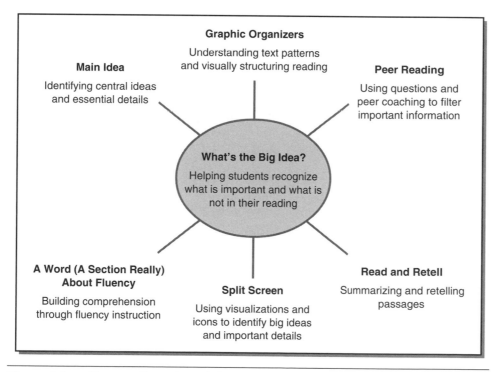

Graphic Organizers

Understanding text patterns and visually structuring reading

Main Idea

Identifying central ideas and essential details

Peer Reading

Using questions and peer coaching to filter important information

What's the Big Idea?

Helping students recognize what is important and what is not in their reading

A Word (A Section Really) About Fluency

Building comprehension through fluency instruction

Split Screen

Using visualizations and icons to identify big ideas and important details

Read and Retell

Summarizing and retelling passages

Figure 1.1 Chapter Overview: Advance Organizer

> *"How does a main idea become a main idea?"*
>
> —Estelle Theander, seventh-grade
> social studies teacher

Imagine you were an idea. Not a great idea. Not an important idea. Something smaller and off to the side. Something other people saw as a detail. You lived in a writer's head, or in a reader's mind, or on a page somewhere in a library. But you were ambitious: you wanted to become something more, something bigger, say, a main idea. What would you do?

Strange question. But it is a question that lies close to the heart of helping students become thoughtful readers. And, as a question, it is not alone. It resides with a number of equally provocative questions, such as:

- Do readers find important ideas, or do they make them up?
- How do authors let you know they think an idea is important?
- How can you tell a main idea from a detail?
- Can an idea be important for one person but secondary for another?
- What if a nonfiction reading has no main idea?
- What about fiction? Do stories have main ideas?

These questions may seem bothersome and overly philosophical, but the readers in your classroom struggle with them every day. Their struggles become your struggles because, as teachers, we want more than anything for our readers to be successful. We all know that separating the important from the unimportant is an essential reading skill. But how do we know what's important and what's not in the first place?

An Experiment

Figure 1.2 contains readings at various levels of complexity. We would like to ask you to read them and identify the important ideas. "What do we mean by important ideas?" you might ask. We mean the key points you find there: what you would tell others about the passage who had not read it so that they got the gist of its content.

Warning: Our point is *not* that an important idea can be whatever you want it to be. Our point is rather to encourage you to look closely at how you determine what is most important in these passages and to ask yourself how this might apply to how you teach your students.

What the Research Says

So, how did you do? How did you determine what was important in each passage?

Reading Selection #1

Definition of a Point

A *point* is the basic unit of geometry. It has no size. It is infinitely small. It has only one location. A physical model of a point would be a pencil tip.

Picture of a Point   P.

You can use a dot to represent a point. You name a point with a capital letter. This point is called point P.

Reading Selection #2

Why Were Roads Important to the Roman Empire?

At the height of Roman rule, Roman roads reached to the farthest corners of the Empire. This vast network made travel much easier and was directly responsible for the great wealth the Empire gained through trade.

Roman roads were built using three layers of firmly packed rocks that were then covered with slabs of smoother stones. The Romans made great efforts to keep their roads flat, but if a hill or mountain had to be crossed, the Romans preferred a short steep climb to the long trudge around a mountain or hill. By keeping roads flat, Roman troops were able to respond more quickly to rebellions or invasions on their borders. Trade and communication were able to move more rapidly and satisfy the needs of the vast Empire.

Reading Selection #3

My final at-bat was nothing like Mighty Casey's ill-fated one. For one thing, no one expected much from me—I hadn't gotten a hit in five straight games. The people in the bleachers certainly didn't stir back to life for me the way the Mudville faithful did for Mighty Casey. There was one similarity, though: both Casey and I were looking at two straight strikes when that third pitch came hurtling in toward us. And then Wham!—no one in Little League had ever hit a ball far enough to clear the municipal lot where they park the ambulances. No one, that is, before me and my 300-foot home run.

Reading Selection #4

The circulatory system circulates blood throughout the body using the heart and three kinds of blood vessels—arteries, capillaries, and veins. The most important part of the circulatory system is the *heart*. The heart is a very strong muscle that pumps blood into the *arteries* when it contracts and takes blood in from the veins when it relaxes. *Blood* is a liquid that delivers oxygen to all the body's parts and carries away chemical waste for disposal. Blood travels away from the heart through the arteries and then crosses through the *capillaries* into the veins. The *veins* carry the blood back to the heart, where it will soon be recycled and used again.

Figure 1.2   Four Readings

Both Pressley and Afflerbach's (1995) study of skilled reading and Keene and Zimmermann's *Mosaic of Thought* (1997) provide us with a deep understanding of what proficient readers do as they try to identify the important information in what they read.

Proficient readers, whether seven or seventy, engage in distinct reading behaviors in order to extract relevant information from a text. As you read the four behaviors described below, keep track of how you read the sample passages. Did you exhibit any of these behaviors in your reading?

- *Proficient readers* use a sense of purpose and especially questions to screen the information in what they read. In this way, they separate information relevant to the question from information that is not. Thus, questions and purposes act like a spotlight, focusing the mind's attention on what is truly important. (Selection 2, for instance, sets up a purpose for reading by providing you with pre-reading question.)
- *Proficient readers* pay attention to patterns in texts by asking, Is this passage comparing and contrasting, is it describing a process, laying out a sequence of events, explaining causes and effects? (You may have noticed this in your own reading of Selection 3, which tells a personal story by using a compare and contrast pattern.)
- *Proficient readers* use the clues authors provide, such as highlighted topics and subtopics, illustrations, phrases such as "most important," and stated and unstated main ideas. (What you may have done with Selection 1 or 4.)
- *Proficient readers* retell and summarize passages as they read or through rereading. Proficient readers do a lot of rereading to check and monitor their understanding. (What you probably did anytime a passage became difficult.)

What This Means for Teaching "Big-Idea Reading"

Most of the skills described here are performed more or less unconsciously by proficient readers. But if we expect our students to become successful at identifying what is important in their readings, we must teach them:

- How to use the questions we give them and how to create questions of their own to guide their reading.
- How to recognize common textual patterns that fiction and nonfiction readings take and how to use these patterns to identify what is and is not important.
- How to use clues an author provides to identify main ideas (or themes in literature) and supportive details.
- How to successfully summarize and retell the important information both during and after reading.

In the remainder of this chapter, we will provide you with five research-based strategies derived from the above four principles.

The Main Idea strategy helps students identify the central or main ideas and the relevant details that support them.

Graphic Organizers help students understand text patterns and use visual representations to structure their reading.

Peer Reading helps students use questions to filter out the most important information in what they read.

Read and Retell helps students summarize and retell passages.

Split Screen helps students use icons and visual representations to identify big ideas and important details.

THE MAIN IDEA

Overview

Much more than simply knowing what a reading is about, understanding a main idea means that students can recognize cues in a text, distinguish between the topic of a reading and its main idea, and identify and assemble the relevant details to support the main idea. Mastering these skills is critical to comprehension, especially as students move into longer and more complex readings in the upper elementary grades. Main Idea is a strategy designed to build these essential skills in young readers.

The Strategy in Action

Marcia Livan's second graders are learning about extinct animals. Today, they are learning about Super-Croc, a huge crocodile that lived more than 100 million years ago. When its full skeleton was uncovered in 2000, paleontologists were awed by Super-Croc's size.

The reading for the lesson is a brief entry on Super-Croc from *Project Exploration®'s* Web site (http://projectexploration.org). Marcia begins the lesson by telling her students, "Sometimes, when I read, I get a little confused about what I'm reading. Does that ever happen to you?"

"Yes," many of her students say.

"It's happening to me right now," says Marcia. "When this happens, I stop myself. Then I start reading again, only this time I go on the lookout for words and phrases that seem important or that jump out at me." Marcia then reads the entry out loud, stopping to write down words on the Main Idea Organizer she has prepared on the blackboard (Figure 1.3). Then she reads the entry aloud a second time, this time letting students add words and phrases to the organizer that seem important to them. As students stop her to highlight words and phrases, Marcia adds them to the organizer.

"Now that I've got some words down, I ask myself, 'Who or what is the focus of what I'm reading?' In this case, everything in this passage seems to be about . . . "

"Super-Croc."

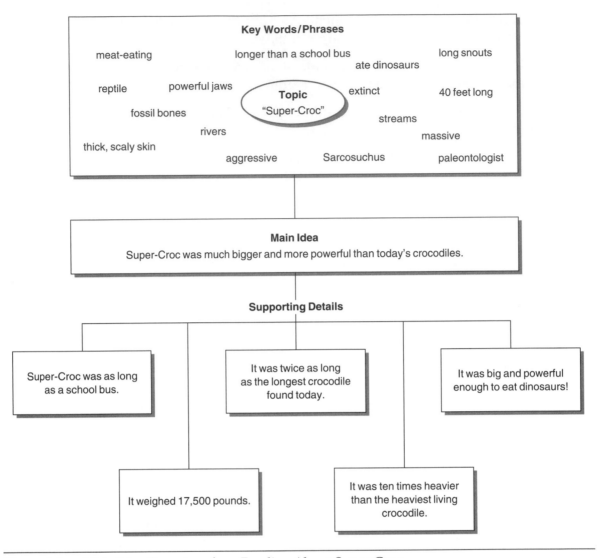

Figure 1.3   Main Idea Organizer for a Reading About Super-Croc

"Right," Marcia says, and writes *Super-Croc* in the oval of the Main Idea Organizer (see Figure 1.3). "Now, I ask myself: 'What is the passage telling me about Super-Croc?' Well, what it seems to be saying is that Super-Croc was like today's crocodiles, but was much bigger and more powerful." Marcia writes *Super-Croc was much bigger and more powerful than today's crocodiles* in the main idea box of the organizer. "Finally, I check my idea by looking to see whether the details in what I'm reading support my idea that Super-Croc was much bigger and more powerful than today's crocodiles. Do you see any clues in the reading that tell us about how big and powerful Super-Croc was?"

"It was as long as a school bus."

"It weighed 17,500 pounds."

"It was twice as long as the crocodiles we have today."

"And 10 times heavier."

"It could eat dinosaurs that came near the water."

As students volunteer their ideas, Marcia records them on the Main Idea Organizer.

When the class has completed filling in the organizer, Marcia reviews the four questions she used to help her find the main idea:

1. What words or phrases seem important?

2. Who or what is the focus of this reading?

3. What is the passage telling me about this topic?

4. What words or clues in the passage support my idea?

Later on as they read their own books during reading time, students practice looking for main ideas using Marcia's four questions and a Main Idea Organizer. Over the course of the year, Marcia uses the strategy with longer and more challenging texts. Students work collaboratively in Main Idea teams, using the four questions to coach one another through the Main Idea process. Marcia also teaches students how to use the Main Idea strategy to find themes in literature and support them with evidence. Figure 1.4

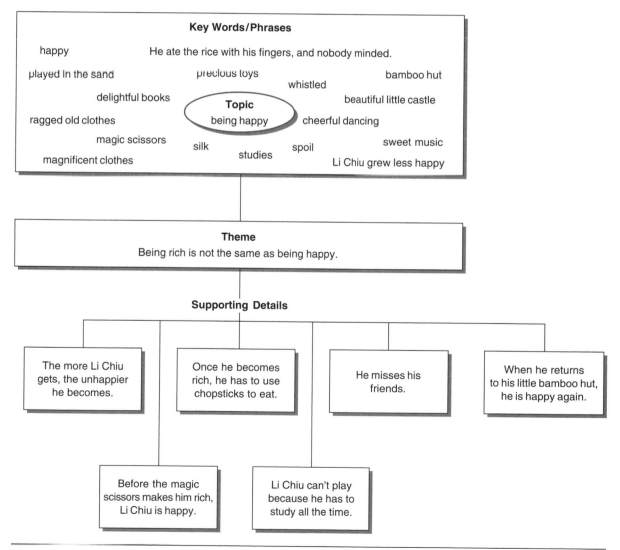

Figure 1.4　Finding Literary Themes Using Main Idea

shows the organizer Marcia and her students created for Loes Spander's fable "The Magic Scissors" (1998), which tells the story of a poor Chinese boy named Li Chiu who is given a pair of magic scissors that make him rich. Once he is rich, Li Chiu longs to have his previous, simpler life back.

Why the Strategy Is Beneficial

Perhaps no element in reading instruction is as confused and muddled as our concept of Main Idea. In their research on how main ideas are conceived in school, Moore, Cunningham, and Rudisill (1983) found that when teachers ask students for a main idea, they may be asking them to:

- Give the *gist* of what they have read.
- Provide an *interpretation*.
- Supply a *key word*.
- Create a *title*.
- Name a *topic*.
- Identify an *issue*.
- Write a *summary*.
- Describe a *theme*.
- Analyze a text and discover a *thesis*.

This confusion is exacerbated by several factors:

- **The absence of a clear developmental curriculum for helping students identify main ideas**. Most schools stop direct instruction in main idea somewhere between the third and fourth grades, exactly at the point that expository texts become more prevalent and the application of main idea strategies more essential.
- **The lack of clear modeling for main idea identification in passages longer than one or two paragraphs.** Usually, and perhaps in deference to standardized tests and SATs, students are asked to identify main ideas only in short, "closed" passages rather than within larger textual structures.
- **The prevalence of inferred (as opposed to directly stated) main ideas in student texts.** For instance, as Baumann and Serra (1984) have discovered, only 44 percent of the paragraphs in student social studies texts contain a clearly stated main idea, and of those only 27 percent use this statement as the opening sentence of the paragraph.
- **Reading programs often inadvertently pose barriers to success.** When Jitendra, Chard, Hoppes, Renouf, and Gardill (2001) evaluated commercial reading programs used in schools, they found that not one program consistently followed a progressive instructional sequence. Instead, 62 percent of the lessons they studied asked

students to construct main ideas as a first step, rather than teaching students a replicable process for finding main ideas. In addition, the mean readability of texts used for teaching main idea analysis often exceeded the level of the intended grade, adding to the difficulties faced by struggling readers.

The Main Idea strategy helps to overcome these difficulties by:

- Beginning with "feel-important" words and phrases. Before students find (or construct) the main idea or even determine the topic of the reading, they are given the opportunity to develop a personal feel for the text and to think about which words and phrases strike them as readers.
- Modeling the clear difference between:
  - Finding the topic (the subject of the reading).
  - Identifying the main idea (a sentence that summarizes the central thought of the reading).
- Showing students how to check findings by assembling and organizing details that support the main idea.
- Providing regular and extended practice in identifying topics, main ideas, and details on progressively longer and more complex passages. This progression should move through collaborative work to independent practice.
- Direct teaching and practice of notemaking using a visual organizer that ensures students gradually develop the ability to record notes that are accurate, well organized, and easy to understand. (See Chapter 2, "From Note Taking to Notemaking," for a variety of other techniques.)

The strategy is typically used with nonfiction texts that follow a main idea structure. (Nonfiction texts that follow other structures such as sequence, comparison, or problem/solution are handled in the Graphic Organizers section in this chapter.) However, the strategy is highly adaptable to fiction, serving as a technique for helping students identify themes. The strategy is also appropriate at all elementary levels. In their work with third graders, van den Broek, Lynch, Ievers-Landis, Naslund, and Verduin (2003) found that young elementary students have the ability to identify main ideas, while a study by Lehr (1988) found that preschoolers can identify basic story themes such as friendship and cooperation. Of course, young students are less successful at finding main ideas and themes than older students—supporting the importance of the Main Idea strategy in the early grades.

How to Use the Strategy

Use Organizer 1-A, "What's the Main Idea?" on page 15.

Incorporate the Main Idea strategy into your classroom using the following steps:

1. Explain and use sample texts to show students the difference between *the topic* of a reading and *the main idea*. The *topic* is the subject of the reading. The *main idea* is a sentence that summarizes the central thought the reading provides about the passage.

2. Model the Main Idea process (collect key words and phrases, identify the topic, state the main idea, assemble the details) through teacher Think Alouds (describing what is happening in your mind while you model the process).

3. Explain to students that when the main idea is not specifically stated in nonfiction texts, they can look for these cues (adapted from Van Dijk & Kintsch, 1983):
   - Print cues—the use of italics, boldface type, and subheadings to indicate important topics.
   - Word cues—the use of words such as *important*, *key*, or *significant* as indicators of the most vital information.
   - Sentence cues—the use of summarizing or previewing sentences (or paragraphs) to highlight the information central to the text.
   - Organization cues—the use of standard expository prose structures (sequence, cause and effect, conceptual, descriptive comparison) to provide a pattern to guide student understanding. (See the section on Graphic Organizers, pages 16–31.)

4. Show students how to check the main idea by identifying and organizing details that support it.

5. Select a reading. Use Organizer 1-A "What's the Main Idea?" to guide students through the process of identifying the four elements central to the main idea (key words/phrases, topic, main idea, supporting details of the main idea).

6. Provide regular and extended practice in identifying the four elements on progressively longer and more involved readings.

7. Over time, move students through collaborative group work toward independent practice in which students use the strategy as they read on their own.

Helping Struggling Readers

The Main Idea strategy, with its emphasis on modeling and its built-in support structure—first working with the teacher, then in collaborative groups, then moving toward independent work—is highly effective with both struggling readers and English language learners. Once students are in their groups, opportunities for coaching abound, which is a huge instructional benefit; Jitendra, Hoppes, and Xin (2003) found that teaching main-idea reading to struggling students in small groups leads to gains in comprehension and fosters independent use of the strategy after instruction.

Both struggling readers and English language learners may need more time and practice illustrating main ideas and details through drawing, sketches, and concept maps (see Information Search, pages 163–168, Split Screen, pages 45–48, and Concept Mapping, pages 72–75 for help in these areas).

Also, these students may have difficulty determining main ideas and relevant details because of gaps in their application of grammatical information to reading. For example, below are two sources of confusion often experienced by struggling readers when looking for main ideas and relevant details (adapted from Burns, Roe, & Ross, 1998):

- **Pronoun Referents**
  "Though many colonists were eager for a conclusive conflict with England, others felt *their* loyalty to *their* mother country came first." (*Their* refers to others.)
- **Adverb Referents**
  "Since reptiles rely more on the sun than mammals do, they will frequently, during cooler periods, find an area free of enemies, fix themselves to a warm rock, and remain *there* until the temperature rises." (*There* refers to the rock.)

Trouble with sentences like these is in no sense the fault of students. Striving to create a classroom in which reading instruction and grammatical concepts are closely linked is the best means of addressing the problem.

For students who have not yet grasped the structure of main-idea paragraphs, a tactile model such as a shoebox often helps them solidify their understanding. You might start with the main idea, "You can find many things at the seashore," by writing it on the box. Then have students guess some of the items you have placed inside. As you take items out of the box (sand, shells, coins, etc.), explain how they support the main idea. Or you can reverse the process by taking items out of the box one by one and ask students to construct a main-idea sentence that supports the contents.

Once students have overcome the abstraction of main ideas and supporting details through the physicality of the shoebox, continue with the analogy by showing them how to use a Shoebox Organizer to identify topics and main ideas and to collect details when they read. Figure 1.5, for example, shows a completed Shoebox Organizer created by a third-grade student on the basis of a reading about the hog-nose snake.

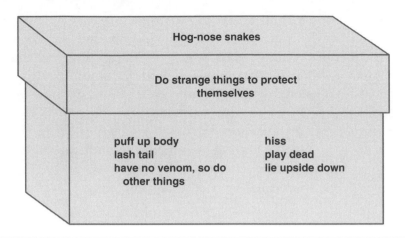

Figure 1.5   Shoebox Organizer

Finally, struggling readers may become confused by the differences between fiction and nonfiction as they work to capture big ideas. In fiction, we call the central idea a theme rather than a main idea. Although the Main Idea strategy can easily be adapted to fiction (see pages 7–8), many struggling readers—even those who can find and support main ideas in nonfiction texts—may need extra help finding themes in literary texts. The reason? Unlike finding main ideas, understanding themes in literature requires students to make two connections unique to narrative texts. First, because themes are derived from character and plot, students must first have these core story elements in place before they can make the connection to the theme. Second, because themes in elementary school are often lessonlike in nature (e.g., *People should work together, It's best to be honest*), a deep understanding of a theme means understanding how the theme connects to real life.

Theme Scheme (Williams et al., 2002) is a strategic reading model designed to address the challenges inherent in helping young readers discover and relate to literary themes. Theme Scheme has proved highly successful with struggling readers as young as second and third graders. In one study (Williams et al., 2002) of 120 second and third graders in inner-city New York City, of which 98 percent received free or reduced lunch and more than 80 percent were minority students, researchers found that regular use of Theme Scheme led to significant gains in comprehension and in students' abilities to transfer themes to new stories from stories that they read.

Driving the Theme Scheme model is a series of eight questions. Figure 1.6 lists these questions and one student's responses for "The Magic Scissors." (For a comparison between the Theme Scheme approach and the adapted Main Idea approach to theme-building, see Figure 1.4.) Notice how these questions move students progressively toward higher levels of thinking by asking them to: identify the main character (Question 1);

1. **Who is the main character?**
   Li Chiu, a Chinese boy

2. **What is the main character's problem?**
   Once he gets rich, he can't do the things he wants to do.

3. **What did the main character do about the problem?**
   He finds the fish who gave him the magic scissors.

4. **And then what happened?**
   He throws the scissors back in the river.

5. **Was what happened good or bad?**
   Good

6. **Why was it good or bad?**
   Because the spell is broken and Li Chiu gets his regular life back.

7. **The main character learned that he or she should . . .**
   Li Chiu learned that he should not be greedy.

8. **We should . . .**
   We should not be greedy and should be thankful for what we have.

Figure 1.6   Theme Scheme Questions and a Student's Responses for "The Magic Scissors"

outline the basic plot (Questions 2–4); form and justify an opinion about the story's outcome or character's action (Questions 5–6); derive a theme from the story (Question 7); and apply the theme to their own lives and experiences (Question 8).

In experimenting with and improving Theme Scheme as an instructional method, Williams (2005) has found that the following suggestions yield the greatest benefits for young readers:

1. Run a series of lessons using texts with clear theme concepts (e.g., greed, courage, the importance of family). Before the first lesson, hold a discussion on the concept of themes—what they are, why they're important, how they relate to our lives.

2. At the start of each lesson, introduce the relevant background information associated with the focus story. Be sure to model the process

of answering the Theme Scheme questions for the first few lessons, giving students time to internalize the questions.

3. For the first few lessons, state the theme concept before reading (Today's story is about courage.). Let students generate the theme concept themselves as they become more familiar with the process.

4. Read the story aloud. At key points, stop and ask a variety of questions, including those that ask students to make connections to their lives (Has anything like this ever happened to you?), make predictions (What do you think will happen to Yuri?), and explain significant episodes (Why do you think Sophie left while Sam was speaking?). Discuss responses. Over time, allow students to pose the questions themselves.

5. Work with students to develop a summary after reading by answering the first four Theme Scheme questions together as a class. (Once again, increase student responsibility for creating the summary with each new lesson.) Allow students to reflect on the summary before answering Questions 5–8.

6. Reinforce the theme by providing students with a highly condensed, one-paragraph vignette with the same theme. Use the eight questions to discuss the vignette, but this time, add two more questions, which are designed to increase transfer from text to real life:
   • When is it important to _____?
   • In what situations is it easy/difficult to _____?

7. Review the lesson, and ask students to generate examples from their lives or ideas for stories that would illustrate the same theme.

8. Provide students with a meaningful way to demonstrate and express their understanding of the theme. Discussion, writing tasks, sketching and drawing, and role-playing are all good ways to enrich and synthesize learning.

ORGANIZER 1-A: WHAT'S THE MAIN IDEA?

Name: _____

What's the Main Idea?

Key Words/Phrases

(Topic)

(subject of reading)

Main Idea (sentence that summarizes the central thought)

Supporting Details (Facts and ideas that support the main idea)

<u>Reflection</u>   How I identified the topic and the main idea:

☐ It was stated in the reading.
☐ I used a cue:
   ☐ Print cue (italics, boldface type, subheads)
   ☐ Word cue ("important," "key," "significant")
   ☐ Sentence cue (summarizing or previewing sentence)
   ☐ Organization cue (sequence, cause and effect, conceptual, descriptive comparison)

GRAPHIC ORGANIZERS

Overview

Being able to "see" text structure is a key skill elementary school students must develop to become proficient readers. Students must be taught to recognize the underlying pattern of a text, understand how ideas are connected, and extract the information from the passages they read. This strategy helps students learn to distinguish among some of the most common text structures and use visual representation to organize information and construct knowledge from their reading.

The Strategy in Action

Gary Tucker is conducting a unit on the Civil War with his fifth graders. "Part of understanding history," Gary explains, "is to understand the personalities and beliefs of the people who helped make it. I want you to focus your attention on two people who were in power during the war: Abraham Lincoln and Jefferson Davis. The next two chapters in our book tell us about the personal history and personalities of these two presidents. As you read about Abraham Lincoln and Jefferson Davis, I want you to focus on how these men were similar and how they were different."

Gary then reminds students how to use a comparison organizer to record and organize the important ideas in their reading. During reading time, Gary moves around the room to help struggling students and to ensure students understand how to use the organizer to gather the appropriate information. Afterward, he reviews the key points on the board with students. Once the organizer is complete (see Figure 1.7), Gary asks his students to write a brief essay explaining how each president was uniquely qualified for his job.

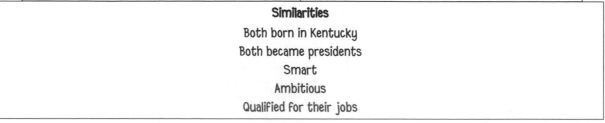

Differences—Lincoln	Differences—Davis
Against slavery, especially as a part of westward expansion	Pro-slavery, owned slaves
Became famous during debates with Stephen Douglas	Became famous as a hero in war with Mexico
Wanted North and South to remain unified	Argued for Southern power, slavery, and right of states to secede
Calm, logical, never mean-spirited	Mischievous boy. Became serious and studious after malaria
1861—took office as president of the United States	1861—took office as president of Confederacy

Similarities
Both born in Kentucky
Both became presidents
Smart
Ambitious
Qualified for their jobs

Figure 1.7   Compare and Contrast Organizer

* * * *

Joy St. Maarten is teaching an art class. She has asked her students to select an artist of their choice from the books in her library and to prepare a brief oral report on their artist. Specifically, Joy wants her students to focus on a single essential question: How has the artist's personal biography affected his or her work as an artist?

To help students prepare, Joy decides to model the process by using a sequence organizer to record major events from the life of artist Georgia O'Keeffe. Using an overhead projection of a selection from Robyn Montana Turner's 1991 biography of O'Keeffe from the *Portraits of Women Artists for Children* series, Joy explains,

> What I do when reading an artist's biography is select the five most important events from the artist's life. To help me determine if an event is significant, I ask myself: Does the author explain how or why this event affected the artist's life and work? Look, for instance, at the bottom of page 7, where it says that when Georgia was 12 years old, she began taking private drawing and painting lessons. Does it say why this is important to Georgia as an adult?

"It says Georgia discovered she liked to paint," one student says.
"She began painting her own imaginary scenes," says another.
A third student says, "It made her realize she wanted to become an artist."
"Great," Joy says. "It looks like we have a very important event that affected her as an artist. Art lessons made Georgia realize she wanted to be an artist in the first place." Joy records this information in the first section of the sequence organizer (Figure 1.8).

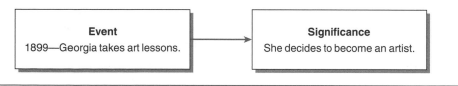

Figure 1.8   Sequence Organizer

Joy continues this modeling process with her students until she has completed the sequence organizer. Students then use this process to conduct research on their chosen artists for their oral presentation.

* * * *

The students in Leo Spinetti's fourth-grade class have been busy learning what makes a story a story. Over the course of their short-story unit, students have been using Story Organizers to "take stories apart" by breaking stories down into their core elements. According to Leo, this process is powerful for three reasons:

1. Students learn how stories are universal and what all stories have in common, which students can transfer to new stories and novels.

2. Students make a strong visual connection to the art of storytelling because organizers lay out the structure of stories in a graphic format. For students who struggle with reading, this gives them another, non-linguistic entryway into understanding a text.

3. Students develop their comprehension skills because story organizers focus attention on the big picture of character, setting, plot, etc., rather than the individual words. This big-picture focus also readies students for the next leaps—into inference and interpretation.

Today, Leo is reviewing the work he and his students have done so far. He reviews the Story Organizers he and the class have created, goes over the steps in story mapping, and tells students that today they will be mapping out a story on their own. As students read and map Cynthia Rylant's "Stray" (1988), a story about a girl who finds a stray dog while shoveling snow (Figure 1.9 shows one student's map), Leo walks around the room to see how students handle the job of breaking down stories on their own and to provide assistance and coaching to struggling students.

Someone (main character) Doris Lacey	Somewhere (setting) The Lacey Home
Wanted (goal) To keep the puppy that she finds in her driveway.	But (obstacle) Doris's parents tell her they can't afford to keep the puppy.
So (how the character tries to reach the goal) Doris begs her parents to let her keep the puppy.	Then (the result of the character's efforts) Her parents say no, and Mr. Lacey brings the puppy to the pound.
Therefore (effect on the main character) Doris cries and wonders if she'll ever have anything that makes her happy.	Finally (resolution) When Mr. Lacey sees the pound, he changes his mind and brings the dog back home.

Figure 1.9   Story Organizer for Cynthia Rylant's Short Story "Stray"

Why the Strategy Is Beneficial

Students will encounter several different types of text structures in their reading, both in and outside the classroom. Nonfiction texts in particular are often organized according to text patterns that are unfamiliar to young readers. For example, a text explaining the difference between frogs and toads might use a structure of comparison (e.g., "Unlike the toad, the frog has teeth in its mouth"), while a reading on how to serve a tennis ball might follow a pattern of sequence (e.g., "First, you should place your feet approximately two feet apart while standing behind and perpendicular to the baseline"). Readings such as these, longer readings that contain a variety of text patterns, and narrative fiction, which has a structure (or grammar) all its own, often make it difficult to use a main-idea structure to find the important information. Different reading strategies are needed to extract the relevant information from these types of texts. But when it comes to understanding texts, especially those that lack clear main ideas, what is it exactly that the proficient reader sees?

Research conducted over the past 20 years has consistently provided one answer to this question. What the reader sees is text structure. Many studies, including those conducted by Pearson and Comperell (1994), Ruta (1992), Derewianka (1990), and Jones, Pierce, and Hunter (1989) all verify this conclusion. Text structure refers to the patterns authors use to organize their writing. Research into text structure regularly notes the following patterns as prominent in the nonfiction readings assigned to students:

- **Topic Description** provides information organized around central concepts and subtopics.
- **Sequence/Cycle** places events into a chronological sequence or a series of steps.
- **Comparison** explores the similarities and differences between related events, people, concepts, or ideas.
- **Problem/Solution** lays out a problem or issue and explores one or more solutions and their effects.

Proficient readers have, through extensive reading, learned to use clues in the text to determine the text pattern. They then use the pattern to help them anticipate what kinds of information the text is likely to provide and what particular aspects of that information are likely to be important.

On the other hand, average and struggling readers frequently are unable to structure what they are learning or determine what is and is not important for them to remember and understand. They feel overwhelmed by the amount of information. The solution is to teach students about text structure, and the best way to teach students about text structure is to make the process visual by showing them how to use Graphic Organizers.

Each of the four most common nonfiction structures has a distinctive organizer as well as a set of cueing words and phrases that help keep the reader oriented as she or he reads (see Figure 1.10).

Narrative text has its own structural pattern, typically called "story grammar" (Mandler & Johnson, 1977). Many children develop a general awareness of story structure before they enter school and can use it to comprehend simple stories. As students read longer and richer stories, their comprehension skills will need to advance to meet this new level of literary sophistication. Figure 1.11 shows three different story organizers at three levels of sophistication.

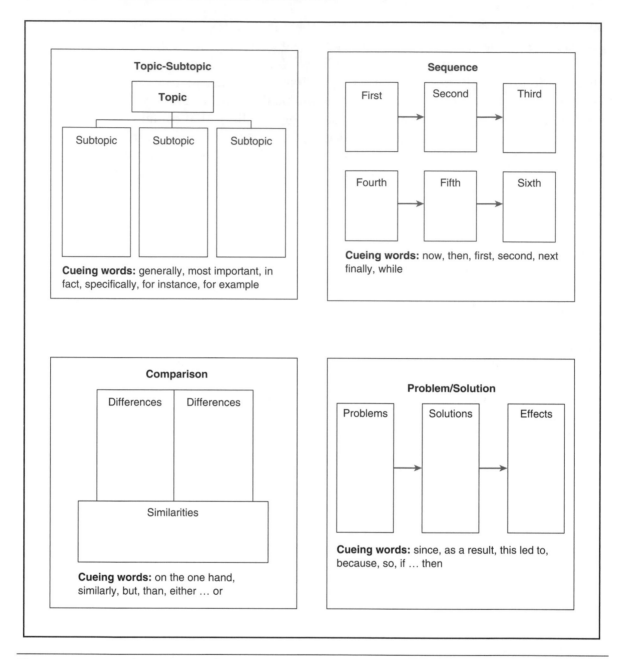

Figure 1.10 Four Common Nonfiction Structures

The effectiveness of using Graphic Organizers to teach students about text structure has been widely validated (Alvermann, 1986; Egan, 1999). Williams and colleagues (2002) report benefits to students as young as second graders. According to Hyerle (2000), when we teach readers how to use and, over time, create their own Graphic Organizers, we foster an evolution in students' thinking: Students first learn how to manage information and then how to use that information to construct knowledge.

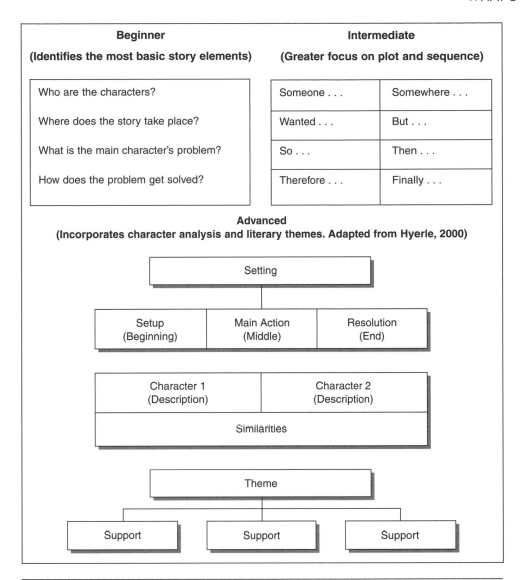

Beginner	**Intermediate**
(Identifies the most basic story elements)	**(Greater focus on plot and sequence)**

Who are the characters?
Where does the story take place?
What is the main character's problem?
How does the problem get solved?

Someone . . .	Somewhere . . .
Wanted . . .	But . . .
So . . .	Then . . .
Therefore . . .	Finally . . .

Advanced
(Incorporates character analysis and literary themes. Adapted from Hyerle, 2000)

Setting

Setup (Beginning)	Main Action (Middle)	Resolution (End)

Character 1 (Description)	Character 2 (Description)
Similarities	

Theme

Support	Support	Support

Figure 1.11   Three Story Organizers

How to Use the Strategy

Use Organizers 1-B to 1-I on pages 24–31: "Topic-Subtopic Organizer," "Sequence Organizer," "Cycle Organizer," "Comparison Organizer," "Problem/ Solution Organizer," "Beginner Story Organizer," "Intermediate Story Organizer," "Advanced Story Organizer."

Incorporate the use of Graphic Organizers into your classroom using the following steps:

1. First, explain how Graphic Organizers work, their purpose, and how they can help students become better readers. Explain that there are several different ways of representing information and that the key

to using Graphic Organizers is to find the organizer that best represents the text's structure.

2. Model what you expect students to do. Create a working model organizer on the board or an overhead and distribute corresponding organizers to students. (Refer to Organizers 1-B to 1-I for samples to use.) For your model and for students' initial practice, choose readings in which the content is familiar to all students (e.g., differences between summer and winter). Also, make sure that the information lends itself to graphic organization.

3. Using your working model organizer, show students how to use their corresponding visual organizers to take notes. Allow them to work on their own while the model is still clear in their heads.

4. Over time, as students master the process, introduce additional organizers and text structures. Model their uses and compare and contrast the different text structures to ensure students can tell the differences between them.

5. Provide students with practice identifying the various text structures and selecting the most appropriate organizer.

6. Encourage students to develop their own visual organizers to fit the organizational patterns of the texts they are reading. For example, one creative second-grade student developed the diagram organizer shown in Figure 1.12 to help him understand a reading on insects.

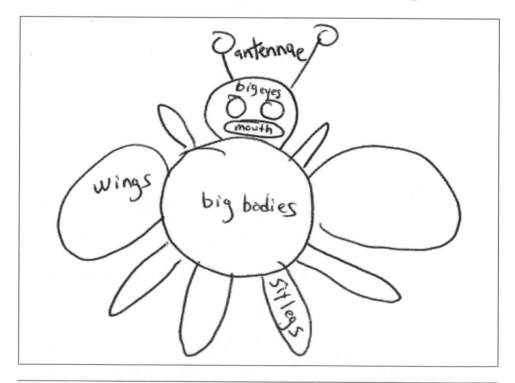

Figure 1.12   A Student's Insect Organizer

Source: Copyright © Thoughtful Education Press. Reprinted with permission.

Helping Struggling Readers

Research on the use of Graphic Organizers to build comprehension shows that they are especially helpful to struggling students (Lehman, 1992) and English language learners (Gersten & Baker, 2000). For narrative reading, Gardill and Jitendra (1999) demonstrated that struggling students who were taught how to organize story elements using a visual framework improved their understanding of story grammar and deepened their comprehension.

Nevertheless, these students may require extra help in learning how to use Graphic Organizers well. Allow struggling readers and English language learners to work with partners or in groups in which they can discuss their difficulties in using Graphic Organizers and can create a complete organizer collaboratively. Work with these groups to help students become aware of their own difficulties and—through coaching and modeling—to see what's involved in overcoming them. Allow other students in the group to explain what works for them when they run into difficulties.

You may also want to develop a list of problem-solving questions to guide students through the process and to help them internalize the steps. For example:

- How does the information seem to be arranged?
- Which organizer best matches the text's organization?
- What cueing words should I look for?
- What's the important information to write on the organizer?
- Does my completed organizer adequately summarize the reading(s)?

To help students reach a comfort level in using organizers, you may want to provide them with a word bank listing the words, phrases, or sentences to be placed in the organizer. When students have access to the key words and phrases, the focus is taken off extracting relevant information and placed on using the concepts and the organizer appropriately. For instance, if your students are using a cycle organizer to understand a reading on the water cycle, you might provide them with key words and phrases such as:

- Vapor condenses
- Water evaporates and rises
- Vapor sticks to dust particles
- Billions of vapor droplets form clouds
- Earth's surface heats up
- Precipitation

This way, students build confidence in using the organizer. With English language learners, it may also be necessary to identify and define any potentially problematic vocabulary words.

ORGANIZER 1-B: TOPIC-SUBTOPIC ORGANIZER

Name: _____

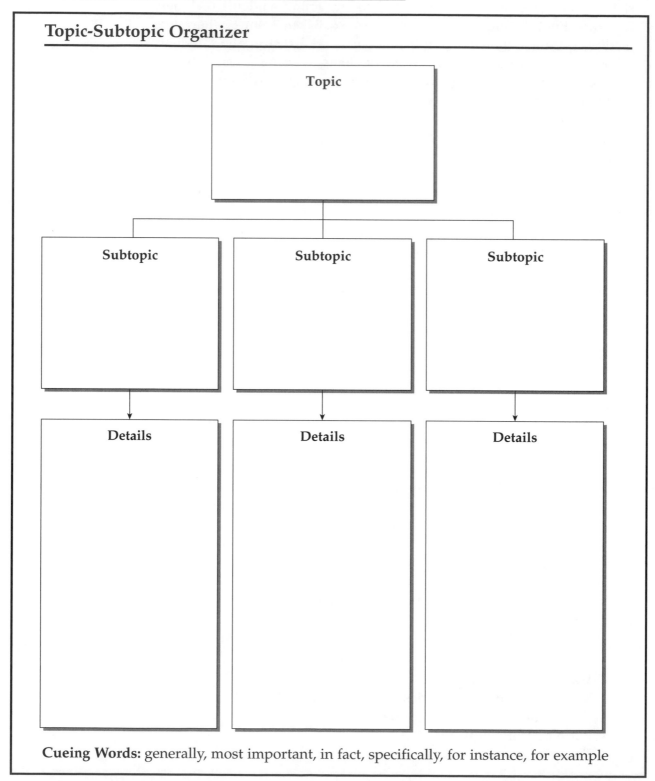

Topic-Subtopic Organizer

Topic

Subtopic   Subtopic   Subtopic

Details   Details   Details

Cueing Words: generally, most important, in fact, specifically, for instance, for example

ORGANIZER 1-C: SEQUENCE ORGANIZER

Name: _____

Sequence Organizer

First	Second	Third

Fourth	Fifth	Sixth

Cueing Words: now, then, first, second, next, finally, while

ORGANIZER 1-D: CYCLE ORGANIZER

Name: _____

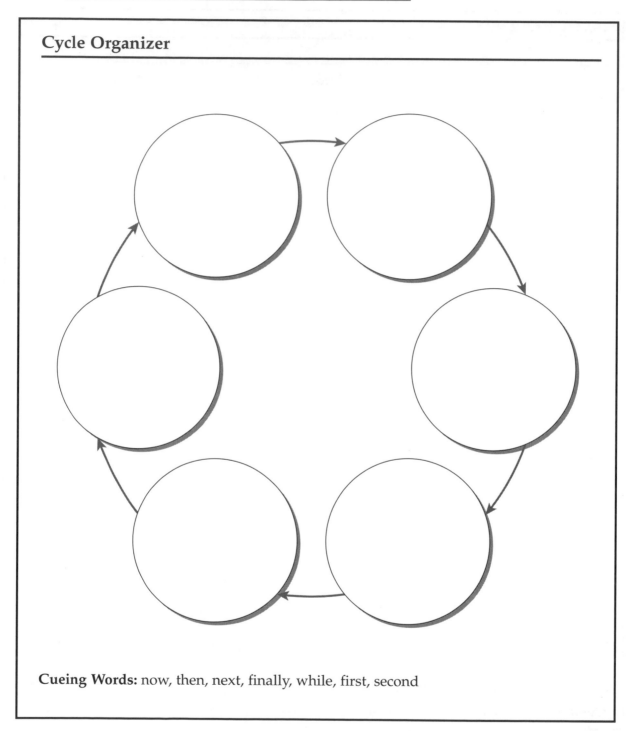

Cueing Words: now, then, next, finally, while, first, second

ORGANIZER 1-E: COMPARISON ORGANIZER

Name: _____

Comparison Organizer

Differences	Differences

Similarities

Cueing words: on the one hand, similarly, but, than, either . . . or

ORGANIZER 1-F: PROBLEM/SOLUTION ORGANIZER

Name: _____

Problem/Solution Organizer

Problem	Solution	Effects

Cueing words: since, as a result, this led to, because, so, if . . . then

ORGANIZER 1-G: BEGINNER STORY ORGANIZER

Name: _____

Story Organizer (Beginner)

Who are the characters?

Where does the story take place?

What is the main character's problem?

How does the problem get solved?

ORGANIZER 1-H: INTERMEDIATE STORY ORGANIZER

Name: _____

Story Organizer (Intermediate)

Someone . . .	Somewhere . . .
Wanted . . .	**But . . .**
So . . .	**Then . . .**
Therefore . . .	**Finally . . .**

ORGANIZER 1-I: ADVANCED STORY ORGANIZER

Name: _____

Story Organizer (Advanced)

Setting

Setup (Beginning)	Main Action (Middle)	Resolution (End)

Character One	Character Two

Similarities

Theme

Support	Support	Support

PEER READING

Overview

Reading a densely packed passage and extracting the relevant information to create a comprehensive yet concise summary is a difficult challenge for readers of all ages. Peer Reading is a collaborative learning strategy that helps students break down readings into manageable chunks and scaffolds the task of summarizing through coaching partnerships and summarizing questions. As they continue to use the strategy, students work toward independence, creating their own summarizing questions to build their comprehension.

The Strategy in Action

As part of their unit on natural disasters, Robert McGill's fourth graders are studying earthquakes. The students have been divided into pairs. Each student in each two-person team has a copy of an article about the causes and effects of earthquakes and the uncanny ability of some animals to predict earthquakes. Robert has divided the article into four short sections, and both members of each team have a coaching sheet (Figure 1.13) with questions keyed to building a brief summary of each section of the reading. Morris, the A reader, will address questions 1, 4, and 5, while Sara, the B reader, will address questions 2, 3, and 6.

As Peer Reading partners, both Morris and Sara read each section independently, marking the text to highlight the information that feels important to them. At the end of the first section, both stop reading, and, after taking a quick look at his marked text, Morris turns the article over so he can't see it. Sara keeps her copy of the article open and asks Morris

---

Peer Reading Coaching Sheet

Section One Question (for Reader A)

1. What causes earthquakes?

Section Two Questions (for Reader B)

2. What happens during an earthquake?
3. What are the effects on people, animals, and the land?

Section Three Questions (for Reader A)

4. What animals are the best earthquake predictors?
5. How do animals behave before earthquakes?

Section Four Question (for Reader B)

6. What do scientists believe are the reasons animals can predict earthquakes?

Figure 1.13 Summarizing Questions for Guiding Peer Reading

> **Earthquakes**
>
> Earthquakes come from cracks in the Earth
> called faults. Shock waves come from the
> fault and make the ground roll and shake.
> Earthquakes can make trees and buildings
> fall. Streets can crack, and pipes can break.
> When things fall or break, people and
> animals can be hurt or killed.
>
> Some animals seem to know when
> earthquakes will come. The best earthquake
> predictors are snakes, lizards, and small
> animals. They run out of their burrows before
> earthquakes. Other animals get angry before
> an earthquake, or they get scared and bark.
> Scientists think animals can hear or sense
> changes in the Earth before earthquakes.
> Humans cannot sense these changes.

Figure 1.14   Sample Student Summary

question 1, "What causes earthquakes?" As he answers, Sara uses her
marked text to coach him toward a more complete answer.

When Morris finishes, both read section 2 and then reverse roles.
Sara puts her materials aside while Morris coaches her toward complete
answers to the questions, "What happens during an earthquake?" and
"What are the effects of earthquakes on people, animals, and the land?"

The partners continue this process of reading and coaching for sections
3 and 4, reversing roles each time. After completing the reading, both
students reread the article and use the question sheet to develop notes that
will help them create a summary. Together, both students in the partnership then develop a comprehensive summary of the article (Figure 1.14).

As students work, Robert circulates around the room. He takes notes on
students' note-taking and summarizing behaviors, looking for strengths
and weaknesses, and he collects data for his own record of students' development. Over the next few weeks, Robert will gradually teach his students
to create their own summarizing questions, which they will use to conduct
independent research into another natural disaster in human history and
how people coped with it.

Why the Strategy Is Beneficial

For many years, the teaching of summarizing involved teaching students
how to:

1. Delete unnecessary ideas and details

2. Replace specifics with more general ideas

3. Select or construct main ideas or topic sentences from a text.

However, several problems plague this procedure. Afflerbach and Johnston (1986) pointed out that the ability to delete trivial or unimportant information presumes that students know how to identify important information. Yet this is exactly the skill most average and below-average readers lack.

In addition, Afflerbach and Johnston noted that the construction of unstated main ideas constituted a second area of difficulty for struggling readers. Complicating the situation further is that most passages are not organized around a main idea and detail structure. Some describe a sequence, others discuss cause and effect, while still others compare information or tell a story. Asking students to search for main ideas in prose that follows a different format establishes a schema that conflicts with the organizational structure of the reading and thus hinders comprehension. Finally, as Cunningham and Moore (1986) pointed out, asking students to read each passage and decide on its main idea tends to be vague and may not focus their attention on any specific information. On the other hand, readers with a concrete problem to solve, such as "What is the ocean floor like?" or "Why did the Roman Empire fall?" have a definite purpose that leads them to specific information.

With these ideas in mind, Silver, Hanson, Strong, and Schwartz (1996) developed a revised model of summarizing. In this version, students work in pairs to answer questions about a central topic. This approach to summarizing, called Peer Reading, yields five distinct advantages over the traditional teaching of summarizing:

1. Peer-assisted reading strategies are proven to build both comprehension and fluency at all grade levels (McMaster, Fuchs, & Fuchs, 2006).

2. The use of summarizing questions scaffolds the task of summarizing by directing students to specific information.

3. Both the oral summary and the presence of a coach heighten the processing of information and provide students with a greater sense of control over the reading.

4. Students process the text in four ways: by answering the questions, by coaching their partners, by taking notes, and by developing a collaborative summary.

5. Students work toward independence, eventually creating their own summarizing questions to build comprehension and as an independent research tool.

How to Use the Strategy

Use Organizer 1-J, "Peer Reading," on page 37.
You can incorporate the Peer Reading strategy in your classroom using a method similar to that employed in "The Strategy in Action" section.

1. Select a reading and break it up into manageable sections.

2. For each section, create a question or a set of questions that will require students to summarize the section. Write these questions on Organizer 1-J, "Peer Reading."

3. Divide students into pairs. Distribute the reading and the summarizing questions to all students.

4. Ask students to read the first section, mark their text, and then engage in coaching partnerships (Reader A puts his reading aside while the coach asks the summarizing questions and uses her marked copy to coach Reader A to a more complete answer).

5. Have students reverse roles for each remaining section of the text.

6. When they are finished, ask students to use the summarizing questions to take notes on the reading and to create a summary collaboratively.

7. Over time, gradually model and coach students through the process of identifying their own summarizing questions and using their new skills to summarize readings and conduct research.

Helping Struggling Readers

Research shows that Peer Reading benefits struggling readers and English language learners. Vaughn, Gersten, and Chard (2000) cite interactive groups or partners, along with opportunities for interactive dialogue between students, as two critical elements of reading interventions that promote positive outcomes for students with reading disabilities. Klingner and Vaughn (1996) found that both peer tutoring and cooperative learning lead to improved learning outcomes with English language learners with learning disabilities. Similarly, Cheung and Slavin's (2005) review of reading programs for English language learners supports the use of partner reading to increase comprehension.

In addition, the teacher's observations and coaching of the individual student teams provide opportunities for diagnosing and interviewing students with particular problems that occur during the Peer Reading strategy.

For students who are still having difficulty summarizing the reading, the Collaborative Summarizing strategy (Silver, Strong, & Perini, 2001) can be helpful. The strategy works like this:

1. After reading, students list three to five ideas they believe to be the most important.

2. Students pair up with a partner and review the guidelines for consensus negotiation:
   • Avoid win-lose statements.
   • Yield only to positions that have sound, logical foundations.
   • Avoid quick and easy solutions.

Using these guidelines, students negotiate with their partner to reach consensus on the most important points in the reading(s).

3. Each student pair meets with another pair, and the four students renegotiate their lists to create a comprehensive list of the most important points (Figure 1.15). Once students have agreed on their lists, the group prepares a collaborative summary.

4. The teams of four then meet with another team, read their summaries, and develop a set of agreed-on criteria for powerful summaries (Figure 1.16).

5. Groups share their criteria with the class and reflect on their understanding of the content and what makes a good summary.

6. Students use these criteria to develop individual summaries of new readings they encounter.

Spanish Conquistadors

✓ The conquistadors were courageous.

✓ The conquistadors were extremely cruel to Native Americans.

✓ The conquistadors led expeditions to Central, South, and North America.

✓ The conquistadors wanted gold.

✓ Weapons and European diseases helped the conquistadors conquer the Native Americans.

Figure 1.15   Negotiated List of Important Points

What Makes a Summary Powerful?

---

1. A powerful summary is accurate and thorough.

2. A powerful summary identifies main ideas and important details (unless a reading has a different pattern—then the summary should follow that pattern).

3. A powerful summary is clear and well organized.

4. A powerful summary correctly applies the rules of:
   • punctuation
   • grammar
   • spelling
   • capitalization

Figure 1.16   Criteria for Powerful Summaries

ORGANIZER 1-J: PEER READING

Name: _____

Peer Reading

Section 1 Question(s) (for Reader A)

Section 2 Question(s) (for Reader B)

Section 3 Question(s) (for Reader A)

Section 4 Question(s) (for Reader B)

READ AND RETELL

Overview

Read and Retell provides students with a powerful model that they can use to handle any type of reading effectively. The strategy engages students in pre-reading activities to activate prior knowledge, give students a preview of the text, and help students organize their thoughts as they approach the reading. Students then read and reread the text several times until they can retell it. The process of preparing a written retelling and sharing it in collaborative context deepens their comprehension and retention of the content.

The Strategy in Action

Amira DeKahn and his sixth-grade students have spent the last three weeks studying tales of discovery in their social studies class. In working their way through this unit, students have:

- Gathered in groups to conduct research around "shared books."
- Discussed what they learned with the whole class and the teacher.
- Brainstormed lists of everything they know about discovery and looked for patterns to organize their learning.

Today, Amira is going to introduce the Read and Retell strategy using a reading on Marco Polo and his travels through the Middle and Far East called "Discovering the Unknown East." He begins by telling his students the title of the reading and asking them to help him predict ideas the reading might contain, as well as some of the words or vocabulary they would expect such a passage to use.

When the class has completed its list of predictions, Amira reads the passage aloud and then asks students to read it on their own silently. Amira then shows students how he continues to read and reread the passage until he knows he's ready to write a retelling of the reading in his own words. The students work for 30 minutes or so, reading and writing their own retellings. Figure 1.17 shows a sample of a student's retelling. The lesson

---

Sample Retelling

In 1271 Marco Polo sailed with his father from Venice, Italy to China at the age of fifteen. It took Marco and his father three years to reach China. When they got there, Marco impressed Kublai Khan, the ruler of China. Kublai Khan liked Marco so much that he made him one of his ambassadors. Marco spent the next seventeen years traveling to countries like India and Persia as the ambassador of Kublai Khan. Finally, in 1292, Marco and his father decided to leave China and return to Venice. It took them three years to get back home, and Marco was now 39 years old.

Figure 1.17 Sample Retelling

closes with students sharing and comparing their retellings and discussing the differences they find in one another's work.

As the year goes on, Amira's students show a progressively better grasp of the content of their reading and greater maturity as writers. Every month their writing, as well as their approach to reading, becomes more organized, more insightful, and more vivid.

Why the Strategy Is Beneficial

In 1987, Hazel Brown and Brian Cambourne (a primary school teacher and a researcher at the University of Wollongong in Australia, respectively) pioneered Read and Retell as an effective technique for helping students develop listening, comprehension, and summarizing skills. The strategy they developed moves through five phases:

1. Immersion—students read texts with a common theme (discovery) or genre (tall tales).

2. Prediction—students predict topics, events, and vocabulary likely to appear in the text.

3. Reading—teacher reads the passage; then the student reads the passage.

4. Retelling—each student writes a retelling of the passage.

5. Share and Compare—students share their retellings, noting the differences.

Brown and Cambourne (1987) noted that the use of this strategy improved student comprehension markedly and that, unexpectedly, the strategy also precipitated the following general improvements in students' language skills:

- Students were using a greater variety of new sentence forms and structures in their writing.
- Students were showing greater confidence in their abilities to read, write, and understand.
- Students were making fewer spelling and punctuation errors.

Brown and Cambourne labeled these surprises *linguistic spillovers* to indicate that the effects they found had spilled over far beyond their initial setting. Over time, these student improvements spread beyond the boundaries of the strategy and served to improve students' overall approach to a wide variety of reading and writing tasks.

The reason for this general improvement is twofold: First, by immersing students in a thematic or genre-based unit, students become less likely to see the strategy as isolated or occasional and instead begin to look for connections, relationships, and further applications of their skills and knowledge within the unit. Immersion also provides students with a context that maximizes their opportunities for using prior knowledge. The second reason for linguistic spillover lies in the postreading task of creating a summative retelling. Borne out by a variety of researchers (Doctorow, Wittrock, & Marks, 1978; Morrow, 1983; Taylor & Beach, 1984), when students are given postreading tasks that are generative in nature (e.g., a summary, a retelling, or an interpretation), their levels of retention and comprehension prove significantly higher than when they are asked to complete less-demanding postreading tasks such as multiple choice or end-of-chapter review questions.

What this research indicates is that demanding postreading tasks such as creating a retelling will lead students to reorganize and refine their reading and writing processes. With modeling and practice, students will develop more flexible schemas that can be applied in many linguistic situations. This finding suggests that scaffolding students' reading by reducing task size to a minimum (e.g., multiple choice, matching exercises) may inhibit reading development.

How to Use the Strategy

Use Organizer 1-K, "Read and Retell," on page 44.

Incorporate Read and Retell into your classroom using the following steps:

1. Ask students to use the title, bold print, or pictures of a text to generate a list of predictions in the space provided on Organizer 1-K, "Read and Retell," about the topics, events, and vocabulary likely to appear in the text.

2. Read the text to the students so that they hear adult use of pauses and inflections, which enhance comprehension.

3. Now ask students to read the text silently on their own as many times as necessary until they feel confident they can produce a retelling. Remind students that their goal is to understand, not to memorize verbatim.

4. Challenge students to write, in the space provided on the organizer (or on a separate page), a retelling of the passage without looking back. Students should try to create a text of their own that could help other readers get the same pleasure and understanding they derived from the text.

5. Ask students to team up with a partner and share their retellings, noting differences in their presentation.

6. Encourage students to identify areas where they might have "muddled the meaning," examine differences in their use of paraphrasing,

and discuss what they might "steal" from one another to improve their retellings.

Helping Struggling Readers

The process of previewing the text, the teacher's read-aloud, and the collaborative nature of the Read and Retell strategy all support struggling readers and English language learners. However, these students may run into difficulty with summarizing tasks. Below are four common sources of difficulty, along with solutions for getting struggling readers on track.

1. The student lacks background knowledge. This problem is much less likely to occur if the retelling is embedded in a unit that explores reading texts linked by common theme or genre. For English language learners who need extra help in accessing appropriate background knowledge, use visuals—photos, pictures, symbols—to help them activate what they already know about a topic. Previewing the text for new vocabulary will also help improve their comfort with the reading.

2. The student does not understand the way the text is structured. Immersion in texts linked by a common theme or genre is also useful here. However, text structure may continue to elude students. Graphic Organizers may prove helpful by supplying students with various structures that they can superimpose on their readings to discover which structure fits. This activity can be explored in groups or alone and should revolve around the idea of structure in texts and why it is important. (For more information, see Graphic Organizers, pages 16–31.)

3. The student does not see how to create a retelling from the reading passage. Help students learn to manage this difficulty by modeling the process as extensively as possible. Pull together a small academically mixed group (five to six students) that contains some adept readers and retellers and some who are experiencing more difficulty. Show the group directly how you put together a retelling, emphasizing how you use structural clues within the piece ("See how each paragraph begins with a number word: 'First,' 'Second,' etc."), and paraphrasing ("How might we say this sentence in another way using our own words?"). Then examine another text together and coach the group toward a shared retelling.

Another way to help struggling readers and English language learners create retellings is through pictures. Picture books, including all-pictures, no-words series such as Mercer Mayer's *Frog* series, allow students to see how a retelling fits together visually before they construct a written version. Build retelling skills further by presenting the pictures in the wrong order and asking students to sequence them correctly.

Finally, the narrative retelling strategy known as SPOT (Kuldanek, 1998) has proved effective in helping young learning-disabled readers build their comprehension skills, develop a strong sense of story, and craft quality retellings. After a period of direct instruction in story elements and practice in completing story organizers using multiple texts, introduce SPOT, which works like this:

1. Read two short stories aloud to students. After each story, model the process of retelling using SPOT:

   S—Setting (Describe where the story takes place.)

   P—Problem (What is the problem faced by the character(s)?)

   O—Order (In what order does the action occur?)

   T—Tail End (How does the story end?)

2. Establish an "author's chair" in which students will retell a story out loud to the group or the entire class.

3. Give students time to read and practice retelling their story in small groups using SPOT. Then have each student sit in the author's chair to retell the story out loud. Each retelling lasts no more than five minutes.

4. Encourage students to retell stories using SPOT regularly—in their reading groups and at home. Invite parents into the process by encouraging them to use SPOT to retell stories with their children at home.

If your struggling readers continue to have difficulty, pull them aside for more systematic work on summarizing (see "Collaborative Summarizing," pages 35–36).

4. The student does not know what a good retelling looks like. Students will benefit greatly by seeing and analyzing exemplary retellings. Use superior retellings as models. Provide students with a double-input rubric that both the student and the teacher can use to assess summaries. Figure 1.18 shows a double-input retelling rubric.

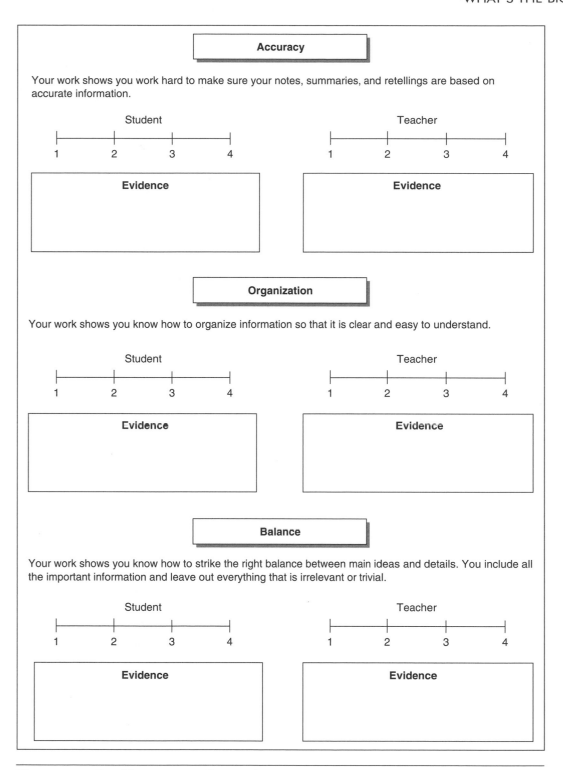

Figure 1.18 Double-Input Retelling Rubric

Source: Copyright © Thoughtful Education Press. Reprinted with permission.

ORGANIZER 1-K: READ AND RETELL

Name: _____

Read and Retell

Title of Reading: _____

Predictions
Before you read the text, use the title of the reading, bold print, or pictures to make a list of predictions about the topics, ideas, events, and words or vocabulary that might appear.

Retelling
After you have read the text, retell what you have read in your own words.

Review
Reread the text. Compare your retelling with the text. Ask yourself:

- Is my retelling accurate?

- Is it well organized?

- Does it show a balance between main ideas and details?

Now, check the box below that best describes your retelling:

☐ Excellent ☐ Good ☐ Okay ☐ Needs Help

SPLIT SCREEN

Overview

The link between image making and high levels of reading comprehension is well documented. The Split Screen strategy teaches students how to capture and represent key information from a text in both visual (symbols and icons) and verbal formats. This "dual coding" of textual information improves students' abilities to remember key information, identify main ideas and relevant details, and summarize texts clearly and concisely.

The Strategy in Action

In response to his state's standards, Lester Grundley helps his students develop proficiency in listening skills and visual literacy with regular use of the Split Screen strategy. Today, for science class, Lester is using Split Screen in conjunction with the class's learning unit on plants by reading *The Reasons for a Flower,* by Ruth Heller (1983).

To begin, Lester reads the book aloud. Students do not take notes; their only job is to listen. Sometimes Lester stops reading to discuss difficult vocabulary words such as *pollen* and *nectar* with his students to make sure that they understand what the words mean. Once Lester has completed reading the book, he reads it again. But this time, he reads it very slowly and with emphasized emotion. During this second reading, students write and sketch their ideas about the text on a form that looks like Figure 1.19.

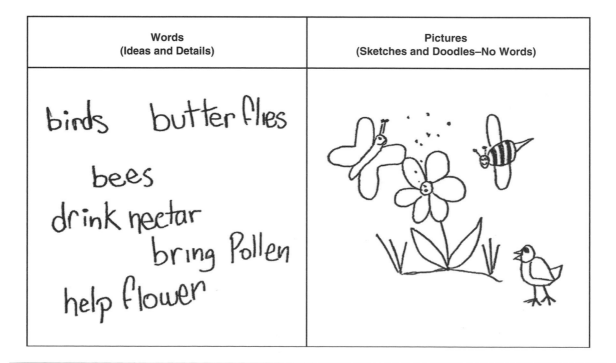

Words (Ideas and Details)	Pictures (Sketches and Doodles–No Words)
birds butterflies bees drink nectar bring Pollen help flower	

Figure 1.19   Split Screen Organizer

At key points in the text, Lester stops reading and asks students to explain their pictures to one another and to identify big ideas and important details with one another. After the second reading, Lester puts students into groups to create posters that tell the story of a flower.

Lester knows that Split Screen builds listening and visualizing skills as well as reading skills. In fact, by this time next month, Lester expects his students to be able to use Split Screen on their own as a tool to help them build visual images of the big ideas in their readings.

Why the Strategy Is Beneficial

Do you ever remember having a hard time with a reading because you couldn't see it? For example, did a passage on how blood flows back and forth between the lungs and the valves and chambers of the heart ever seem impossibly abstract to you? Similarly, much of children's reading difficulty lies in seeing or creating the right images for the content they are studying. Even young children examining something as basic as a bean plant frequently have trouble with the concepts they need to master. Why is sunlight important? Where does the water go? What's the difference between pollen and seeds?

Of course with narrative reading, it is equally important for students to be able to imagine the settings and characters, and to visualize their actions and the events that unfold as a result. Because "seeing" is so integral to deep reading, it should come as no surprise that training students how to develop images while reading enhances their ability to make inferences, form predictions, and recall the content of their reading (Gambrell & Bales, 1986; Sadoski & Paivio, 2004).

Split Screen (adapted from Brownlie, Close, & Wingren, 1990; and Siegel, 1984) is designed to help students see and refine the images they naturally create while reading and listening. The strategy works well for any reading (e.g., science, social studies, literature, math word problems) where images or imagery are important. It also works well as a notemaking procedure: the linguistic element facilitates the skill of separating essential and nonessential information, while the nonlinguistic or visual component helps students summarize and condense information.

How to Use the Strategy

Use Organizer 1-L, "Split Screen," on page 48.

Incorporate the Split Screen strategy into your classroom using the following steps:

1. Read a book or passage aloud while students listen. If the emphasis is on reading rather than listening, ask students to read the passage to themselves. Along the way, identify and discuss difficult vocabulary words.

2. Distribute a Split Screen organizer (Organizer 1-L) to each student. Tell students that you will reread the passage aloud and that they

are to take notes and draw pictures or icons to represent ideas. Encourage sketches over refined scenes.

3. Reread (or have students reread) the passage aloud slowly and with emphasized emotion so that pauses, inflections, and tones are more easily used as cueing devices. Pause during rereading to give students time to create their visualizations on the organizer.

4. Ask students to pair or team up to explain their pictures and to identify big ideas and important details.

5. Have students work together or in pairs to create a product (e.g., a poster, an organizer) that uses both words and pictures to explain and summarize the reading. If the passage describes a sequence or procedure, you might ask students to use a comic book format—one frame for every step in the process.

6. Encourage students to use Split Screen as an independent note-making technique.

Helping Struggling Readers

The ability to visualize information enhances and improves reading. Good readers form mental images in their heads to better understand the material and to improve their ability to recall details later. However, this vital skill can be difficult for many readers, particularly when working with image-laden passages.

Below are some additional ways to adapt the strategy to help struggling image makers:

- **Progressive Imaging:** Begin with younger students by showing them how to create images for words, then sentences, then paragraphs, and then larger passages.

  Word—Can you think of an image that represents "love"?

  Sentence—Can you draw a picture for this sentence: "Alligators have rough, scaly skin, powerful jaws, and long tails"?

- **Icons:** Discuss icons that students are familiar with (No Smoking signs, restroom gender markers) and how they are useful. Show students how icons are helpful as a shorthand tool when taking notes and discuss their value in helping students remember ideas from reading.

- **Visualizing Questions:** The right questions can help guide students to visualize information. For instance, asking students to think of things they know that are rough or scaly can help them imagine what an alligator's skin looks and feels like.

- Use the *Mind's Eye* and *Image Making* strategies on pages 137–142 to help students build visual skills.

ORGANIZER 1-L: SPLIT SCREEN

Name: _____

Split Screen	
Notes About the Text	
Pictures, Symbols, Icons	Big Ideas, Important Details
Pictures, Symbols, Icons	Big Ideas, Important Details
Pictures, Symbols, Icons	Big Ideas, Important Details

A WORD (A SECTION, REALLY) ABOUT FLUENCY

One of the most recent and most important developments in reading research has been the increased emphasis on fluency. Fluency is the ability to read a text:

- accurately
- at an age-appropriate pace
- with proper phrasing (paying attention to punctuation cues and making meaningful text chunks)
- expressively

The difference between a fluent reading and a nonfluent reading is the difference between

Three blind mice. Three blind mice.	and	Three/ blind/ mice. Three/ blind mice.

The fluent reader knows that "Three blind mice" represents a meaningful chunk of text and puts the pause between the two repeating chunks. The reader who lacks fluency sees a list of individual words and labors through each word individually. In this case, when the nonfluent reader sees the word *Three* for the second time, he recognizes it and, liberated from having to sound it out, rushes through it, thus missing the one break he should have made while making inappropriate breaks everywhere else.

A recent large-scale study conducted by the National Assessment of Educational Progress (2003) found that almost one-half (44%) of fourth graders in the United States struggle with fluency. This is bad news for more than one reason. Obviously, readers' struggles in fluency are trouble in and of themselves. When students have continued difficulty reading texts accurately, quickly, and well, they become frustrated readers, and their motivation to "take the plunge" into new texts decreases. What's more, fluency is linked inextricably to comprehension. Pikulski and Chard (2005) call fluency "the bridge between decoding and reading comprehension," while Rasinski, Blachowicz, and Lems (2006) identify fluency as "a necessary precondition for good comprehension" (xi). It should come as no surprise, then, that the NAEP study found that the students with low fluency also tended to have among the lowest ability in comprehension. The reasons behind the fluency-comprehension link are fairly obvious: Nonfluent readers must devote the great majority of their mind's attention to reading individual words; their ability to attend to larger units—sentences, paragraphs, characters, ideas—is therefore compromised.

Now that we have the bad news, here's the good news. The research also shows that reading fluently is a highly teachable skill. As Vaughn and

Linan-Thompson (2004) tell us, "It is natural for beginning students to read slowly and laboriously at first. As they rehearse passages, they will get more and more comfortable reading words quickly" (p. 51). Even better news can be found in the results of fluency instruction, especially when applied to our most challenged readers. For example, fourth-grade teacher Lorraine Griffith (Griffith & Rasinski, 2004) found that in her classroom, strategies such as Readers' Theater and other forms of oral reading instruction produced an average annual gain of three grade levels in achievement among her lowest-achieving Title I students.

So, Why Is This Section on Fluency Here?

The strategies found in the earlier part of this chapter help students separate critical from less relevant information in the texts they read. They develop students' abilities to figure out how texts are structured, and they teach students how to compress their emerging understanding into meaningful retellings. In a word, these strategies emphasize deep *comprehension*.

We have seen how comprehension is tied to—and even depends on—fluency. This means that many students' struggles with understanding what they read are actually struggles with fluency. In the remainder of this section, we provide a set of tips and strategies for helping students develop the often-neglected skill of fluent reading. One note before we launch into the tips: You'll notice that we have not incorporated sustained silent reading into our list of suggestions. Although independent reading is clearly beneficial on many fronts, new research (including the 2000 National Reading Panel Report) shows that when it comes to fluency, more direct forms of instruction that include oral repetition produce the greatest gains.

Seven Tips for Increasing Students' Fluency

Tip One: Make time for reading aloud. Reading aloud is about more than fostering the love of stories. Reading aloud is critical to the development of fluency among young and developing readers, who benefit from hearing regularly how fluent reading sounds and how adult readers articulate and inflect their voices while reading texts. But readers who struggle with fluency need to do more than listen to adult reading; they need to learn how to imitate it by reading the same text out loud and on their own, often several times. One simple and highly effective read-aloud strategy that improves students' speed, accuracy, and expression is known as Listen-Follow-Read, or LFR. LFR works like this:

1. Distribute copies of a brief text or excerpt (no more than 250 words) to a student or small group of students.

2. Read the text aloud at a steady pace. (Remember, you want students to match your reading, so be careful not to go too fast or too slow.) Be sure to put some expression in your reading so students can hear the questions, exclamations, pauses, etc. Ask students to listen carefully to how your reading sounds.

3. Read the text aloud again. This time, students should follow along, pointing to each word in the printed text as you read it.

4. Have the student(s) read the text aloud back to you. Each student should read separately and should attempt to duplicate the rate and expression of your reading.

5. Allow struggling students to read the text again.

Aside from L-F-R, there are a number of other effective read-aloud strategies that improve students' fluency.

Choral Reading means reading aloud together as a group. Begin by distributing a short text to all of your students. Model a fluent reading, and then read the text a second time, this time encouraging students to join in by reading aloud with you as they recognize words on the page. Over the course of the next few days, conduct two or three more choral readings of the same text. Then have students read the text independently.

This technique works especially well when it revolves around a text with a predictable narrative pattern or a sing-song style. Once students pick up the pattern or rhythm of the text, they will be more enticed to join in the choral reading.

Echo Reading is similar to Choral Reading but can be used for slightly longer texts because it breaks the modeling and read-aloud sessions into two-to-four-sentence sections. After reading two to four sentences of the text, have students try to imitate you by reading the same sentences aloud. Work through the remainder of the text two to four sentences at a time, first by conducting a fluent reading of the sentences and then by having students attempt to match your rate and articulation.

Partner Reading puts students into pairs who work together to read a text aloud, paragraph by paragraph or section by section. Typically, Partner Reading pairs a more-fluent reader with a less-fluent reader. The more-fluent reader provides a model for the less-fluent reader by reading the paragraph first. Then the less-fluent reader reads the same paragraph. If the less-fluent reader struggles, the more-fluent reader should be encouraged to help by rereading difficult sections of the paragraph until the less-fluent reader can read the paragraph fluently. When using Partner Reading in this way—pairing a more-fluent with a less-fluent reader—make sure that the text you select is at an appropriate level for the weaker reader. Of course, with a technique like this, a high level of sensitivity is in order. Make sure that partners know what a productive partnership looks and sounds like. Use modeling to show students how to praise efforts and successes. Remind students that partners should always be encouraging and that their interactions should be respectful and positive.

You can also use Partner Reading to enhance instructional activities in which you—the teacher—have already provided a model of a fluent reading. After your reading, students can work together as partners to help each other reread the same passage aloud. For this variation on Partner Reading, reading partners should be evenly matched rather than broken into pairs of more-fluent and less-fluent readers.

With any read-aloud strategy that involves teacher modeling, it is a good idea to call attention, at least periodically, to why you're reading certain parts of a text in a particular way. For example:

> Were you able to hear how my voice changed when I read the sentence "How could a soccer-playing Dalmatian be real?" My voice went up a little bit at the end of the sentence because it's a question—you can tell by the question mark at the end. See? [The teacher has the students point to the question mark in the reading.] When we read questions, our voices change to show that someone is asking something. Here, listen to the difference between how the sentence with the question mark sounds when compared to the next sentence, which ends with a period . . .

Of course, too much interruption for teacher talk disrupts the flow of the text, so pick your spots.

Last but not least, in making time for reading aloud, try to incorporate as many models of fluent readings as possible into your classroom. Keep in mind that nearly all major publishers—including children's publishers—have committed a large number of titles to audio (tape, CD, downloadable MP3s), thereby giving you and your students the chance to listen to actors, professional readers, and other masters of expression work their magic on texts. Don't be afraid to invite parents, other teachers, and older students into your classroom to read. The more models students can use to develop their fluency and their own unique style as readers, the better.

Tip Two: Help students make the connection between speaking and reading. Readers who lack fluency often read aloud in a monotone, missing natural pauses and failing to capture any of the expressiveness of language. In their wonderfully concise *Guided Reading Coaching Tool*, teachers Daphne Byrd and Polly Westfall (2002) recommend that teachers help students overcome this kind of expressionless reading through fluency coaching. Fluency coaching helps students take what they know naturally about expression from their everyday lives as speakers and apply that knowledge to reading. Byrd and Westfall offer six simple prompts that teachers can use to coach their students toward greater fluency:

- Read the text for me and point to the words.
- Read it now without using your finger. Did your eyes have any trouble keeping their place on the page?
- Read the text again, but now try to read it as if you are talking.
- Point to the important punctuation marks that show you when to slow down.
- What should your voice do when you see a comma, a period, a question mark, or an exclamation mark?
- Listen to my voice as I read the next sentence. Am I reading at a fluent pace? Now, you try it. (From "Fluency Coaching," in Byrd & Westfall [2002].)

Tip Three: Capitalize on the motivational power of "You're on in five minutes!" Nowhere is fluency more important than on the tens of thousands of stages and billions of movie and television screens across the globe. To do their work, actors read and reread and reread their lines, getting each word exactly right and finding those places nestled among the words where a shout or a whisper or a waver of the voice can create a new level of meaning.

Readers' Theater is a strategy that uses the dynamic of dramatic performance to motivate students to read and reread texts until they know they can "nail" them for an audience. Students assume the roles of characters from a story or play and work cooperatively to help one another until they can all read their lines fluently. Students also help one another commit their lines to memory and then rehearse together. Finally, they perform their play in front of an audience, usually of other class members, although other classes and parents may also be invited.

Readers' Theater can also be pared down in scope without sacrificing the motivational core of performance that lies at its heart. Students may be asked to read a few lines of dialogue expressively without having to get up from their desks or concern themselves with memorizing the lines.

Tip Four: Help students get control over difficult or "trip-up" words before reading. In any text, certain words are more likely to trip up students than other words, whether by virtue of their rarity, length, or relative strangeness to students. Help students overcome the challenge of difficult words in a text by identifying and helping students master them beforehand. Use a Vocabulary strategy such as See It, Say It, Show It, Store It (see pages 101–102) or Word Walls (page 97) before reading. This way, students will already be comfortable and familiar with difficult words when they encounter them in the text. Or, try using a strategy such as Inductive Learning (page 123), which gives students the opportunity to define important words before reading, explore the relationships among the words by putting them into labeled groups, and use their groups of words to make a set of predictions about the text.

Another way to help students gain control over difficult words before reading is to use the technique called Flashlight. Flashlight is easy to implement and highly engaging for students. It focuses on small units of text (usually only a few sentences), allowing students to pre-identify and master difficult words and then read them aloud, fluently and in context. To use Flashlight, follow these five steps:

1. Write two to five potentially difficult vocabulary words from a short reading (no more than a page) on the board or on a piece of poster paper.

2. Turn off the lights. Spotlight each word one at a time using a flashlight. As you point to each word, say it out loud, along with a brief definition. Have students repeat the pronunciation and definition several times.

3. Turn the lights back on and provide students with a copy of the brief reading that contains the words you spotlighted.

4. Allow students to work in small groups to practice reading the passage aloud.

5. Conduct a Choral Reading in which you and the students read the text aloud together.

Tip Five: Frontload comprehension. Fluency serves as a bridge to comprehension, which means that a lack of fluency is an impediment to comprehension. But there may also be some instructional advantages to putting comprehension first—before fluency. Why? Think of it this way: If students already understand a text before they read it, both the teacher and student have increased their capacity to focus on fluency when it comes time to actually read.

To get a better understanding of how this frontloading works, take a look at the steps in the strategy known as Do You Hear What I Hear? (page 142). Notice in these steps how much has happened before students read the actual text. Before they ever lay eyes on the reading, students have listened to it twice, made notes about it, retold it to a partner, coached their partner to another retelling, and formulated some initial responses to the guiding questions. When the text finally arrives, students already understand it. With comprehension largely out of the way, the reading of the text presents a wonderful opportunity to concentrate on fluent expression.

A similar example is the Split Screen strategy found in this chapter (pages 45–47). During Split Screen, students listen to a text multiple times, create notes and sketches to represent big ideas, and discuss their sketches and big ideas, all before reading the text themselves.

Tip Six: Build fluency into reading instruction. It doesn't take the research community to tell us that too much focus on reading skills can adversely affect students' attitudes toward literature and reading. None of the authors of this book has ever seen students leaning forward in their seats, their eyes wide with wonder, waiting in anticipation for the next timed reading activity. Good reading instruction incorporates skills but does not sacrifice the joys of reading to the skills. So here are two more pieces of good news as you work to build students' fluency. First, reading instruction in general and, more specifically, every single strategy in this book can easily be modified to include reading aloud and to scaffold fluency. For example, Literature Circles (pages 178–184) can serve as a group fluency-building technique, with students in their reading clubs taking time to read aloud sections of the text that they liked (a natural motivator). Meanwhile the teacher and other students in the reading club can work as fluency coaches. Now, here's the second piece of good news: second- and third-grade teachers need to spend only 20 minutes on fluency-related activities a day for students to reap the significant benefits associated with fluency development (Vaughn & Linan-Thompson, 2004).

Tip Seven: Keep assessment simple. Assessing students' fluency need not be some protracted process. The easiest way to assess fluency is to listen to your students read aloud. Students who are struggling with fluency will sound choppy or read very slowly or adopt a monotone voice. More formal assessments, including timed reading, should also be conducted but, once again, keep things simple. For example, Armbruster, Lehr, and Osborn (2003) suggest basing more formal assessment of fluency on three factors:

- Is the student reading at an appropriate rate?
- Is the student able to read orally with expression?
- Is the student able to comprehend what he or she reads orally?

2

From Note Taking to "Notemaking"

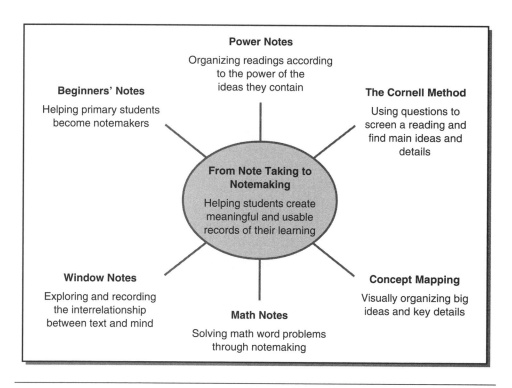

Figure 2.1   Chapter Overview: Advance Organizer

> *"I want my notes to be tools for thinking."*
>
> —Lucy Calkins, *Living Between the Lines*

WHY ARE NOTES SO IMPORTANT?

Ask the average teacher, the average parent, the average American, "Is note taking an important skill?" and they will probably answer "Yes" all the way down the line. Most would probably say they want it taught in schools, they want it to be an important part of the curriculum, and they want students to become proficient in taking notes.

Despite the ever-increasing technological applications used in classrooms today, taking notes, by hand, with pen and paper, still remains a significant part of students' academic experience (Kobayashi, 2006). Marzano, Pickering, and Pollock (2001) have found note taking to be one of the most powerful skills students can cultivate for academic success, and it's easy to see why. After all, consider for a moment what you can't do if you can't take notes:

1. You can't conduct research effectively.

2. You can't keep track of the main ideas and important details in your textbook.

3. You can't remember in May what you read and learned in October.

4. You can't track themes, patterns, and ideas that run through a month or a year.

5. You can't plan effectively for long-range projects.

6. You can't practice condensing and compacting information and deciphering what is and is not important in what you read.

7. You can't collect ideas from different sources and perspectives and see how they relate.

8. You can't keep track of the thoughts and questions that occur to you as you read.

9. You can't personalize your learning, keep a record of what it means to you, or return to ideas and questions you've had before and use them as sources for new books to read, new projects to pursue, or new pieces to write.

10. Eventually, maybe not today or tomorrow, but sometime in middle or high school, in college, or on your first or your third job, you won't be able to learn something as well as someone who knows how to take good notes.

FOUND PETS, KITCHEN SINKS, AND NOTES

As important as notes are to many people, notes and notebooks are a bit like found pets and kitchen sinks: Lots of people think they're a good idea, but it's hard to find anyone who wants to care for them. Many students might like to buy new notebooks and decorate them, but few enjoy taking care of what's inside them. Similarly, many adults view note taking as part of the drudgery of learning, associating it with the hours they lost copying from the board, paraphrasing articles from an encyclopedia, and scurrying their pens over lined paper trying to catch up to a professor's last words. Many teachers dislike teaching note taking as well. In fact, many teachers see teaching the skill as a struggle whose only joy is in seeing student papers that are neat and organized. All of this brings us back to where we started: Almost everyone agrees notes are an essential but repetitive and routine task. But what if everyone's wrong? What if taking notes is a deep and dynamic form of thinking? What if taking notes is a personal and creative act?

Note Taking to "Notemaking"

Making notes is a deeply creative act of learning. If this simple fact is difficult for most people to see—from the student who likes the notebook's colorful cover but not its insides, to the adult remembering impossibly long lectures with professors who spoke like machines guns, to the teacher feeling that vague sense of dread while preparing to teach students how to take notes—it is probably because they have never made notes. All of them have spent hours upon hours "note taking." "Notemaking" is something else entirely. Let's listen to three people who know the difference between note taking and notemaking (Figure 2.2).

"How could anyone ever get bored with notemaking? There are so many different ways to make notes. And then there's figuring out which way works best in which situation. We talk about it all year long."

Stan Silverman
Third-Grade Teacher

"I begin the year with notemaking. Notes are what young children write. They make these little marks on the page, and when you ask them what they mean, they tell you worlds. Worlds in just a little mark or scribble."

Maddy Lefferts
Primary-School Teacher

"Without my notebooks, I'd be lost. My whole year, everything I learned, is in there. Notes help me a lot. We have to create a one-act play about people in the Depression. My group was using the textbook plus some sources from the library to get ready. So I suggested to my group that we make Concept Maps to keep track of our ideas. It's great—we put 'Depression' in the middle, and the ideas just kept coming. Soon, our whole project was organized for us."

Yan Huo
Fifth-Grade Student

Figure 2.2   Three People Describe Notemaking

Maddy, Stan, and Yan have very different ideas about notes from the people we described earlier. Maddy, Stan, and Yan understand there are different noting techniques that make reading more meaningful. They know how notes can and should produce a personal, abbreviated text that mirrors the big ideas in the texts they read. No, Maddy, Stan, and Yan do not believe in taking notes; they believe in *making* them.

In her recent book, *Active Literacy Across the Curriculum*, Heidi Hayes Jacobs (2006) provides us with a precise and practical way of thinking about the distinction between note taking (which Jacobs calls copying) and notemaking (which Jacobs calls creative note taking). According to Jacobs, there are four forms of creative notes that spur deep learning, deep thinking, and deep reading: (1) notes that ask students to gather and categorize information; (2) notes that allow students to make comments and ask questions; (3) notes that identify key relationships using visual organizers; and (4) notes that outline or sequence sets of information.

Now that we have a better sense of what notemaking is, the question becomes: Why is it important? Notemaking is an extremely important skill for three reasons:

1. Through the act of notemaking, students create a shorter, more personal record of their own learning to which they can return to recall, rehearse, and revisit yesterday's learning.

2. The very act of notemaking requires students to consider a text more deeply in elaborating and developing its personal and literal meanings.

3. The process of notemaking is a far more appropriate method of practicing and applying comprehension skills than traditional worksheets or after-chapter questions.

In this chapter, we describe a variety of notemaking tools that students can use to separate the significant from the insignificant, deepen meaning, and build a record of learning.

Before we lay out these specific tools, let's take a moment to explore how students learn notemaking tools in general. Notemaking tools are best acquired through a three-step learning cycle, described in Figure 2.3 below.

Step One	Step Two	Step Three
The teacher models the process by thinking aloud, letting students see how her mind works as she approaches the task.	The teacher asks students to practice using a notemaking tool on texts they have selected to fit their own interests or a common text that is part of their current study. As the students work, the teacher circulates, observing and coaching students and helping them adapt the strategies to their own situation and their own personal style.	The teacher regularly pulls the whole class together to discuss their adaptations and the problems they faced while trying to apply the techniques to their own reading.
How it sounds in the classroom: *"First, I skim the passage, trying to get a general sense of what kinds of questions the text is trying to answer. So when I come to a subheading like this, I try to rewrite it as a question."*	**How it sounds in the classroom:** *"You know, I often have trouble coming up with good questions as I read or skim my texts, so here's a little trick I use . . ."*	**How it sounds in the classroom:** *"In the beginning I was having trouble finding out what was really important. Then I remembered what you showed us about drawing our ideas. I found that if I sketched out my ideas first, it helped me see what was really important."*

Figure 2.3   Three-Step Learning Cycle for Notemaking

By moving back and forth between modeling, practice, coaching, and discussions of application, the teacher helps students adjust and adapt particular notemaking tools to their own personal styles and to the demands of different texts and research situations.

In the following pages, six teachers introduce their favorite notemaking tools and discuss how they use these tools to help their students become successful notemakers. This chapter of the book is similar to the previous one in that each notemaking tool is divided into five sections: Overview, The Notemaking Tool in Action, Why the Notemaking Tool is Beneficial, How to Use the Notemaking Tool, and Helping Struggling Notemakers. In the second of these five sections, The Notemaking Tool in Action, however, each teacher speaks in the first person about his or her experiences with the notemaking tool, while sample student notes appear with each teacher's discussion.

The six notemaking tools discussed are:

Beginners' Notes, which helps our youngest students learn to create simple notes.

Power Notes, which assists students in organizing their notes, from the main idea to specific details.

The Cornell Method, which calls for students to create questions about a reading, then find details and main ideas that answer the questions.

Concept Mapping, which helps students group information and see connections.

Math Notes, which helps students analyze word problems and break them down into manageable "chunks" before they begin solving them.

Window Notes, which provides students with a simple and powerful framework for collecting facts, asking questions, and expressing their own thoughts and feelings about what they are reading.

BEGINNERS' NOTES

Overview

This strategy puts young students on the path to effective notemaking, a skill they'll need throughout their academic careers. Beginners' Notes allows students to use both visual and verbal representations and follows a progressive structure that teaches students how to make different kinds of notes to organize different kinds of information. The strategy culminates in a group project that draws on all the notemaking skills students have learned.

The Notemaking Tool in Action

Mary Daley says that students need to learn how to make notes early, as part of their learning, not as an isolated skill. Here's how she does it with her primary students:

"In September, I introduce my students to notemaking by discussing the ways people make memories. Students talk about diaries, photographs, videos, and online photo albums. Then I explain that notemaking also is a way to make memories. To demonstrate this, I ask students at the end of the day to review what they learned and what they did, and to use words and pictures to record and list what they remember. Students share their lists with their parents to see how the notes have helped them make memories. For the rest of September, we focus on making simple lists. Often, we'll brainstorm lists together: colors, toys, animals, holidays, etc. During brainstorming, I write students' ideas on the board, or I draw a picture of the idea. Sometimes, we also look for ways to group our notes, such as circling all the winter holidays or putting a star next to all the animals that are pets.

"By October, students are making their own lists, and that means it's time to teach them how to find notes in their reading. For example, as they read stories and books, they list things like the places Pooh goes, the ways Frances shows she loves her little sister, or the types of foods that the pilgrims ate at the first Thanksgiving. Again, we often look for ways to group the information they list. By the end of the month, students can usually make fairly comprehensive lists from their reading.

"By November, we've already talked quite a bit about how information can be grouped, so now students are ready to learn how to systematically organize information using concept webs. While creating basic webs with my students on topics such as what makes a good friend, I see lightbulbs lighting up in their heads. Suddenly, they get it—they see how lots of information can be chunked. Sometimes, students ask if they can go back to old lists and make concept webs out of those.

"Once students are comfortable making simple webs, we use what we've learned for a whole-class investigation. This year, we took a field trip to the local maritime museum. To prepare for our trip, I read two books about the seaside, and we brainstormed and listed things we could investigate at the museum. Figure 2.4 shows the results of our brainstorming, which we organized into a set of notes incorporating words and pictures.

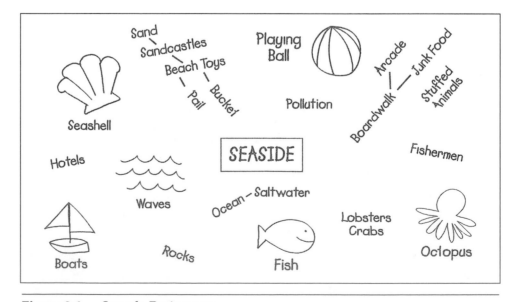

Figure 2.4　Sample Brainstorm

Source: Copyright © Thoughtful Education Press. Reprinted with permission.

"Students formed groups and used their notes to create concept webs as I walked around the room and helped them. From the webs the groups created, the class came up with three topics for investigation: animals at the seaside, businesses at the seaside, and people at the seaside. Each group took notes on one of these topics. When we got back, the groups looked through their notes to find as much information as they could about their topics. Each group created a collage of words, drawings, and clippings from the museum pamphlets. They had a great time, and so did I!"

Why the Notemaking Tool Is Beneficial

Notemaking means teaching students to create a record of their learning so they can look back, remember, and use what they know. Although study skills, including notemaking, have traditionally been reserved for older students, the primary and early elementary grades are the ideal time to begin building notemaking skills, which will become essential to student success in higher grades.

Based on Bobbi Fisher's (1995) work with primary students, Beginners' Notes follows a progressive structure that allows students to build skills over several months and then apply their new skills to an inquiry-based project. The notes that students create need not be too detailed and can include both simple words and pictures. As they practice and develop their skills of listing, finding information in books, making concept webs, and using notes for research, students continually share ideas with partners. This collaboration helps students get better at recognizing what important information looks like.

Students' ability to become novice notemakers depends a great deal on their prior knowledge of the subject they are studying. For example, many students, after developing basic skills, feel comfortable making notes about clothing or a book about dogs but will not have the knowledge base to make notes on Native Americans if the topic is new to them. However, if the teacher directs and focuses a brainstorming activity, reads a book aloud, and shows a cartoon about Native American life, students will develop the knowledge needed to create and organize notes. Incorporating notes into a learning unit in this manner also will help students gain confidence in their ability to make notes.

How to Use the Notemaking Tool

Beginners' Notes follows a progressive plan to build student competence in notemaking through slow and gradual steps. Incorporate the tool into your classroom using these suggested steps:

Lists (September)

1. Introduce notemaking by explaining to students that they are going to "make memories."

2. Challenge students to list all the things they can think of for a category or topic. Direct the brainstorming and write each idea on the board for students to see and include on their own lists.

3. Encourage students to draw simple pictures as well as to use words. Include pictures on the board so students feel comfortable sketching ideas. Label sketches to foster vocabulary development.

4. After generating a list, work with students to find ways to identify related items (e.g., a list of foods can be broken into vegetables, meats, dessert foods). Have students record the relationships as you write them on the board.

Notes from Books (October)

1. Read a book aloud to the class.

2. Lead students in making notes on different kinds of information contained in the book (e.g., buildings in a community, people in a community, things in a community).

3. Ask students to make notes individually as you write on the board. Over time, students should begin to make notes on their own or in groups, using simple picture books.

4. Ask students to share notes in groups to help them fill in the gaps and identify missing information from their notes.

Concept Webs (November)

1. Introduce students to concept webs by webbing a simple, controlled topic such as seasons. (If you need help with this step, see Concept Mapping, page 72.) Explain that webs let us see how information can be organized.

2. Move toward webbing broader topics, using Organizer 2-B, "Concept Map," on page 75, or a simplified version. Here are two ideas for using concept webs:

   • Tell the class the topic is clothes. Ask students to list different types of clothing, which you or a student can write on one side of the board. When the class reaches a dead end, ask a question such as, Why do people wear clothes when other animals don't? Ideas about warmth, modesty, and not having any fur or feathers may arise. You or a student can write these ideas on another section of the board. This can be continued for a number of topics.

   • Another possibility is to scatter ideas from the brainstorm randomly across the board and then draw lines to connect related ideas (e.g., for a brainstorm on food, dessert foods could be connected with yellow lines, meats with white lines). Students can then turn these into more comprehensive webs using the organizer.

Culminating Projects (when students are ready)

1. Provide questions or a topic organizer to help students see large categories (e.g., What did you learn about the colonists? Native Americans? The first Thanksgiving?) that they will use to structure their group project.

2. Ask students to organize ideas from one set of notes or combine and organize several sets. Advise group members to help one another fit information into the categories and fill gaps in their notes.

3. Have students use the newly organized notes to complete a group project such as a collage, poster, skit, or newspaper.

4. As students' skills develop, guide them in using more advanced notemaking techniques (e.g., bullets, numbering, Power Notes, Concept Mapping [page 72] to organize their learning).

Helping Struggling Notemakers

Because of its progressive skill-by-skill structure, Beginners' Notes is an excellent strategy to use with struggling readers and English language learners at various grade levels. Here are some suggestions for helping students who need further help:

Retelling: Ask a student who is struggling with identifying what to draw or write down to orally retell what happened in a story or picture book before taking his or her notes.

Questions: Overly detailed or random notes can be focused with questions. Before reading a book about tigers, for example, tell students you want them to take notes afterward. Ask them to concentrate on three questions: What do tigers look like? What do tigers eat? Where do tigers live? Or, you may ask students what they want to learn about tigers and choose a few of their questions to focus on before reading.

Cooperative Learning: Have timid or confused notemakers work in groups while making notes or during an encompassing project. Seeing the work of others helps struggling students notice what details they may have missed or included mistakenly.

POWER NOTES

Overview

Power Notes builds and reinforces students' skills in identifying the differences between main ideas and supporting details. Students learn a basic system for organizing information according to the specificity of the information in a particular passage or text. The strategy follows a traditional outline format but simplifies it by converting the complex Roman numeral system into four "powers," or levels of specificity, numbered 1, 2, 3, and 4.

The Notemaking Tool in Action

Fourth-grade teacher Jim Aacker teaches his students how to become independent users of Power Notes.

"I like to introduce Power Notes to my students using basic concepts. For example, I usually teach the technique to students using something like sports as a model. After I write *sports* on the board, I say, 'Sports is our topic. What are some sports?' The kids rattle off a half dozen sports and I write them on the board, explaining that each one is a Power 1 topic called *types of sports*. Then we look at a specific sport such as *baseball*, and I ask students for some ideas that would fit under that sport. After I get a number of responses, such as *bat*, *ball*, *glove*, I write them beneath *baseball*, and so on, until we have a complete set of Power Notes for sports. By January, my students are creating elaborate Roman numeral outlines—without Roman numerals."

Figure 2.5 below shows a set of Power Notes for a reading on Native American clothes created by a student named Janelle.

Reading Passage:	Student's Power Notes:

While Native Americans wore highly decorated clothes for special occasions, they usually wore simple clothes for everyday use. They designed their clothes to suit their climate, from rainforests to deserts, where they wore clothes as a way to keep cool. Native Americans' clothes were also designed to be loose so that they could move more easily. Men usually wore shirts, loincloths, leggings, and tunics. Women wore skirts and dresses.	Topic: Native American Clothes
	
	1. Everyday clothes
	  2. Dressed to suit climate
	    3. rain forest
	    3. desert
	      4. wore very little, to keep cool
	  2. Clothes fit loosely for movement
	    3. men wore
	      4. loincloth
	      4. shirt
	      4. tunic
	      4. leggings
	    3. Women wore
	      4. skirts
	      4. dresses

Often, people wonder how Native Americans made all their clothes. Native Americans used the things around them to make their clothes. From animals, they used skin for cloth, sinews to make thread, and bones as needles. They also wove cloth from special kinds of plants . . .	1. How they were made
	  2. From things around them
	    3. Animals
	      4. skin for cloth
	      4. sinews for threads
	      4. bones for needles
	    3. Plants
	      4. wove cloth from

Figure 2.5   Janelle's Power Notes

Why the Notemaking Tool Is Beneficial

Power Notes (Sparks, 1982) teaches students the essential skills of extracting and discriminating between main ideas and the details that support them. By breaking down textual information into various levels, or "powers," of specificity, students produce a set of highly organized notes. Unlike traditional Roman numeral outlining, which requires students to remember a complicated organizational system, Power Notes is simple for students to learn and use: the only components students must remember are the numbers 1, 2, 3, and 4.

In a set of Power Notes, the ideas that most closely connect to the topic of a reading are the Power 1 ideas, or the main ideas. Powers 2, 3, and 4 designate information that is increasingly specific. For instance, if the topic of a passage is outer space, a set of simple Power Notes might look like Figure 2.6.

Topic: Outer Space

Power 1: Solar systems
    Power 2: Planets
        Power 3: Earth
            Mars
            Venus
            Power 4: Revolve around stars
                Usually have moons
                Don't give off light

    Power 2: Stars
        Power 3: Sun
            North Star
        Power 4: Give off light
            Give off heat
            Very large

Figure 2.6   Power Notes on Outer Space

Because Power Notes produces such a highly organized set of information, it is an ideal method for teaching students how to bring structure to their reading, as well as to their writing tasks and study sessions.

How to Use the Notemaking Tool

Incorporate Power Notes into your classroom using the following steps:

1. Model Power Notes with your students, starting with well-known topics that have clear structures. You may begin by showing students an example such as the one on outer space, above.

2. Clarify the concept of powers by adding more levels with students. For instance, as new items such as "asteroids" and "black holes" are generated, ask students to determine which power they belong to and to explain why.

3. To further model the strategy, ask students to generate and organize sets of Power Notes as a class. Use well-known topics such as games, hobbies, movies, seasons, etc., and write class-generated Power Notes on the board (see Figure 2.7 for an example).

4. Move students to using Power Notes on their own as a way of organizing their reading.

Topic: Food
1. Mexican food
1. Fast food
1. Italian food
   2. Pasta
      3. Lasagna
      3. Spaghetti
      3. Ravioli
         4. Meat ravioli
         4. Cheese ravioli

Figure 2.7   Introducing Power Notes Using Well-Known Topics

Helping Struggling Notemakers

The most difficult aspect students encounter in learning Power Notes is learning how to organize information according to the tool's structure. The following suggestions from Santa, Havens, and Maycumber (1996) can help struggling notemakers overcome this difficulty:

1. Ask students to arrange index cards on which you have written Power 1, 2, 3, and 4 words. Or, give each student in a group a single card and ask them to physically arrange themselves into 1, 2, 3, and 4 ideas.

2. Practice selective underlining with students by showing them how to underline key words and ideas and to assign each underline a power on the basis of its relationship to the main idea.

3. Place a selected portion of text on an overhead. Model the process of creating Power Notes using Think Alouds (explaining your thinking process as you model the tool), selective underlining, and text marking.

4. Start with simple 1 and 2 power structures. Add 3 and 4 ideas as students' skills become more sophisticated. As skills develop, have students use their Power Notes to create written or spoken paraphrases of the original text.

5. Use class challenges in which you put two blank Power Notes structures on the board, provide a topic, and ask teams to compete against each other by filling in the blanks as quickly as possible.

THE CORNELL METHOD

Overview

The Cornell Method is a time-tested notemaking procedure that helps students use questions to break down a reading into main ideas and supporting details. Creating notes according to the Cornell Method has the added benefit of giving students a ready-made study sheet to review key content and prepare for tests.

The Notemaking Tool in Action

Roger Dixon, a fifth-grade teacher, says he's always been partial to the Cornell Method, a simple way of reinforcing good reading and study skills.

"In my class, first we skim the text to get a sense of the topics and subtopics. Then we convert these into questions. For example, if the heading says 'Parts of the Circulatory System,' we write, 'What are the parts of the circulatory system?' in the left-hand column of the organizer (see Figure 2.8). Then we read the passage and jot down the details and main ideas that answer our questions in the corresponding columns. I make sure that students are just writing down words and phrases—never sentences and never straight copying.

Parts of the Circulatory System		
Questions	**Details**	**Main Idea**
What are the parts of the circulatory system?	Heart—pump Arteries—carry blood out Veins—bring blood back Blood—nourishes body, contains oxygen	All parts work together to nourish body

Figure 2.8   Sample of the Cornell Method Notemaking Tool

"When it comes time to study, the students just cover up the main idea and supporting details columns and there are the questions they need to know for the test, along with the answers. When students are unsure, they peek at the answers they created for themselves. After students have practiced answering the questions without looking at their notes, they put a check mark (✓) next to the question if they know the answer, a question mark (?) if they have a question about it, and an asterisk (*) if they need more review."

Why the Notemaking Tool Is Beneficial

The main idea/detail format of the Cornell Method (Pauk, 1974) is especially effective with expository texts in which the information is fairly well organized and the goal is for students to master the information. The Cornell Method organizer also makes a great tool for studying and reviewing. By adapting the strategy to include an extra column for questions, as Roger Dixon did above, students learn how to direct their search for specific information in a text.

How to Use the Notemaking Tool

Use Organizer 2-A, "Cornell Method," on page 71.

Incorporate the Cornell Method into your classroom using the following steps:

1. Guide students in surveying the text for topics and subtopics.

2. Show students how to convert topics and subtopics into questions. Have students write their questions in the Questions column of Organizer 2-A, "Cornell Method."

3. Have students read the text and stop periodically to collect details and main ideas that answer the corresponding questions.

4. When they have completed a full set of notes, have students review their notes.

5. Ask students to cover up the details and main-idea columns and to answer each question in their own words.

6. After students have reviewed their notes, allow them to assess their understanding using the following reader's punctuation:

   ✓ I know this.

   ? I have a question about this.

   * I need to review this more.

7. Once students have taken a test or applied their learning to a synthesis task, have them reflect on the process. You can do this with questions such as: How well did you do on your test? Did the Cornell Method help you? What did you do to learn the material?

For example, Darlene Freeman asked students in her third-grade class to reflect on the process by restating all they did to prepare for the test. Darlene kept track of the responses on the board:

1. We figured out how the author organized the text.

2. We identified critical questions.

3. We scanned the text for main ideas and details.

4. We studied our notes by testing ourselves.

5. We predicted the types of questions that would probably be asked on the test.

After listing the students' reflections, Darlene asked them what ideas they would use to study for their next test.

Helping Struggling Notemakers

If students have difficulty identifying main ideas and important details, practice the Main Idea strategy to help students learn how to find key words, main ideas, and supporting details (see Main Idea, pages 5–14). Take a good look at the "Helping Struggling Readers" section of Main Idea, which provides specific tips and strategies for overcoming common difficulties that struggling readers and English language learners face in identifying main ideas.

ORGANIZER 2-A: CORNELL METHOD

Name: _____

Cornell Method		
Questions	Details	Main Idea
		Self-Assessment Key ✓ I know this ? I have a question about this * I need to review this more

CONCEPT MAPPING

Overview

Concept Mapping combines linguistic and nonlinguistic forms of thinking to deepen students' understanding of how textual information is presented and how it can be organized to better understand reading. When students "see" a concept and how its subtopics and details interrelate, their ability to engage in higher-order thinking (e.g., writing about that concept, applying it, or connecting it to other learning and ideas) increases significantly.

The Notemaking Tool in Action

"I guess Concept Mapping is as old as the hills," says teacher Janice Zatricia, "but it really works when my third graders have trouble seeing how information is related and grouped into topics, subtopics, and details. The strange thing is, every time we use it, I seem to learn something new about how it works."

"We begin by placing our topic in the center of the paper. Then we draw lines out from that for subtopics or questions we want to explore. As we gather details and main ideas from the reading, we connect them to their subtopic or question.

"Lately, we've added a new wrinkle: When their maps are finished, I ask my students to draw lines connecting details under one subtopic to details under another. I ask the students to label this relationship by writing down on the line what led them to make this connection." (See Figure 2.9.)

Why the Notemaking Tool Is Beneficial

Maps force students to pay attention as they read, reread, and study. Muth (1987) reports that mapping, because it makes hierarchical patterns of text explicit, is highly successful in helping students manage expository reading tasks.

As a diagram, a map is a visual tool that capitalizes on spatial intelligence and promotes visual literacy. Maps effectively double the power of learning because they marry linguistic information to nonlinguistic information by situating words and phrases within a visual framework. For students who tend to get lost in their reading, a map provides a way for them to see the text and its inner relationships in their entirety. Maps are especially helpful to younger students for this reason.

Finally, maps build students' reflective capacity. Hyerle (2000), a renowned expert on the use of visual tools in the classroom, explains that by mapping out what they are learning, "students are constantly *reflecting* on the configuration of their maps, and thus, seeing how their frames of reference and mental models are influencing their perceptions" (pp. 86–89).

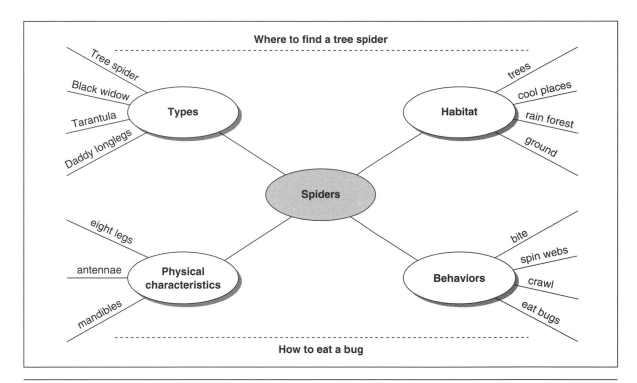

Figure 2.9   Sample of Concept Mapping Technique

Source: Copyright © Thoughtful Education Press. Reprinted with permission.

How to Use the Notemaking Tool

Use Organizer 2-B, "Concept Map" on page 75.

Incorporate Concept Mapping into your classroom using the following steps:

1. Identify a topic, main idea, or central question relevant to a reading or unit. Ask students to use Organizer 2-B, "Concept Map," to write this central idea in the circle at the center of the organizer.

2. With your students, identify secondary categories they would like to explore and have them connect the categories to the main idea, using the spaces provided on the organizer. (They can add circles as needed.) Model the process and describe your thinking as you identify the subtopics and details.

3. Guide students in using this "conceptual skeleton" to collect supporting details as they read. Show them how to connect each supporting detail to the subtopic it supports. (Students can add lines as needed.)

4. Students may then add to this map with further readings, explore connections between details, or use it as an aid for studying and recalling information.

5. Allow students to practice using maps on their own as a way to organize their readings.

Helping Struggling Notemakers

Because of Concept Mapping's visual component, it is an excellent strategy to help struggling readers and English language learners improve their notemaking skills, particularly as they move onto more complex readings.

As with other forms of notemaking, the most difficult aspect of mapping is for students to identify a reading's structure, topics, subtopics, and details. Here are some helpful ideas:

- Provide maps in which subtopics are already established for the students.
- Have students work collaboratively before working independently to help them build confidence.
- Provide generic concept maps for students to record their ideas, or introduce student-friendly mapping software such as Kidspiration® or Smart Draw®, which allow students to create and print their own maps.
- To stimulate hands-on kinesthetic learning, have students create three-dimensional Concept Maps in the form of mobiles or sculptures.

ORGANIZER 2-B: CONCEPT MAP

Name: _____

Concept Map

Note: Feel free to add lines or ovals as needed.

MATH NOTES

Overview

Mathematical word problems represent a falling-off point for many students. Rather than following a set of algorithmic steps, students are suddenly being asked to read text and figure out what to do on their own. Faced with a new and more complex form of problem solving, many students jump to a solution rather than focusing on what they are being asked to do. Math Notes curtails this impulsivity and teaches students how to examine the components of word problems, gain control over them using both words and pictures, and think through the problem-solving process carefully and strategically.

The Notemaking Tool in Action

Fifth-grade teacher Sarah Shays says, "My students have a lot of trouble coming to grips with word problems, so we use Math Notes to help them take notes and deepen their reading and understanding of math problems.

"We begin by listing the relevant facts in the upper left hand corner of the window. Then we restate the problem in the lower left box and draw a picture or diagram in the lower right. Finally, we list the steps we are going to follow in the upper-right-hand corner. Then we solve the problem on the back.

"My students keep each Math Notes sheet in a special section of their notebook. That way, when they get stuck, they can go back and leaf through problems they have already solved to see if they have ever solved a problem like the one they're stuck on."

Figure 2.10 shows a set of Math Notes Maya developed with her students for the following problem:

Maya took a flight from Austin, Texas, to Milwaukee, Wisconsin. The plane had two sections: A first class section with eight rows of six seats, and a main cabin with 15 rows of nine seats. Maya noticed that the plane was almost full, so she asked the flight attendant how many people were on the flight. "180," the flight attendant told Maya. How many open seats were on the plane?

Why the Notemaking Tool Is Beneficial

The introduction of word problems into the math curriculum represents a major shift in the way we ask students to think about math. Unlike the algorithmic nature of adding, subtracting, multiplying, and dividing, word problems require students to think analytically and to become problem solvers rather than problem doers.

Suddenly, for the student being introduced to word problems, math involves reading, determining the problem for oneself, identifying the problem's components, and developing a problem-solving plan—all new skills for most elementary students. These new and complex operations can be a

The Facts	The Steps
What are the facts?	What steps can we take to solve the problem?
• 180 people on the plane. • First Class has 8 rows of 6 seats. • Main cabin has 15 rows of 9 seats. What is missing? • The number of people the plane holds.	1. Add 48 + 135 to find out how many people the plane holds. 2. Subtract 180 from the total number of people the plane holds. 3. The number you get by subtracting will be the number of open seats on the plane.
The Question	**The Diagram**
What question needs to be answered? • How many open seats are on the plane? Are there any hidden questions that need to be answered? • Before we can answer the question, we need to know how many people the plane holds.	 $8 \times 6 = 48$ $15 \times 9 = 135$

Figure 2.10 Sample Math Notes

Source: Copyright © Thoughtful Education Press. Reprinted with permission.

source of anxiety and frustration for many students (Thomas, 2003), even as they have become increasingly central in most states' testing systems.

Math Notes, which is adapted from Thomas's *Styles and Strategies for Teaching Middle School Mathematics* (2003), provides students with a systematic means of analyzing, dissecting, visualizing, and solving word problems. Because both state standards and the National Council of Teachers of Mathematics recognize the need for students to reason their way through nonroutine problems based on real-world contexts, it is essential that students be taught early on how to become strategic problem solvers.

Math Notes encourages students to spend most of their time preparing to solve the problem. This pre-solution thinking is especially important as problems become more complex and less routine, ensuring that students break the problem down and see the big picture (i.e., what the problem is asking and what it looks like) before they try solving the problem.

How to Use the Notemaking Tool

Use Organizer 2-C, "Math Notes," on page 79.
Incorporate Math Notes into your classroom using the following steps:

1. Present students with a word problem that they must solve. Have students use Organizer 2-C, "Math Notes," to break down the parts of the problem in this sequence:
   • In "The Facts" box, they identify the facts of the problem and determine what is missing.

- In "The Question" box, they isolate the main question that the problem is asking, and they search for hidden questions or assumptions.
- In "The Diagram" box, they visualize and draw the problem as they see it.
- In "The Steps" box, they determine what steps should be taken to solve the problem.

2. Challenge students to solve the problem by following the process in "The Steps" box on the organizer. They may use the back of the organizer to solve the problem.

3. Instruct students to check their work for accuracy (did I add, subtract, multiply, divide, etc., correctly?), reasonableness (does the answer make sense?), and appropriateness (does my solution answer the question?). (Make sure students know basic checking techniques such as estimating, guessing and checking, and working backwards.)

4. Have students keep the problems and solutions in a special notebook or folder. This collection of problems serves as a reference guide for students: When students encounter difficult word problems, they can refer to this collection, look for any similar problems, and use them to help solve the new problem. Over time, students will begin to identify and categorize different types of word problems and, more important, be able to apply the most useful problem-solving process to new problems.

Helping Struggling Notemakers

Often, students about to solve word problems leap before they look. To make matters worse, traditional problem-solving approaches often emphasize finding solutions over internalizing and understanding the problem. One of the most important ideas of Math Notes is that of slowing students down and engaging them in four powerful pre-solution thinking strategies. Modeling and practice sessions play an important role in breaking the habit of impulsive problem solving. Focusing one by one on the four strategies that make up Math Notes and moving progressively toward finding solutions can also help students focus their attention on getting prepared to solve the problem.

ORGANIZER 2-C: MATH NOTES

Name: _____

Math Notes	
The Facts What are the facts? What is missing?	**The Steps** What steps can we take to solve the problem?
The Question What question(s) need(s) to be answered? Are there any hidden questions that need to be answered?	**The Diagram** How can we represent the problem visually?

Now use the back of this page to solve the problem.

WINDOW NOTES

Overview

Although the benefits of notemaking are beyond dispute, what is less clear is how teachers can get students interested in the process. Enter Window Notes. Developed as part of a two-year investigation into the causes of student boredom, Window Notes invites students directly into notemaking, giving them the opportunity to capture their own ideas, feelings, and questions about what they are reading. The simple window-shaped framework of Window Notes also deepens comprehension by asking students to think as they read and develops students' capacities for reflection and metacognition.

The Notemaking Tool in Action

Ellie Beck Carter's fourth-grade class has just begun reading Betsy Byars' *The Pinballs* (1977), a novel about three children learning about dependence and independence in foster care. In today's reading, students are introduced to Carlie, a central character with a very strong personality. Ellie uses Window Notes to help students better understand Carlie's character as well as their reactions to her as readers.

"Before we begin reading, I like to let students get comfortable with Window Notes. So I start by modeling. But I don't use a text to model. I choose something simpler, something every student, regardless of reading level, can understand in a snap. This way, students are free to focus their attention on the process, rather than the reading. For example, I'll model how to make a set of Window Notes on the board using my dog Sparky as the topic. I collect facts, questions, ideas, and feelings about Sparky in each quadrant of the Window Notes organizer (see Figure 2.11). As I record each

Facts	Feelings
1. Sparky is a German Shepherd.	1. I feel sad when we leave Sparky to go on vacation.
2. Sparky slobbers when he's hungry.	2. I don't care if he has bad breath. I still love him.
3. Sparky doesn't like it when we go on vacation and don't take him.	
Questions	**Ideas**
1. Why is Sparky's breath so bad?	Sparky really likes my brother. Maybe if I have my brother take care of Sparky while we're gone, Sparky won't get so upset.
2. How will Sparky do when we go away to Vermont this summer?	

Figure 2.11   Modeling Window Notes

note, I talk out loud, explaining how I decide what's a fact, what's a question, what's an idea, and what's a feeling.

"Then I tell students that I've created a set of Window Notes on something that's important to me. Now it's their turn to create a set of Window Notes on something that's important to them (Figure 2.12 shows the Window Notes Aidan made for the topic, "Playing basketball with my brother"). As they work, I walk around the room to see how students are working and to help those who are having difficulty.

Facts	Feelings
1. I play one-on-one basketball with my brother. 2. Our driveway is being paved so we play at the Middle School.	1. It's no fun losing to your brother. 2. Even though he's older than me, I still think I can beat him. 3. It will feel great when I finally win.
Questions	**Ideas**
How can I get better at my free throws?	My brother practices by shooting with one hand. Maybe I should try that.

Figure 2.12   Aidan's Window Notes for "Playing Basketball With My Brother"

"Next, I review with students the critical idea that we've been busy discovering: There is more than one way to pay attention. We can pay attention to facts, such as what kind of dog Sparky is or where we play basketball with our brother. We can focus on questions we have by recording the things we wonder about, such as where bad breath comes from or how to become a better free-throw shooter. We can pay attention to the interesting ideas and connections that pop into our heads as we learn or think about a topic. Or, we can let our feelings decide what's important by paying attention to our personal responses and reactions.

"This is when I feel that students are ready to make the connection to the reading. So I tell students that in the next two chapters of *The Pinballs* they will be introduced to one of the stars of the novel, a girl named Carlie. Then, I ask them to read the chapters on their own. As they read, they use the Window Notes framework to collect facts, questions, ideas, and feelings about Carlie while I walk around to get a feel for the kinds of notes students make naturally and which kinds of notes cause them to struggle.

"Brianna's notes show that she is adept at all four kinds of notes. I love the way she made up a new simile for Carlie in the 'Ideas' quadrant!"

Facts	Feelings
1. Carlie's stepdad was very cruel to her. 2. Carlie is hooked on TV. 3. She acts like she is really independent.	At first I thought Carlie was mean, but by the end of the chapter, I kind of liked her. She makes me laugh.
Questions	**Ideas**
1. Why does Carlie act so tough? 2. Why does Mrs. Mason think Carlie can help Harvey?	It's interesting how Carlie sees herself as a pinball. I see her more like a wild cat, but without claws.

Figure 2.13 Brianna's Window Notes for the Character "Carlie"

"After students have completed their Window Notes, I draw a big Window Notes organizer on the board and ask different students to offer up one of their notes. Together, the class and I decide what kind of note each response represents, and I record it in the appropriate quadrant. With each new note, I ask students, 'What does this tell us about Carlie?' After some discussion about Carlie's habits, how she treats people, and what motivates her, I give my students an assignment: I ask them to write a letter in which they tell Carlie what they admire about her and what personality traits they think might get Carlie into trouble.

"As we continue to read *The Pinballs*, I use Window Notes several more times to help students get a handle on key chapters. Which brings me to what I like best about Window Notes: By the third or fourth time, students' preferences as notemakers become clear. I ask students to add up how many facts they recorded, how many questions, etc., and we talk about how these totals might be seen as a 'window' into students' minds. It all makes for a wonderful discussion about how readers use their preferences to interpret literature."

Why the Strategy Is Beneficial

Ask any researcher—from Kobayashi (2006) to Marzano, Pickering, and Pollock (2001)—who has looked into the benefits of notemaking, and you'll hear the same thing over and over again: Students who know how to make good notes outperform their peers consistently and by wide margins. But then come the "And yets." And yet students yawn when teachers focus instructional time on how to make notes. And yet teachers seem to talk more about the struggle of teaching notemaking than the successes. And yet if you ask almost any adult what he or she remembers about taking notes in school, the most typical responses come in one of the following forms: A wince, a shudder, a "How-could-you?" look, a sudden desire to talk about the weather.

Notes do wonders for students' academic careers. And yet, and yet, and yet . . .

When it comes to notes, it seems that the majority of Americans fit under the category of "reluctant learners." Window Notes is designed for that reluctant majority, who stand to gain the great benefits of notemaking if only their teachers could find ways to get them actively engaged in the process. Strong (2005) explains how Window Notes helps teachers overcome student reluctance toward notes:

> Reluctant learners believe no one's interested in what they think . . . [Window Notes] asks them what they think and lets them have their own opinions. Kids get bored when what they're learning doesn't relate to their lives or isn't deep enough . . . Window Notes challenge [students] to go beyond the basic facts of what they're learning and push further, into self-discovery. The window-shaped structure explicitly lays out what they need to share. (p. 2)

What's even better about Window Notes is the insight it provides teachers about different students and how their minds work. Observe students at work and fold discussion about students' preferences into your Window Notes lesson. Use questions to focus discussion on the different ways students can pay attention and the uses of Window Notes in other contexts:

- If your mind paid attention mostly to facts, why might that be good for you as a reader?
- What if you focused your attention on feelings? What skills would that give you?
- How might a preference for asking questions or generating ideas benefit a reader?
- How is Window Notes like a window into your mind?
- How can you use Window Notes in other classes?

As you and your students learn more about their preferences as learners, you can work collaboratively to help students capitalize on their learning strengths and minimize their weaknesses. Chapter 7, "Reading Styles: The Key to Reading Success" discusses this topic in-depth.

How to Use the Notemaking Tool

Use Organizer 2-D, "Window Notes" on page 85.
Follow these six steps to incorporate Window Notes into your classroom:

1. Introduce and model Window Notes by showing students how you collect facts, questions, ideas, and feelings related to a particular subject.

2. Ask students to divide a blank sheet of paper into a window shape of four quadrants and label the quadrants *Facts*, *Questions*, *Ideas*, and *Feelings*. Or, you can use Organizer 2-D, "Window Notes."

3. Introduce the text to be read. Have students collect different kinds of notes and responses on their organizers as they read the text.

4. Invite students to share their notes with the class and conduct a discussion on what students have learned about the content and about their personal preferences as notemakers.

5. Assign a task that requires students to use their notes.

6. Over time, teach students how to use the strategy independently, as a way to help them break new learning into meaningful sets of information and as a way to help them pay attention to the inner workings of their own minds.

Helping Struggling Notemakers

The Window Notes strategy was designed with the struggling student in mind. We have seen how it alleviates the drudgery associated with notes by putting students' curiosity, insight, and emotions at the center of the notemaking process. Nevertheless, the novelty of Window Notes and the typical difficulties associated with collecting specific kinds of information can be sources of difficulty for some learners. For students who struggle with the process, try these suggestions:

- Introduce Window Notes by using it in a context that does not involve reading (modeling and allowing students to practice with well-known topics such as the Statue of Liberty or personal topics like "My summer vacation.")
- Try letting students work together and then conduct peer reviews on each other's notes. A student who is adept at asking questions stands to both teach and learn by being paired with a partner who struggles with questions but loves to explore personal feelings.
- Conduct a Window Notes lesson with the entire class. Read the text aloud, then lead students through it a second time. During the second reading, collect students' responses, pose questions, and help students determine which type of note each response represents.

ORGANIZER 2-D: WINDOW NOTES

Name: _____

Window Notes

Facts	Feelings

Topic

Questions	Ideas

3

Cracking
Vocabulary's CODE

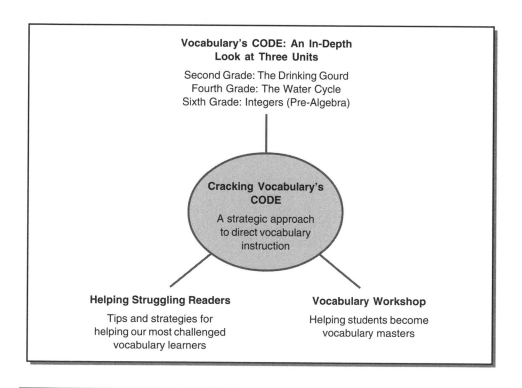

Vocabulary's CODE: An In-Depth Look at Three Units

Second Grade: The Drinking Gourd
Fourth Grade: The Water Cycle
Sixth Grade: Integers (Pre-Algebra)

Cracking Vocabulary's CODE

A strategic approach to direct vocabulary instruction

Helping Struggling Readers

Tips and strategies for helping our most challenged vocabulary learners

Vocabulary Workshop

Helping students become vocabulary masters

Figure 3.1   Chapter Overview: Advance Organizer

> *"It is the business of thought to define things, to find the boundaries; thought, indeed, is a ceaseless process of definition."*
>
> —Vance Palmer, twentieth-century
> Australian novelist

We all know that one of the hallmarks of good readers is their ability to master new vocabulary. But did you know that the correlation between rich vocabulary and good reading is so high that some researchers (Carver, 2003; Thorndike, 1974) have claimed that word knowledge and reading comprehension are virtually indistinguishable? Statistically and cognitively speaking, these researchers have identified something that amounts to a kind of reading law: poor vocabulary, poor reader; average vocabulary, average reader; rich vocabulary, proficient reader.

Obviously, students' knowledge of words is critical to their power as readers, but we also know that vocabulary affects much more than reading. Nearly all aspects of learning hinge on vocabulary—on critical academic concepts (think *equation, community,* and *living* vs. *nonliving*), ideas (think *independence, friendship,* and *responsibility*), and terms (think *character* and *plot, bar graph,* and *planet*—whose scientific definition has recently changed, by the way). *In fact, teaching vocabulary directly to our students is one of the most important instructional decisions we can make.*

But don't students develop rich vocabularies by reading a lot? Or is vocabulary really something that should be taught directly?

As recently as 10 years ago, these questions would have been more difficult to answer. After all, students who spend more time with their favorite authors develop more robust vocabularies than students who spend that same time with their televisions and PlayStations. Thus, in the 1980s and 1990s, a number of researchers (Adams, 1990; Nagy & Herman, 1987) questioned the value of teaching vocabulary directly. The best way to improve students' vocabulary knowledge, according to these researchers, was to promote wide reading. These researchers also pointed to the time difficulties inherent in direct vocabulary instruction, considering that students encounter thousands of new words each year—far too many to be taught directly.

More recently, however, the research on direct vocabulary instruction has put these doubts to rest. Beck, McKeown, and Kucan (2002), for example, show that wide reading, while important, is an inadequate way to address students' vocabulary development. The researchers suggest focusing instruction on roughly 400 words each year, making the work of direct instruction manageable for the teacher and productive for the student. The case for direct instruction is made even more forcefully by Marzano (2004), who shows that direct vocabulary instruction, when focused on essential academic vocabulary (rather than high-frequency word lists) leads to an average improvement of 33 percentile points on subject-area tests. And that's not all that building students' vocabularies and developing their word sense will do for students. Not by a long shot. Consider:

• **Vocabulary is more than the words we say; vocabulary represents what we know**. Vocabulary correlates very strongly with our background knowledge (Marzano, 2004). This means that the richer our vocabulary becomes, the more background knowledge we acquire. The more words and background knowledge we have in our memories, the more we bring to each new learning experience. So why does this matter? Simply stated, by increasing our students' academic vocabularies, we expand their ability to comprehend new information.

• **Good oral and written communication depends on a robust vocabulary.** This statement is so self-evident that it needs no further explanation. However, we all like a good story, so here's a true story that Heidi Hayes Jacobs (2006) tells about Mr. Davidson. Mr. Davidson taught high school science for more than 30 years when he decided to make a change. After consulting with his fellow teachers about the poor quality of many students' writing, he posted in his classrooms a word bank for each new unit of study. The word bank was a collection of "vivid, precise, and engaging words that embellish and give power to thinking in print and in speech . . . In short, Mr. Davidson stepped up his role as a science teacher to that of a science teacher who gives his students a critical tool for better science: better words" (p. 33).

And the results? As Jacobs explained in her recent workshop on literacy (2006):

> By asking students to use at least five words from the word bank in their lab reports and allowing students to revise their reports to make them more engaging, Mr. Davidson saw students who began the year writing "It went down the test tube" end the year with sentences that sounded like this: "The viscous blue fluid oozed down the side of the test tube."

• **A rich vocabulary fuels more powerful and more precise forms of thinking.** Although it is rather obvious that a good vocabulary improves both written and oral communication skills, the relationship between word knowledge and powerful thinking may be less clear. Yet "knowing the vocabulary" is one of the prerequisites of sophisticated thought. Why? Well, imagine this scenario: You've been asked by your school board to decide which computer model to purchase for the entire school. In your brain's bank of "computer words" are terms such as processor, hard drive, operating system, gigabytes, and RAM. Now, take those words away. Erase them and their meanings from your vocabulary. How insightful will your recommendation be without them? Would you trust a recommendation for a purchase of several thousand dollars from someone who doesn't know what a processor is or why it's important to know how many gigabytes of information the hard drive can hold?

Now imagine two fifth-grade students about to take an end-of-unit test on the American Revolution. One student has mastered the 12 critical terms from the unit; the other has not. Whose work will show greater depth of thought?

- **Students with rich vocabularies do better in school and go further in life than students with inadequate vocabularies.** Although this statement may not be fair, it is certainly true. Study after study shows that a rich vocabulary correlates significantly with higher test scores, greater academic opportunities, increased earning power, even higher intelligence. Although a good deal of students' word knowledge is formed at home and inherited by teachers, it is also true that high-quality instruction makes a significant difference in students' linguistic development (Dickinson & Smith, 1994; Snow, Barnes, Chandler, Goodman, & Hemphill, 1992). Which brings us to . . . Vocabulary's CODE.

Vocabulary's CODE is a strategic approach to direct vocabulary instruction that helps students master critical concepts and terms by engaging them in a progressive series of learning activities. In working from initial exposure to in-depth understanding, students learn to "crack" Vocabulary's CODE by:

- **C**onnecting with new words.
- **O**rganizing new words into meaningful categories.
- **D**eep-processing the most important ideas and terms.
- **E**xercising their minds through practice and review.

Vocabulary's CODE is based on three principles:

Principle 1: Not all vocabulary terms are equal. To get a sense of the different kinds of vocabulary terms that students encounter in their subject-area reading, read the following brief passages:

- Selection 1: An excerpt from "Hoops," Richard Burleigh's (1997) poem about the beauty and energy of the game of basketball.

  Feel your throat on fire.

  Feel the asphalt burning beneath your shoes . . .

  The watching and waiting to poke and pounce.

  The fox on the lurk.

- Selection 2: An excerpt from a social studies textbook.

  The bus riders included blacks and whites of all ages. They became known as the "Freedom Riders" because they rode all through the South to show that they stood together against segregation.

- Selection 3: A math word problem.

  Write an equation for this word problem:

Mark worked for two hours at the ice cream store. He received $3 in tips and earned $15 altogether.

Students across the country struggle with passages like these every day, and the main cause behind their struggle is unfamiliar vocabulary. Although the words in these passages may be second nature to us and our educated, adult minds, to our students—even our brightest students—some words may seem every bit as foreign as *gestalt* or *chiaroscuro*.

In selection 1, for example, the average fourth grader may have trouble with the words *asphalt* and *lurk*. Without an understanding of these words, the student may still be able to pick up the excitement and sense of anticipation in the moments before the player drives to the basket. What the student will miss are the details that bring imagery into focus and the finer layers of meaning that lend richness and beauty to poetry and prose—the way the hot *asphalt* implies color (black), setting (outdoor court), and even a strong sun, whose heat the black surface has absorbed; the idea that players must keep their strategies for scoring hidden from defenders by *lurking*.

The word *segregation* in selection 2 presents an even greater challenge to student comprehension. How could a student who doesn't know what *segregation* is appreciate what the Freedom Riders were doing? How could the student understand the severity of the injustice African Americans faced or why these multiracial bus rides were such historic events? Without important words such as *segregation* in their academic vocabularies, students miss critical connections and will have a hard time making inferences.

Finally, imagine the horror in a fifth grader's eyes when, upon reading selection 3 on a test, realizes that he can't respond because he doesn't exactly know what an *equation* is! When a student lacks a firm understanding of core content words such as *equation*, that student is doomed to struggle for weeks, and perhaps even a whole year. Future attempts to build new learning will be futile if the initial foundation is weak.

In the previous three passages, we can discern a certain hierarchy of vocabulary, not unlike the hierarchy Wiggins and McTighe (2005) outline in their model for establishing curricular priorities. Wiggins and McTighe seek clear distinctions between indispensable knowledge and that which is simply nice to know. In the classroom, where content is considerable yet time is limited, such distinctions are essential. By applying their evaluative method to vocabulary instruction, we get a useful filter for determining the importance of different vocabulary and how much time might be spent on each type (see Figure 3.2).

The best time to prioritize and select essential vocabulary is during unit planning, when the teacher is naturally focused on the task of separating the essential from the nonessential content. By tapping into this natural link between content and vocabulary and then designing the lesson sequence with both in mind, the unit is made more powerful, while the teacher's work burden is reduced significantly.

	Level 1	Level 2	Level 3
Type of Word	**Core Content**	**Important**	**Nice to Know**
What the word does	Concepts or ideas that lay the foundation for entire units of study or disciplines.	Concepts, events, people, or places that deepen understanding and facilitate connections between content.	Nouns, verbs, adjectives, adverbs, specialized vocabulary, etc., that enrich language but are not central to understanding.
Suggested time spent mastering words	Anywhere from one lesson to an entire unit, depending on the importance and complexity of the concept.	From fifteen minutes to a couple of class periods, depending on importance.	From one to ten minutes, depending on student comprehension speed.

Figure 3.2   Vocabulary Importance Chart

Source: Adapted from Thoughtful Education Press. (2004). *Word Works: Cracking Vocabulary's CODE, Teacher Planning and Implementation Guide.* Ho-Ho-Kus, NJ: Thoughtful Education Press.

Principle 2: Vocabulary instruction should be designed around how the brain learns, processes, and retains new information. Four essential interactions must occur between our brains and new information if we expect to master that information. Specifically, we must:

Connect to new words by searching our memories and examining the word and its context.

Organize new words into meaningful categories and frameworks.

Deep-process the most important words by visualizing or elaborating on their meanings

Exercise our vocabularies by revisiting and practicing our new words.

Applied specifically to vocabulary, these four interactions give us a clear framework for designing vocabulary-based lessons and units. Viewed in this light, effective vocabulary instruction means:

1. Providing opportunities for students to CONNECT to new words, typically through word-immersion strategies such as Word Walls or word-attack strategies such as Power Decoding.

2. Helping students ORGANIZE words into a meaningful big picture, using organizers, prioritizing techniques, and grouping and labeling strategies.

3. Allowing students to DEEP-PROCESS the most important words by using visualization, elaboration, and critical thinking strategies.

4. Making sure students get plenty of EXERCISE through frequent usage, word games, and review strategies.

Principle 3: Teachers need a repertoire of instructional techniques to teach vocabulary. There are three reasons why this is true. First, there's the research, which tells us that vocabulary learning improves dramatically when students are exposed to words multiple times and given the opportunity to work and play with those words in a variety of ways (Marzano, 2004). Second, different kinds of words call for different kinds of instructional techniques. Sometimes we want students to identify with terms (think *endangered species*); some words scream for classification (think of the instruments in the orchestra); some words (say *reptiles* vs. *amphibians*) are best understood when set against each other for comparison. Other words lose their abstraction once students make a visual connection (for example, *cube*). Because different kinds of words call for different kinds of instruction, only a repertoire of techniques will allow you to find the ideal fit between the words you teach and the many ways you can teach them. Finally, there's the issue of implementation, of what to do in the actual classroom to make all of this stuff work. Although the four phases of CODE provide a basic framework for vocabulary instruction, the question of what specific strategies and tools teachers can use to help students Connect, Organize, Deep-Process, and Exercise their words remains.

For these reasons, we have developed the Vocabulary Matrix (Figure 3.3). The Vocabulary Matrix presents a variety of vocabulary tools and strategies organized according to the four phases of CODE. As you design vocabulary lessons or units, refer to this matrix to help you select appropriate techniques for each phase and to ensure deep learning for all students through multiple and diverse exposures to new words.

RESEARCH, TRADITION, AND PRACTICE: PUTTING IT ALL TOGETHER IN THE CLASSROOM

In this introduction to vocabulary, we can find two distinct traditions. The newer tradition, represented by Marzano (2004) and his work in connecting vocabulary to background knowledge, emphasizes academic vocabulary—the critical concepts and terms that make up the disciplines. But there is another, older tradition exemplified by Mr. Davidson and his insistence on more vivid and more engaging lab reports. This tradition places a higher premium on interesting words, or words that help students become better speakers and writers. Thoughtful teachers look for a balance between these approaches. In this chapter, we introduce you to three different teachers who use the Vocabulary's CODE framework to honor the intent in both of these approaches. What all three teachers have in common is their use of Vocabulary's CODE to:

- Prioritize and select critical words when designing their units.
- Develop vocabulary-based units built on the four phases of CODE.
- Select appropriate strategies for each phase of CODE using the Vocabulary Matrix (Figure 3.3).

PRACTICAL TOOLS FOR CRACKING VOCABULARY'S CODE

C	O	D	E
Word Walls A collection of words organized into categories and posted on the wall for students to use in their reading and writing.	**Prioritizing Vocabulary** Teacher or students determine which words are essential, important, and good to know.	**Visualizing Vocabulary** Creating visual images, sketches, or icons with brief explanations to demonstrate understanding.	**Vocabulary Games** Using Bingo, Jeopardy, Word Baseball, etc. to review vocabulary in a competitive and fun manner.
Power Decoding Teaching students attack skills for new words: prefixes, suffixes, roots, context clues, substitutions.	**Key Vocabulary Organizer** A concept definition map that establishes the largest categories that key concepts fit into, critical attributes, examples, and related concepts.	**Multisensory Processing** A technique that encourages students to explore important words using words, feelings, sensory information, and visualization.	**Write to Learn** Students are asked to use a specific number of new words in their writing assignments.
Word Spiders Teacher introduces eight words that are associated with a mystery, one word for each leg of the spider organizer. Students try to guess the mystery word.	**Categorizing** Teacher or students place a list of words into specific categories.	**The Four R's** Students *R*evisit their words, *R*eview them, and either *R*efine or *R*evise their definitions in light of new understanding.	**Teams-Games-Tournaments** Students are divided up into heterogeneous study groups to review words, then compete in homogenous groups to earn points for their team.
Associations Students generate words, pictures, feelings, physical reactions to words. There is no right or wrong, just what comes to mind.	**Concept Maps** A technique used to create visual representations of hierarchical relationships between a central concept, supporting ideas, and important details.	**Metaphors/Similes** Students learn words deeply by exploring their relationships to other words/concepts (e.g.,How is democracy like baseball?).	**Vocabulary Carousel** Teacher sets up 5 or 6 stations. Students work in small groups at all stations. Stations include a variety of vocabulary activities.
See It, Say It, Show It, Store It Students look at the word, pronounce it slowly, record its meaning, draw a picture with a brief explanation, and store the word in their Vocabulary Journals.	**Fist List** Teacher provides a category in the "palm" of a hand organizer; students generate 5 words that fit the category, one for each finger of the hand organizer.	**Defining Characteristics** Students build multi-layered definitions by focusing on essential characteristics: What is it? What is it used for? Why is it valued? What kind is it? Where does it come from? What does it look, feel, sound, smell like? etc.	**Effective Practice** Teacher instructs students in the principles of effective practice, including how to mass and distribute review sessions, use words often, and make stronger connections.
Glossary Students keep a glossary of new words by defining words and including icons or pictures.	**Word Banks** Students examine a list of words and place them into the appropriate slots in a visual organizer.	**Etymologies** Students investigate word histories, analyzing how original meaning is intact and how it has changed.	**Three's a Crowd** Students decide which word of three doesn't belong and explain why.

PRACTICAL TOOLS FOR CRACKING VOCABULARY'S CODE

C	O	D	E
Concept Attainment The teacher presents yes and no examples of a concept in order to help students determine its critical attributes. Students use the critical attributes to distinguish among examples and generate their own examples. Excellent for rich concepts with clear attributes, like "mammals" or "nouns."	**Group and Label** Students examine a list of vocabulary words and place them into groups based on common characteristics. For each group that students create, they devise a label that describes what all the grouped words have in common.	**Cinquains** A five-line poem used to define a term: • **noun:** coal • **two adjectives:** black and shiny • **three action verbs:** smolder, burn, pollute • **four-word sentence or phrase:** a source of energy • **ending word:** limited	**Peer Practice** A reciprocal learning strategy in which students work as peer partners. One student serves as a coach, the other as a player. While the player works to define key terms from the unit, the coach provides assistance, feedback, and praise. Students then reverse roles.
Unit Diagram An illustrated Word Wall that puts all the terms in the unit into a visual framework and is posted at the front of the classroom.	**Three-Way Tie** Students select three words from a unit's vocabulary and arrange them in a triangle. They then connect the words with lines and explain the relationship between each pair of words by writing along the lines.	**Compare & Contrast** Students set two rich concepts against one another and describe each separately. They then use their descriptions to draw out the deep similarities and differences between the two concepts. Finally, students must decide if the two concepts are more similar or more different, and explain why.	**Boggle** After independent study, students retrieve all the vocabulary they can. Students join a group of 3–5 students, compare lists, and add any words or meanings they missed. Students then leave their team to "Boggle" with other students, gaining points for terms and meanings that appear on their list but not on their competitors' lists.
Word Catcher Students are asked to "catch" a new word each day.	**A Diagram to Die For** Students are asked to create a diagram that shows the relationship among the words on a Word Wall.	**Crazy Connections** The student picks a word out of one hat, then a household, classroom, or odd object out of another. The student's job is to generate as many similarities as possible.	**Para-Writing** Students write a paragraph or short piece using between five and fifteen vocabulary words. Each word must be embedded meaningfully into the text, or it doesn't count.

Vocabulary Notebook. A notebook in which students collect important words while reading. In their notebooks, students record their initial "educated" definitions. They then look up the word and select the dictionary definition that best fits the word as it is used in the text. Students compare their initial definitions with the actual definition, and describe briefly what differences they note between them. Finally, students create a visual icon to help them process and remember the word's meaning. The notebook also serves as a great tool for review.

Please note: This strategy includes all phases of CODE.

Figure 3.3 The Vocabulary Matrix

Source: Adapted from Thoughtful Education Press. (2004). *Word Works: Cracking Vocabulary's CODE, Teacher Planning and Implementation Guide.* Ho-Ho-Kus, NJ: Thoughtful Education Press.

Then we will meet a teacher who conducts regular Vocabulary Workshops, modeling techniques from the Vocabulary Matrix (Figure 3.3) and then providing time for practice, coaching, and discussion so that students learn how to apply vocabulary strategies to their independent reading. Finally, we include a set of tips and suggestions for helping struggling learners and English language learners master new vocabulary terms.

VOCABULARY'S CODE: AN IN-DEPTH LOOK AT THREE UNITS

Vocabulary's CODE Unit 1: *The Drinking Gourd,* Second Grade

Note: This unit is adapted from Eva Benevento's curriculum unit, *The Drinking Gourd: A Curriculum Resource Guide,* 1998. Used with permission of Eva Benevento.

1. **Identify essential vocabulary.**

    Each winter, Maria Costa reads *The Drinking Gourd,* F. N. Monjo's (1993) chapter book about the Underground Railroad, with her second graders. In selecting vocabulary for her unit, Maria keeps three goals in mind:

    - She wants to highlight words that support the themes of the book—words such as *freedom, abolitionists,* and *morals.* Maria calls these kinds of words Big-Idea Words.
    - She wants students to learn the vocabulary associated with the culminating task: writing a single-paragraph thesis essay, which Maria calls an I-Think Essay. Thus, terms such as *main idea* and *supporting details* also make Maria's critical vocabulary list.
    - She wants students to collect and master the new and interesting words they encounter during reading—words that the author uses to bring characters and situations to life and that students can learn to use as well. Maria decides to leave the selection of words associated with this goal open ended. Instead of working off a predetermined list, she builds in time during her unit when she and her students can select and discuss the new words they find in each chapter of *The Drinking Gourd.*

2. **Decide how to help students CONNECT with new words.**

    Maria decides that the best way to help students connect to new words while maintaining her three vocabulary goals is to develop a Word Wall. Maria creates her Word Wall (Figure 3.4) on extra-large poster paper and posts it prominently at the front of the classroom.

    Maria likes using Word Walls in this way for two reasons. First, the Word Wall is interactive. As Maria and her students encounter new and interesting words, they work together to figure out what they mean, and they collect the words in the "Interesting Words"

Big-Idea Words	Words that will help us write our I-Think essays
Freedom: The right to do what you want. *Slave:* A person forced to do hard work away from home without being paid. *Lawbreakers:* People who don't follow the law. *Abolitionists:* People who worked hard to end slavery. *Morals:* A person's beliefs about what is right and wrong.	*Main idea:* The first sentence of an I-Think essay. It tells what you think about the topic. *Supporting details:* Sentences that help you prove your main idea. *Sequence:* The order of the sentences in your essay. *Conclusion:* The final sentence or sentences of your essay. The conclusion lets the reader know your essay is ending.

Interesting words in *The Drinking Gourd*

Figure 3.4   Word Wall

section. Maria keeps definitions for these words very brief, using synonyms such as *reward* for the vocabulary word *bounty* or clipped definitions such as *person who helps lead a church* for *deacon*.

Second, Maria likes how the Word Wall pulls extra weight in the CODE model. Not only does the Word Wall immerse students in critical vocabulary and facilitate the introduction of new words (CONNECT), it also:

- Organizes new words into three separate categories (ORGANIZE).
- Makes important words conspicuous for the duration of the unit, thereby making it much easier for students to practice incorporating words into their writing and speech (EXERCISE).

3. Establish a method for helping students ORGANIZE new words.

Thanks to the design of her Word Wall, the organization of vocabulary words is already built into Maria's unit. To reinforce this organizational scheme, Maria holds a series of discussions about each of the different kinds of words on the Word Wall. Discussion topics include the following: What Makes a Big-Idea Word a Big-Idea Word? When Is a Word Worth Collecting? and, Now That You Think It, How Can You Prove It?

4. Activate DEEP-PROCESSING of key words.

At the heart of *The Drinking Gourd* lies a rich and controversial question for second graders and adult readers alike: When is it acceptable to break the law? Maria feels that without a personal understanding of the unit's Big-Idea Words—*freedom, slavery, lawbreakers, abolitionists,* and *morals*—students may be unable to think deeply about this theme.

Because these Big-Idea Words carry a high level of abstraction with them, Maria decides to have students deep-process them using the tool known as Visualizing Vocabulary. Visualizing Vocabulary works like this:

Step 1: Students define the word.

Step 2: Students draw a picture or several pictures that represent the word.

Step 3: Students explain why the pictures they drew are good representations of the word.

Figure 3.5 shows the work of a student who used Visualizing Vocabulary to deep-process the word *freedom*.

5. Search for opportunities for students to EXERCISE and revise their understanding of new words.

Throughout the unit, Maria provides students with practice and review activities, including synonym searches, Which one doesn't belong?, and word banks.

Also, for their final writing assignment (a simple I-Think essay in which students take a position on whether the characters were right or wrong to break the law by helping the runaway slaves),

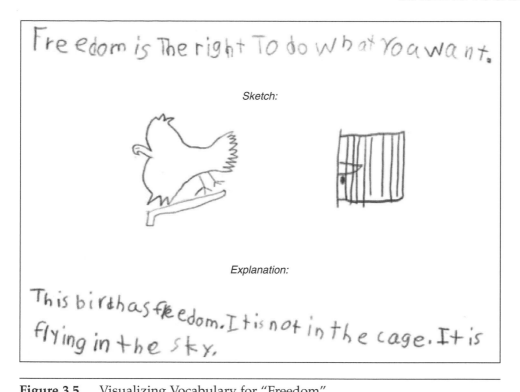

Figure 3.5 Visualizing Vocabulary for "Freedom"

Source: Copyright © Thoughtful Education Press. Reprinted with permission.

students are asked to refer to the Word Wall and to incorporate at least four new vocabulary words into their essays.

Vocabulary's CODE Unit 2: The Water Cycle, Fourth Grade

Source: This unit is adapted from Joyce Jackson's curriculum unit, *The Water Cycle*, 2005. Used with permission of Joyce Jackson.

1. Identify essential vocabulary.

Sarjena Reddy focuses her unit on water around three essential questions:

a. Why is water important to us?
b. How does water behave (the water cycle)?
c. How can we conserve water?

Because an in-depth understanding of the water cycle is so critical to her unit, Sarjena selects the following terms for concentrated vocabulary study:

condensation	infiltration	water vapor
evaporation	pollution	ground water
transpiration	water cycle	responsibility
precipitation	water table	consequences

2. Decide how to help students CONNECT to new words.

At the front of the room, Sarjena posts a unit diagram (see Figure 3.6), which shows the role of each term in the water cycle within a visual framework.

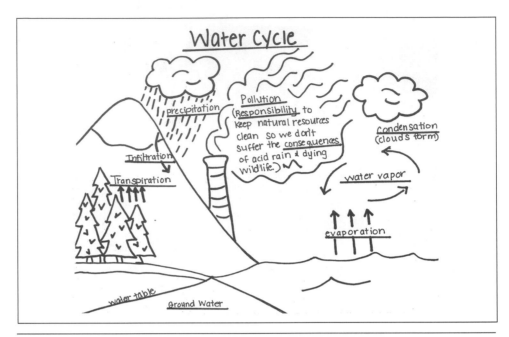

Figure 3.6   Unit Diagram (Water Cycle)

Copyright © Thoughtful Education Press. Reprinted with permission.

3. Establish a method to help students ORGANIZE new words.

Sarjena's diagram goes a long way in organizing the terms for the unit. To make the organization process more active for students, Sarjena presents students with a blank version of the diagram (illustrations only, no words) and asks them to place the key terms in their correct place.

4. Activate DEEP-PROCESSING of key words.

Sarjena uses two kinds of activities to help students forge deep and personally meaningful connections to critical vocabulary terms. First, she asks students to develop and explain similes/metaphors for key concepts. Sarjena provides some of the similes herself (e.g., How is the water table like a farm?) and then challenges students to create two more of their own.

The second way Sarjena activates deep-processing is by asking her students to select the most important term from the list and to write a poem or rap for the term. Jorge's cinquain sounds like this:

> Precipitation
>
> Wet and falling
>
> Rain, snow, sleet
>
> It keeps Earth alive.
>
> Essential

5. **Search for opportunities for students to EXERCISE and revise their understanding of new words.**

Near the end of the unit, Sarjena has students engage in a Vocabulary Carousel. During the Vocabulary Carousel, student teams move around the room to complete five vocabulary review activities at five different stations. Station activities include collaborative story-telling in which each group adds two sentences to the story while using the vocabulary terms; a priority pyramid that asks students to rank-order six terms according to their relative importance; and this mini-task:

> Examine the three sample comic strips you'll find at this station. Quickly (in two minutes or less) generate three things you notice about how the comic strips tell their stories. Then, create your own comic strip that explains the water cycle as a whole, explains an important element of the water cycle, or tells the story of how the water cycle affects you.

Vocabulary's CODE Unit 3: Integers (Pre-Algebra), Sixth Grade

1. **Identify essential vocabulary.**

Keith Warren examines his state standards to determine the essential vocabulary for his pre-algebra unit on integers. Keith identifies the following critical terms for the unit:

integers	number line	order
absolute value	positive	plot
point	negative	inequalities
coordinate	compare	zero pair

2. **Decide how to help students CONNECT to the new words.**

To help his students form a strong initial link to the new words, Keith introduces the terms using the tool known as See It, Say It, Show It, Store It. He provides students with a list of the terms, then walks them through the steps in the tool.

- First students *see the word*. Keith reminds students to note how the word is spelled and what it looks like on paper. He also tells students, "Too often, we forget to stop and concentrate, yet the simple act of focusing on a written word helps your mind make a stronger connection than you might think."
- Next, Keith and his students *say the word*. Keith explains, "Saying the word out loud creates a connection between your mouth and your brain. Repeat it a few times and the connection gets stronger. Oh, and if you're using this technique on your own (which I highly recommend) and you don't know how to pronounce a word, ask someone who does or check for pronunciation in the dictionary."
- Then, Keith has students *show the meaning of the word*. Students check the definition of the word and write the definition in their Vocabulary Notebooks. When glossary definitions prove too

abstract for students, Keith provides examples, clarifications, or explanations to help students get a solid grip on the meaning. "Next," Keith tells students, "comes the really important part of defining the word—showing the meaning in a way that works best for you. You can create a simple sketch, write the definition in your own words, list some examples and nonexamples of the concept—whatever will help you to remember it." To ensure students understand the different ways they can personalize meaning, Keith models the process with a familiar term, *fraction.* He shows students how he can represent a fraction visually, linguistically (in his own words, of course), using examples (1/2, 2/5, 8/13) and nonexamples (10, 2.5, 5 2/7), or by employing a combination of all three techniques.

- Finally, students *store the word.* Students record the word, its glossary definition, and their personal representation of the word's meaning in their Vocabulary Notebooks, which become, over the course of the year, the ultimate study guide for each unit. An excerpt from one student's Vocabulary Notebook appears in Figure 3.7. Notice that the last box of the vocabulary notebook (labeled The Four R's) is left blank. This is because students will revisit their terms later in the unit to deep-process them.

3. **Establish a method to help students ORGANIZE new words.**

In addition to helping students create a grid in their Vocabulary Notebook, Keith organizes students into teams and challenges them to develop a simple categorization system for all the words using the

Word	Definition	How I'll Remember It	The 4 R's
Integer	A whole number that is not a fraction or a mixed number.	Examples: 2, 7, 445 Nonexamples: $\frac{1}{3}$, $4\frac{5}{8}$	
Absolute value	The numerical value of an integer without regard to whether the sign is positive or negative.	$+\ \ \ \begin{array}{c} \\ - \end{array}\Big[\ 8\ \Big]\begin{array}{c} +\ \ + \\ - \\ + \end{array}$ $+\ \ \ \ \ \ \ \ \ \ \ \ \ \ \ +$ $-$ The bars on each side of the number are shields that protect it from positive and negative signs.	

Figure 3.7   Excerpt From a Student's Vocabulary Notebook

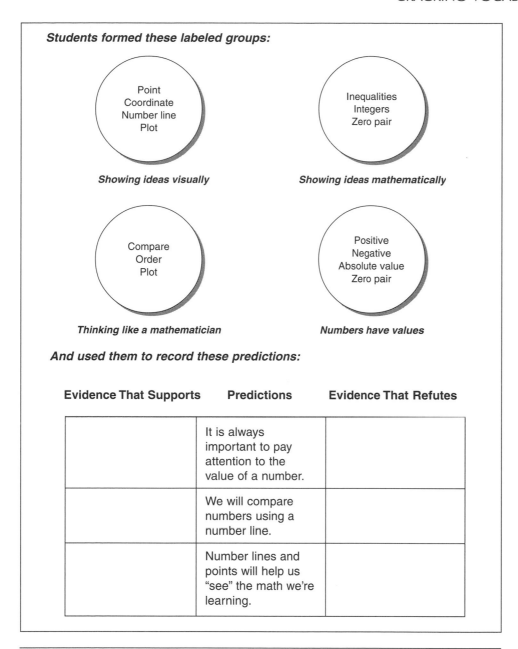

Students formed these labeled groups:

Point
Coordinate
Number line
Plot

Showing ideas visually

Inequalities
Integers
Zero pair

Showing ideas mathematically

Compare
Order
Plot

Thinking like a mathematician

Positive
Negative
Absolute value
Zero pair

Numbers have values

And used them to record these predictions:

Evidence That Supports	Predictions	Evidence That Refutes
	It is always important to pay attention to the value of a number.	
	We will compare numbers using a number line.	
	Number lines and points will help us "see" the math we're learning.	

Figure 3.8   Group and Label Leads to a Prediction Organizer

Group and Label tool. Students then use their labels to generate a set of predictions about what they will learn during the unit. Students refine their predictions as the unit progresses, collecting evidence that either supports or refutes their original predictions. Figure 3.8 shows how one group decided to group and label the unit vocabulary. It also shows the predictions the group generated using a simple three-column Prediction Organizer.

4. Activate DEEP-PROCESSING of key terms.

Four days into the unit, Keith instructs students to return to their Vocabulary Notebooks. "What we're going to do," says Keith, "is spend some time on The Four R's of deep vocabulary learning: Revisit, Review, Refine, Revise."

Keith then models with students how he applies The Four R's to the first term in the notebook: *integer*.

So, what I do is first *revisit* (there's the first R) what I've written and recorded in my notebook. After I *review* (the second R) my definition and my way of helping myself remember it, I ask myself, 'What have I learned about integers that I didn't know before we started the unit and that I can use to help me understand integers even better?' Of course, there are lots of different ways I can *refine* or even *revise* (R's three and four) my understanding. I can draw a new picture. I can create a metaphor. I can rewrite my original definition now that I understand it better. I can add new examples or non-examples. I can include a real-world application of the term that shows how it is actually used by people in their lives and careers. So, for example, one way I might use a real-world application to help me deep-process the terms *positive, negative*, and *number line* is to relate these mathematical ideas to temperature. A thermometer is really a vertical number line, and temperature can be recorded as a positive number or—on the days that make me wish I lived in Florida—as a negative number. So what I'll do is I'll use words, pictures, and a real-world application to help me make an even stronger connection to these three terms, like this (see Figure 3.9):

Word	Definition	How I'll Remember It	The 4 R's
Number line	A line labeled with the integers. At the center is zero.	$-4\ -3\ -2\ -1\ 0\ 1\ 2\ 3\ 4$	A number line is like a horizontal thermometer: 100° Hot! 75° 50° °F 25° 0 −25° Freezing!
Positive	Positive integers appear to the right of the zero and increase in value as they move right.	Positive integers	Most of the time, the temperature is above zero degrees. Temperature is usually a positive number.
Negative	Negative integers appear to the left of the zero and decrease in value as they move left.	Negative integers	It's pretty rare for it to go below zero. When it does, it's really cold. We haven't had a negative temperature in a while.

Figure 3.9 Excerpt From Keith's Vocabulary Notebook (After the Four R's)

5. **Search for opportunities for students to EXERCISE and revise their understanding of new words.**

To help students review and practice their vocabulary learning, Keith uses rapid-fire games, including *Jeopardy* and *Word Baseball*.

VOCABULARY WORKSHOP: HELPING STUDENTS BECOME VOCABULARY MASTERS

Sixth-grade teacher Marcus Hendrickson also designs his vocabulary instruction around CODE. But he takes a more direct approach to the teaching of vocabulary skills. Marcus' aim is to turn his students into "vocabulary masters"—learners who have an arsenal of vocabulary-learning tools at their disposal and can use those tools to attack, process, and store new words and their meanings. To accomplish this goal, Marcus conducts a series of Vocabulary Workshops. A Vocabulary Workshop is a 20-to-30-minute skill-building session broken up into three separate phases:

Phase 1: Modeling. The teacher selects a vocabulary skill and models how to use it. Modeling is more effective when the teacher conducts a Think-Aloud, verbalizing the internal thinking process being used while applying the skill.

Phase 2: Coaching. Students practice the skill either individually or in small groups while the teacher circulates, observes students, and provides coaching.

Phase 3: Sharing. The teacher and students discuss the difficulties students encountered, brainstorm potential solutions, and share insights on how they addressed particular difficulties.

Here's how Marcus puts each of these three phases into action:

Modeling: Today, Marcus is teaching students how to "attack" new words by scouring for context clues, examining word parts, and using personal associations and word substitutions to generate working definitions. This set of word-attack techniques is called Power Decoding. To model how Power Decoding works, Marcus selects the following paragraphs from John Gardner's short story "Dragon, Dragon" (1975):

the dragon lunged and swallowed him in a single gulp, sword and all, and the eldest son found himself in the dark of the dragon's belly. "What a fool I was not to listen to my wise old father!" thought the eldest son. And he began to weep bitterly. (p. 10)

While the students follow along in their books, Marcus conducts the following Think Aloud:

"OK, so when I'm reading this passage, I realize that there's a word that strikes me as a little odd, that I'm not exactly sure that I understand, at least not the way it's used here. That word is *bitterly*. So I start by asking myself, 'Is there anything in the sentence or surrounding sentences that might help me figure out what the word means?' Let's see, I know the son is feeling very foolish about not listening to his father because he calls himself a fool and has been swallowed by a dragon. Also, the author uses an exclamation point, so he must really be carrying on as he is crying.

"Next, I see if I can find any meaningful prefixes, suffixes, or root words in the word. If I take a look at my Quick Reference Chart for Prefixes and Suffixes, it reminds me that words that end in -ly are usually adverbs, which makes perfect sense because *bitterly* would be describing how the son wept. That would make the root of the word *bitter*.

"My associations with the word *bitter* have more to do with food than the way someone acts. I've heard it used when something tastes terrible or too strong, which kind of makes sense for the way someone can cry.

"OK, next I want to substitute another word in the place of *bitterly* to see if the sentence makes sense. . . ."

Coaching: Marcus asks his students to practice Power Decoding the new words they find while reading "Dragon, Dragon." As he circulates around the room, he notices that one group of students seems to be breezing over the step of using context clues and going right to looking for prefixes, suffixes, and roots. Marcus joins the group and, after listening, says: "I really like the way you guys are attacking the words by analyzing word parts so closely. But sometimes we can learn more about a word by how an author uses it than by looking at the word itself. Take *ravaged* in this sentence, for example. What clues are in the sentence and surrounding sentences that might hint at what this word means?"

Sharing: During the discussion phase, one common complaint is that sometimes using the context and the prefixes, suffixes, and roots doesn't really help students establish a preliminary definition. After surveying the class, Marcus finds that about half of the students agree. Those who disagree say things such as, "I was at least able to figure out the part of speech each time," and "I got a rough definition almost every time. I wasn't always right, but just the fact that I was able to do that much says something, I think."

Marcus continues the sharing session and bridges it to the next Vocabulary Workshop by saying:

It turns out that you're both right. Usually, you can use Power Decoding to figure out at least something about the word. But sometimes you can't get quite enough information to generate a useful preliminary definition. Each time you use the tool, you do get a little bit better at figuring out what words might mean, so it's important that we keep practicing it. But the next tool we're going to cover, which is See It, Say It, Show It, Store It, is perfect for those times when you can't get a firm grip on a word using Power Decoding. And that's going to be what we focus on for next week's Vocabulary Workshop.

Each Tuesday for eight weeks, Marcus conducts a new Vocabulary Workshop with his students. By the end of eight weeks, students have eight new tools in their "vocabulary toolkits"—two tools for each phase of CODE. Thus, by the second marking period, Marcus' students know how to:

Connect to new words by:

- Employing Power Decoding skills: approximating definitions by using context clues, personal associations, substitution, and word parts (prefixes, suffixes, and roots).
- Using See It, Say It, Show It, Store It to form strong multisensory memories of new words. (To see how another teacher uses See It, Say It, Show It, Store It, see pages 101–102.)

Organize words by:

- Creating Concept Maps that lay out the relationships among the words associated with a topic or unit (see Figure 3.10).
- Using Group and Label to categorize newly introduced words according to common characteristics and to use these categories to make predictions about the reading or unit (see Figure 3.8 above).

Deep-Process critical words by:

- Explaining metaphors or similes. For example:
  A search engine is like a librarian because both a search engine and a librarian help you find specific information. Both are able to search through a lot of information quickly. When you work with a search engine and a librarian, you need to be very specific about what you're looking for. Both a librarian and a search engine do their work quietly.
- Using Compare and Contrast to first describe two critical concepts separately, and then identify similarities and differences using a Top Hat Organizer (see Figure 3.11.)

Exercise their words by:

- Developing an effective practice schedule
- Using Write to Learn to develop short written pieces that incorporate at leave five new vocabulary words in a meaningful way.

HELPING STRUGGLING READERS

Frequent practice with and exposure to unfamiliar words cannot be stressed enough with respect to struggling readers and English language

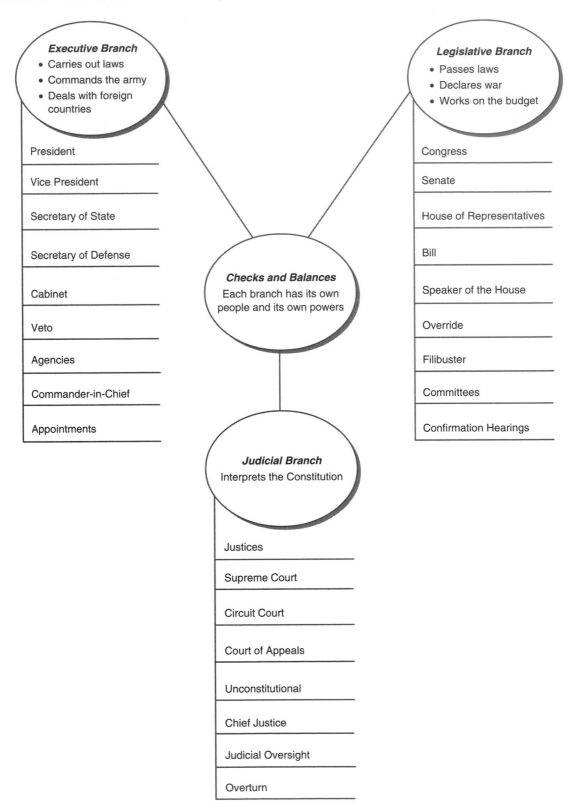

Figure 3.10   Vocabulary Concept Map

Nonrenewable Energy	Renewable Energy
• Examples are coal, oil, natural gas.	• Examples are solar cells, wind farms, and hydroelectric power.
• Supplies are limited, will run out one day.	• Replenished by nature; will not run out.
• Most of our energy comes from nonrenewable fossil fuels.	• Produces much less pollution.
• Easier to transport, store, and use than renewable energy.	• Must be converted into usable energy. Difficult to transport, store, and use.

Similarities

• Produce energy for people to use.

• Come from nature.

• Help people live better lives.

Figure 3.11   Top Hat Organizer

learners. One way to increase familiarity with new words for all students is to use the Word Wall strategy. Word Wall works like this:

1. **Step 1:** Students read a text, either for homework or class work, and identify any words that are new or unfamiliar to them.

2. **Step 2:** When they finish reading, students come together as a class to share some of the words they identified as new or unfamiliar. The teacher records these words on a poster or the chalkboard.

3. **Step 3:** The class defines each word the teacher records and then generates one, two, or three synonyms for each word, which the teacher also records on the poster or chalkboard (generating the Word Wall).

4. **Step 4:** Individually, students work through a synthesis activity by writing a summary of, personal response to, or a thesis essay about the text they read. Students must use between five and ten of the words from the Word Wall correctly in their writing.

To maximize student practice with new words, the Word Wall should be displayed for an entire unit (in some cases, the entire year). Each time students engage in a writing task, they should draw on words from the Word Wall to master the unit vocabulary and to enrich and enliven their writing.

Here are some other ways to help struggling students and English language learners increase their proficiency with new vocabulary:

Use metaphors. All students, regardless of their achievement levels or primary language, have a storehouse of well-known concepts in their memories. One of the great powers of metaphors is that they give students the chance to use concepts they're familiar with (anything from *family*, to *a spider web*, to *the ocean* will do) to make sense of and deeply process new and unfamiliar ideas.

Tap into the power of visualization. Images are universal and language-independent. Images help students cut through abstraction (think of the difference between the formal definition of a *sphere* compared to an image of a sphere). Images are stored in a different part of the brain than words and help students form stronger connections to—and memories of—new terms (Paivio, 1990). For all of these reasons, visualization strategies are powerful techniques for teaching vocabulary—especially with struggling students and English language learners.

Teach simplified mapping techniques. Fist Lists (see Figure 3.12) and Spider Organizers (see Figure 3.13) are great ways to introduce concept

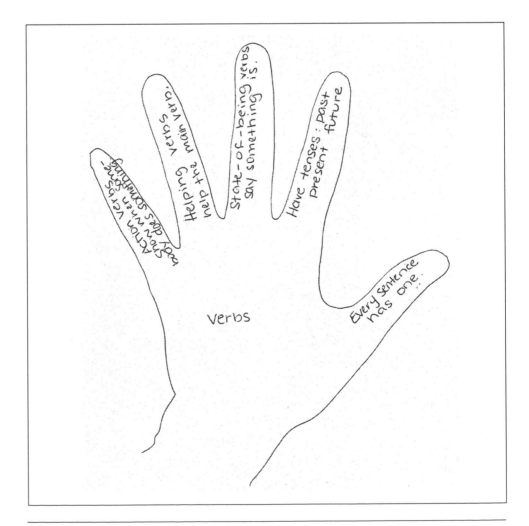

Figure 3.12   Fist List

Source: Copyright © Thoughtful Education Press. Reprinted with permission.

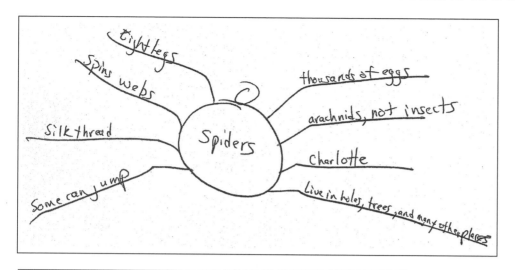

Figure 3.13   Spider Organizer

Source: Copyright © Thoughtful Education Press. Reprinted with permission.

definition mapping to struggling learners. These techniques provide a memorable structure for collecting and recording information about a concept and establish a clear goal for how many details students need to collect (five for Fist Lists, eight for Spiders).

Use your experience—and your common sense. In addition to these techniques, frequent independent and group practice, as well as vocabulary games that borrow the structure of popular games (such as Outburst and Pictionary), will facilitate storage and recall among all learners. So will acting out words, choral review, and repeating words and their definitions with emphasized emotion.

4

Eyes-On, Minds-On Reading

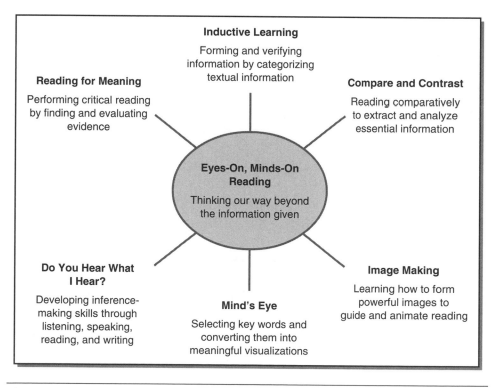

Figure 4.1 Chapter Overview: Advance Organizer

> *"Reading is the creation of ideas out of the invisible."*
>
> —Ann Lute,
> High School English teacher

Writers ask a lot of readers. They expect us to see the invisible. After all, the only items in our sight when we read are the white page and the black letters. The lions of the savannah, the motivations of soldiers, the rhythms of the heart, and the structure of an argument all happen elsewhere—off the page. If we are to understand them we will have to supply them, create them out of the machinery of our minds.

Yet many traditional reading programs have left the role of thinking about reading until after students have read the text. We now know that good readers think not only after reading, but also before, and especially during reading—whether five, nine, or ninety years old. Proficient readers do this naturally. Take this example:

> Far from being an impenetrable jungle, the forest floor is often spacious, open, and easy to walk through. Trees rise like giant columns, their bark smooth and trunks branchless nearly all the way up to the canopy. The biggest are propped up by stabilizing roots that flare out of the base and snake across the ground. (Marent, 2006, p. 25)

When proficient readers read this passage, for instance, their minds show them the surprisingly wide open space of forest floor. They feel their relative smallness as they encounter the thick-shafted tree trunks pushing their way up to the lush canopy overhead. They see in their mind's eye the flaring, snaking network of roots. These images supply much of the meaning and most of the pleasure they find in reading. Now read this example:

> Richard loved to hear his grandfather tell about the war, how he ran away from his master and fought the rebel army. (Miller, 1997)

When proficient readers read a passage such as this excerpt from the biography of the great African American writer Richard Wright, their minds look for word clues like "war," "master," "rebel," and "army." Using these word clues as mind activators, they connect the new reading to their own relevant prior knowledge to infer that Richard's grandfather was a slave who fought with the North during the Civil War. Finally, read this example:

> "That's not me!" a person will say when he hears himself on tape for the first time. The reason your voice sounds weird on tape is because you're finally hearing it the way other people hear it—after it's traveled a few feet or yards. When you hear your voice during normal conversation, the sound travels only a few inches "inside-out," from your head to the inside of your ears! (Strauss, 2005, p. 154)

With a reading passage such as this one, proficient readers notice that the text follows a pattern: Result (our own voice sounds unrecognizable on tape) comes before the cause (we're hearing it from a few feet away instead of a few inches). They then reverse the pattern to piece the whole sequence together:

When we talk, the sound travels "inside out" from our mouth to our ears.

When we listen to a tape of ourselves, the sound travels a few feet through the air.

This is why our voice sounds strange on tape.

This ability to reason while reading helps proficient readers focus on and work through difficult passages or areas of text.

Thus, to move beyond the literal—to become eyes-on, minds-on readers capable of making inferences—proficient readers engage in four distinct forms of thinking:

1. They create images out of the author's words, pictures, feelings, and sounds that bring life and meaning to the text (as with the rain forest reading).

2. They make connections between what they are reading and their relevant, objective knowledge (as with the excerpt from Richard Wright's biography).

3. They apply their reasoning skills to focus on patterns and clues in the text that can help them make inferences or predictions about the text (as with the passage on why our voices sound different on tape).

4. They are aware of their own reading processes as they read. They know when they understand a text and when the reading has become confusing or lifeless. In the case of the latter, proficient readers take one of the three actions above to improve their understanding (as you may have done with any or all three of the readings).

Although expert readers perform the above actions easily, fluently, and largely unconsciously, school-aged children must be taught how to apply these thinking strategies explicitly.

Students need modeling and practice—lots of practice—to become the proficient readers we long for them to be. In this chapter, we explore six strategies that foster the development of these essential skills:

Reading for Meaning, which helps students forge connections between what they already know and what they are reading and builds the skills of evidence-based reading.

Inductive Learning and **Compare and Contrast,** which help students become sensitive to patterns in text and reason their way to successful inferences and predictions.

Image Making and **Mind's Eye**, which help students use their imaginations to construct images and derive meaning and pleasure from what they read.

Do You Hear What I Hear? which scaffolds and builds the core skills needed for deep, inferential reading and allows students to expand their inference-making skills over time.

READING FOR MEANING

Overview

Reading for Meaning addresses the challenges that young readers face in finding and using textual evidence to support their ideas and develop thoughtful interpretations. In a Reading for Meaning lesson, students are given a set of statements that help them preview and make predictions before reading, search actively for evidence during reading, and reflect on what they learned after reading.

The Strategy in Action

Second-grade teacher Eliot Resnick loves reading good stories aloud to his students. Today, Eliot is reading Marni McGee's and Ian Beck's *Winston the Book Wolf* (2006), a humorous story about a wolf who learns that books are better for reading than for eating. Behind him is an easel on which Eliot has written four statements in a particular format (see Figure 4.2):

Proof For		Proof Against
	Winston doesn't understand what books are for.	
	Rosie is a good friend to Winston.	
	You don't have to eat words to know they can be delicious.	
	Learning how to read doesn't make much of a difference in Winston's life.	

Figure 4.2   Eliot's Reading for Meaning Easel

Both before and as Eliot reads the book aloud, he asks students to think about the statements he has written and to see if they can make any predictions about what the book will be about. Then, at key points in the reading, Eliot stops and asks students if they notice anything in the story that might help them decide whether the statements are true or false. If the students' information suggests that a statement is true, he writes it in the

"Proof For" column. If the information suggests that a statement is false, he writes it in the "Proof Against" column. After completing the chart, Eliot and his students discuss the reading and the statements to see how the reading has changed students' initial ideas about reading, words, and the story's main character, Winston the book wolf. In this way, Eliot is helping his students develop the crucial skill of collecting evidence and using it to interpret literature.

* * * *

"Collecting and making good use of evidence," explains Kirsten Hardaway to her fifth graders, "is one of the most important reading and research skills there is." Like Eliot Resnick, Kirsten also uses Reading for Meaning to promote evidence-based reading, but with a yearlong emphasis on building student independence. At the beginning of the year, Kirsten provides students with statements to use in analyzing a reading.

As the year progresses, Kirsten shifts responsibility for using the strategy to her students. For some readings, Kirsten asks students to create their own statements and then to trade these statements with a partner. Each student uses his or her partner's statements to conduct the reading. Partners then meet to discuss each other's statements and, if necessary, to rewrite them so they are keyed to essential information.

To further build student independence, Kirsten shows students how to use the strategy to manage difficult readings. When students become confused by what they are reading, she explains that they can stop reading and instead focus on creating a statement that they believe tells what the passage is about. Students can then use this statement to check whether the reading supports their belief.

Why the Strategy Is Beneficial

Strategic reading is a goal in every classroom where reading takes place. But what exactly is meant by the term "strategic" when it comes to reading? Herrmann (1992), in her work on strategic reasoning, defines the application of strategic reasoning to reading and writing as the "complex thinking processes used before, during, and after reading and writing to construct meaningful interpretations of text and to create meaningful texts" (p. 428). Central to Herrmann's formulation is the idea that the strategic reader interacts with the text at three distinct points: before reading, during reading, and after reading. Of course, Herrmann is not alone in this idea. For example, after evaluating over 60 studies on skilled reading, Pressley (2006) concludes that "in general, the conscious processing that is excellent reading begins before reading, continues during reading, and persists after reading is completed" (p. 57).

Reading for Meaning (Silver, Hanson, Strong, & Schwartz, 1996) is adapted from Herber's (1970) work with Reading and Reasoning Guides and is designed specifically to make students active participants in the three-part structure of strategic reading through three phases: prereading, active reading, and postreading.

- In the prereading activity, students preview statements about the text prior to reading it and anticipate what the text might be about, thus helping them to intuitively develop an image of the text's structure and content. Students may also be asked to decide whether each statement is true or false before reading, which forces students to convert their prior knowledge into predictions and hypotheses. (This option works best when statements are not text-specific. Making predictions about text-specific statements such as "Rosie is a good friend to Winston" amounts to blind guessing. However, general statements such as "Spiders are more helpful than harmful" or "Being brave means you are never afraid" ask students to use their prior knowledge to stake out a position—which will be either confirmed or challenged by the text). As Tierney and Cunningham (1984) report, both of these prereading activities (previewing and predicting) make reading more manageable for students.
- In the active reading stage, students read with a purpose, searching for evidence to support or refute the statements.
- Postreading activity is stimulated by asking students to look back at their statements and consider how their understanding has changed or evolved as a result of the reading.

In addition to its three-phase structure, one of the greatest benefits of Reading for Meaning can be found in the flexibility of its statements. Statements can be crafted so that they focus on specific reading skills and help students overcome common reading challenges. Figure 4.3 shows how you can use statements to build nine distinct reading skills and provides sample statements keyed to each skill.

Focus Skill	*How to Build It*	*Sample Statements*
Vocabulary	Incorporate synonyms, near-synonyms, (or antonyms) for difficult words into your statements.	• Astronomers couldn't agree on whether Pluto should be called a planet. (A statement designed to help students figure out what *consensus* means in this sentence: *But astronomers couldn't reach consensus on the issue of Pluto's claim to planethood.*)
Main Idea Comprehension	Design statements that require students to consider the overall meaning.	• The author's main point is that pollution has a greater effect on amphibians than other animals. • A good title for this would be "Teamwork Helps Everyone Win."

Focus Skill	How to Build It	Sample Statements
Interpretation/ Inference	Craft statements that force students to "read between the lines."	• We can tell that Frog and Toad have been friends for a long time. • There are probably more reptiles in New York than in Alaska.
Case building	Develop statements that ask students to take a position.	• Bats are more helpful than harmful. • Being brave means never being afraid.
Visualization/ Image-Making	Draw students' attention to image-rich sections of the reading.	• The author's language helps me to imagine what the inside of a Pharaoh's tomb looks like.
Exploring Metaphors	Create statements that use metaphors or similes to help students develop new insights.	• Being a scientist is a lot like being a detective.
Appreciating Style and Technique	Use statements to help students see how authors achieve their intended effects.	• The author's description of the house makes the story scarier. • The author's examples are not very persuasive.
Empathizing	Give students the opportunity to identify with characters', subjects', or authors' positions and feelings.	• Mario was deeply hurt by the incident on the playground.
Developing a Personal Perspective	Allow students to examine the content from their own lives and points of view.	• My life would be very different if there were no computers. • My ideas about conservation are a lot like the author's.

Figure 4.3   Using Reading for Meaning Statements to Build Reading Skills

How to Use the Strategy

Use Organizer 4-A, "Reading for Meaning," on page 122.

Incorporate the Reading for Meaning strategy into your classroom using the following steps:

1. Provide students with three to five statements keyed to major ideas in a reading. Have students copy the statements onto Organizer 4-A, "Reading for Meaning." Allow students to preview the statements and anticipate what they think the reading will be about. Depending on how text-specific the statements are, you may also ask students whether they think the statements are true or false.

2. Instruct students to read the text, looking for evidence that corresponds to each statement and recording it on their organizer, either in the "Evidence For" or "Evidence Against" column.

3. After reading, ask students to meet with other students to discuss their evidence and to try to reach consensus for each statement.

4. Lead a discussion in which you survey positions and discuss the role of textual evidence in defending positions.

5. To extend the learning, you may want to challenge students to elaborate on their new knowledge or to use their new knowledge to create a summary or interpretation of the reading.

6. Teach students how to use the strategy independently by developing statements and using them to verify understanding.

Helping Struggling Readers

The primary difficulty students experience during a Reading for Meaning lesson is finding and using appropriate evidence to support or refute the statements. For example, Cataldo and Oakhill (2000) found that poor comprehenders have a harder time locating specific information in text than good comprehenders. English language learners are also prone to struggle with the task of finding specific information, given the added challenge of their limited English vocabularies and their different sources of background knowledge.

How should you address these problems? Obviously, teacher modeling is essential. Beyond modeling, however, the following suggestions can help students develop competence in evidence gathering:

1. Be literal at first. The first time you use Reading for Meaning with students, begin with literal statements that are explicitly addressed in the reading. Over time, you can make the statements more inferential, but by beginning with the literal, you can greatly boost students' confidence in their ability to track down evidence. It is also a good idea to identify potentially challenging vocabulary words or gaps in background information to help English language learners.

2. Encourage text-marking or text-posting. If the students are able to write directly on their readings, let them underline, highlight, and mark up the text to help them find relevant information. If they can't write on their text, provide them with Post-it notes they can use to mark essential information. Or, teach them to use reader's punctuation, such as the following:

   + This supports a statement.

   − This refutes a statement.

   ? I think this is important, but I'm not exactly sure why.

3. Practice using evidence in everyday activities. Accustom students to the idea of using evidence before they begin reading. For example, a fourth-grade teacher from New York began a class by saying, "The New York Yankees are a great baseball team." Then she asked students to provide evidence for or against this statement. Students' responses included: "They've won the World Series more than any other team." "They have lots of All-Stars on the team." "They always win their division." In this way, students were able to see what it means to gather evidence before being asked to do it in conjunction with a text.

4. Use statement strips. Give students a sheet of strips containing facts about a topic (e.g., Spiders eat insects that carry diseases). Then, provide students with a statement such as, Spiders are helpful to humans. Ask students to cut up their strips and to determine whether the information supports or refutes your statement. Students can paste their strips onto an organizer or piece of poster board divided into "Supports" and "Refutes" columns. This activity is a fun, hands-on way for students to evaluate evidence.

5. With English language learners, it may be helpful to use visuals to model the process of prediction and evidence gathering. Gibbons (2002) suggests showing students a key visual from the book—a photo or illustration—and having them predict the topic or story line. If the students will be reading a text about hurricanes, for example, you can show a picture of the devastation caused by recent hurricanes and ask them to guess what happened. Gibbons recommends introducing new vocabulary words that will occur in the text at this point, as most English language learners will be able to quickly connect the new vocabulary to familiar first-language words. Visually anchoring students to the topic and process in this way will make it easier for them to look for evidence to support or refute their initial predictions.

ORGANIZER 4-A: READING FOR MEANING

Name: _____

Reading for Meaning		
Proof For	**Statement**	**Proof Against**

INDUCTIVE LEARNING

Overview

Proficient readers make inferences during reading by filling in the gaps between their prior knowledge and the information they encounter in the text. This process deepens students' understanding and provides a strong conceptual framework for future learning. Inductive Learning capitalizes on and builds students' natural inference-making potential by asking them to:

- Examine key terms from the text before reading.
- Group and label terms according to what they have in common with other terms.
- Use their labeled groups to generate a set of predictions about the reading.
- Collect evidence that supports or refutes their predictions.

The Strategy in Action

Teacher Maggie O'Hagan knows that when students make predictions about a text, their reading becomes an active search, an inquiry spurred by curiosity about whether they were right. This is why Inductive Learning is one of her favorite instructional strategies.

Currently, Maggie is using Inductive Learning as part of her unit on colonial America. Using a reading on the way colonial New Englanders lived, Maggie selects approximately 30 words and phrases from the reading that support the generalizations she expects students to make. For instance, one of the essential ideas in the reading is that colonial New Englanders were very religious. To support this idea, Maggie selects the following words from the reading:

sin

minister

Sabbath

Bible

faith

prayer

congregation

Once she has completed selecting key words for each big idea in the reading, Maggie gives the words to students and asks them to analyze the words. Then, students work in teams of three to group the words into categories on the basis of common attributes. Once students have grouped the words, they must devise a descriptive label for each group that succinctly identifies the common relationship between the words. Figure 4.4 shows one student team's groupings:

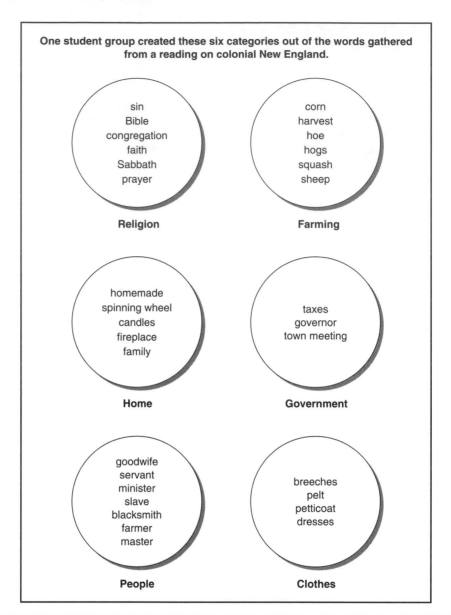

One student group created these six categories out of the words gathered from a reading on colonial New England.

sin
Bible
congregation
faith
Sabbath
prayer

Religion

corn
harvest
hoe
hogs
squash
sheep

Farming

homemade
spinning wheel
candles
fireplace
family

Home

taxes
governor
town meeting

Government

goodwife
servant
minister
slave
blacksmith
farmer
master

People

breeches
pelt
petticoat
dresses

Clothes

Figure 4.4 A Student Team's Labeled Groups

Students then use their groupings to make three hypotheses about life in colonial New England. Among the most common predictions Maggie hears from her students are:

"Life was hard."

"They were very religious."

"Farming was how they got food."

"They had simple clothes—not a lot of extras like jewelry."

"Family was very important."

Once students make their three hypotheses, they read the selection and use it to find out whether they were correct or mistaken. Using a

Support-Refute Organizer (Figure 4.5), students jot down evidence from the selection that supports or refutes each hypothesis in the appropriate space.

Hypothesis	Support	Refute
Colonial New Englanders were very religious.		
They lived simple lives.		
They farmed for their food.		

Figure 4.5   Support/Refute Organizer

To move her students toward independence, Maggie explains that this process is especially helpful when a reading becomes difficult. By starting with the words that seem important and then grouping those words to build a meaningful set of categories, the reader can work through the reading and develop a general understanding of its important ideas. This gives the student a reading framework he or she can use to "crack" the difficult text.

Why the Strategy Is Beneficial

In Marzano, Pickering, and Pollock's (2001) meta-analysis of instructional strategies, they found that generating and testing hypotheses was one of the most effective ways to raise students' levels of academic achievement. Few strategies put greater emphasis on generating and testing hypotheses than Inductive Learning. Inductive Learning is based on the time-honored work of Taba (1971), who found that if students were asked to enumerate and examine related items, group these items into meaningful categories, provide descriptive labels for each group, and make predictions on the basis of those groups, they were better able to make generalizations and find big ideas in the content they were learning.

By asking students to search for patterns, think flexibly about possible relationships, summarize these relationships through labeling, and use these self-created relationships to find meaning, Inductive Learning taps into students' natural potential for making inferences.

Four elements of Inductive Learning make it particularly powerful as a reading strategy:

1. It introduces students to the skills of identifying key words and phrases in a reading.

2. It asks students to form a conceptual framework by developing groups before they read.

3. It asks students to make predictions about what the reading will contain.

4. It asks students to search for relevant evidence.

How to Use the Strategy

Use Organizer 4-B, "Support/Refute," on page 128.

Incorporate the Inductive Learning strategy into your classroom, using the following steps:

1. Identify key words and phrases from the text and distribute them to students. (You can also work with students to enumerate words and phrases from the text, especially after students are comfortable with the process.)

2. Model the process of grouping and labeling.

3. Have students form small groups to analyze the words and to explore the different ways information can be grouped.

4. Ask students to devise a descriptive label for each of their groups.

5. Have students use their labels and word groupings to make several predictions or hypotheses about the reading. Students should write their hypotheses in the appropriate space in Organizer 4-B, "Support/Refute."

6. Instruct students to read the text using Organizer 4-B to search for evidence that supports or refutes their hypotheses.

7. Ask students to reflect on the Inductive Learning process and lead a discussion on what they have learned from it.

8. Teach students how to use the process of identifying words, creating groups, and generating predictions as an independent reading strategy.

Helping Struggling Readers

Although struggling readers have a more difficult time generating inferences (Cain & Oakhill, 1999, Oakhill, 1982, 1984), they face a particular challenge in making elaborative inferences. Elaborative inferences require students to access and integrate prior knowledge to interpret text (Cain, Oakhill, Barnes, & Bryant, 2001), and include such activities as predicting possible outcomes and generating hypotheses about readings. The cause of these difficulties had previously been linked to low background knowledge or poor memory, but when Cain et al. (2001) used a procedure to control for general knowledge differences, they found that struggling comprehenders still generated significantly fewer inferences than their more skilled peers. The researchers concluded that children who struggle with comprehension were unable to select the relevant information from the text on which to base the inference. Bowyer-Crane and Snowling (2005) found a similar trend: less skilled comprehenders had more difficulty making what they call "gap-filling inferences" than their more skilled peers.

The Inductive Learning strategy capitalizes on several proven methods that help struggling readers make the leap into inferential reading, including small-group work, the use of graphic organizers to collect and manage information, and an active process for interacting with the text before, during, and after reading. Below are several additional recommendations for helping struggling students become independent users of this strategy:

1. First, read the passage aloud and highlight key vocabulary words that may be unfamiliar. Then, model the different processes that make up the strategy (generating, grouping and labeling, predicting, collecting evidence). Allow time for guided practice.

2. For students who are struggling while trying to group information from a text, you may want to use concrete objects such as fruits, vegetables, money, toys, etc., to help them develop classification skills through hands-on grouping activities. You can help students gain confidence in their abilities to classify information by providing them with the labels and a set of specific terms or items and asking them to create groups accordingly.

3. Because grouping is a process that uses specifics to help students discover more general (and more abstract) ideas, it is a good idea to expose the different patterns that this specific-to-general relationship can take. Talk with students about their reasons for grouping, for example:
   • Is the reason for grouping categorical? Are the members of the group all examples of one thing (e.g., France, Chile, India, and Kenya are all countries)?
   • Is the reason for grouping descriptive? Are the members of the group connected by similarities in shape, appearance, color, texture, material, etc. (e.g., cotton, feathers, pillows are all soft)?
   • Is the reason for grouping based on a part-to-whole relationship? Are the members of the group all part of something larger (e.g., door, window, kitchen, living room are all parts of a house)?
   • Is the reason for the grouping relational or inferential? Are items grouped according to an abstract quality shared by the whole group (e.g., rain, cloud, mild, and foggy all have to do with the weather)?
   • Is the reason for the grouping mixed? Does it use some combination of the above? Or does it follow another pattern altogether?

In terms of trouble students may encounter in gathering relevant evidence to support and refute their hypotheses, refer to the "Helping the Struggling Reader" section in Reading for Meaning (page 120).

ORGANIZER 4-B: SUPPORT/REFUTE

Name: _____

Support/Refute		
Hypothesis	**Support**	**Refute**

COMPARE AND CONTRAST

Overview

Comparison is one of the most natural and most powerful ways of learning that we have at our disposal. Putting two items, ideas, or texts side by side gives us "double sight," allowing us to see deeply into each by using the other as a frame of reference. Recently, researchers have demonstrated that instructional strategies that capitalize on the comparative power of "double sight" represent the single most effective way to increase students' comprehension and achievement levels. As a reading strategy, Compare and Contrast builds on and refines the natural drive to compare by:

- Asking students to first describe each topic or text separately.
- Having students record similarities and differences on a graphic organizer.
- Engaging students in discussion and asking them to draw thoughtful conclusions.
- Developing student independence in conducting quality comparisons of their own.

The Strategy in Action

Amy Wheeler is teaching her third graders about spiders. When she began her unit, she found that most students think spiders are insects. Today, to help them overcome this misconception, Amy is going to show her class how to distinguish between two objects in order to make careful observations and draw thoughtful conclusions.

Amy begins by asking her students to think about cats and dogs. She asks them to think about what makes a dog a dog and what makes a cat a cat. "How do they look? What do they eat? What are some things they do?" she asks. She asks the class to use these three criteria to describe each animal separately. As students respond, she records their ideas on the board. Once each animal has been adequately described, Amy draws a Top Hat Organizer on the board. She labels the top left column "Cats" and the top right column "Dogs," and uses the information from the description to record the key differences with her students. Then, Amy asks her students what characteristics both animals share and records student responses in the "Similarities" field of the organizer (see Figure 4.6).

After Amy discusses this process of comparing and contrasting, she turns to the two selected readings: one on spiders and one on insects. Before the reading, she hands out pieces of paper on which the students draw their own Top Hat Organizers for recording similarities and differences. Once again, she asks students to first describe each separately by focusing on what each looks like, eats, and does. She reads each text twice, asking her students to listen the first time without writing and then to write down their observations the second time as she reads more slowly. After this

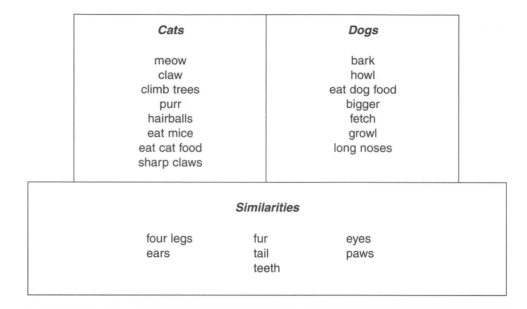

Figure 4.6 Top Hat Organizer

description phase, students use their Top Hat Organizers to discriminate between spiders and insects by recording similarities and differences.

When the students are finished, Amy checks their comprehension of the readings and the accuracy of their organizers by asking what makes a spider a spider, what makes an insect an insect, and what characteristics they both share. She lists student responses on the board and then asks them to decide if spiders and insects are more alike or more different. For a final activity, Amy asks her students to write a brief response to this question: "Would you rather be a spider or an insect? Why?"

Lately, Amy has been using Compare and Contrast to help students develop their skills of literary interpretation as well. She finds that the strategy is an ideal way to help students learn how to conduct close comparative readings of short texts. For example, today students will read two fables about a weaker animal that helps a more powerful animal, Aesop's *The Lion and the Mouse* and a Korean fable called *The Ungrateful Tiger*. Through comparison, students will not only discover the similarities and differences in characters and plot but will also begin a yearlong inquiry into what readers can learn about what different cultures value by paying close attention to the stories that different people tell.

Why the Strategy Is Beneficial

In their comprehensive investigation into the effects of various instructional strategies on student achievement, Marzano, Pickering, and Pollock (2001) found that strategies requiring students to identify similarities and differences represent the single most effective way to raise student achievement, with students exhibiting percentile gains well over 35 points in several studies. In surveying this research on comparison strategies, Marzano and his team went on to identify the "salient generalizations," or the characteristics of highly effective comparison strategies. Among their findings:

- Comparison strategies work best when they include direct instruction in identifying similarities.
- Students need opportunities to identify similarities and differences on their own. Teacher-directed learning is important, but so is student-directed learning. When students have the chance to conduct their own comparisons, their understanding of content and their comfort with the process increase significantly.
- The power of comparative thinking is amplified through the use of graphic organizers.

Compare and Contrast takes these findings and applies them specifically to reading instruction. First, it builds in teacher modeling sessions for two separate processes: one in which students are taught how to describe two topics or two texts separately using clear criteria to guide their descriptions, and one in which they are taught how to use their descriptions to record similarities and differences. Second, after modeling, students describe and compare new topics or texts on their own. Third, both teacher modeling and students' self-directed activity are anchored by a graphic organizer. Compare and Contrast lessons end by asking students to use their comparisons to draw and justify conclusions.

How to Use the Strategy

Use Compare and Contrast Organizers 4-C, 4-D, or 4-E (pages 134–136): "Top Hat Organizer," "Venn Diagram," or "Side-by-Side Diagram."

Incorporate the Compare and Contrast strategy into your classroom using the following steps:

1. Introduce the process of comparison by first describing separately and then comparing simple, everyday objects that students know already—cats and dogs, apples and oranges, summer and spring. Collect the similarities and differences on one of the organizer formats (Organizer 4-C, 4-D, or 4-E).

2. Select and distribute Compare and Contrast Organizer 4-C, 4-D, or 4-E. Choose two separate readings or a reading describing two different topics that students will compare and contrast.

3. Establish the purpose for comparison by answering the question, Why are we conducting a comparative reading?

4. Provide students with criteria for analyzing the two items (e.g., What do they eat? What do they look like? How do they behave?).

5. Have students use the criteria to describe each item separately.

6. Show students how to use Organizer 4-C, 4-D, or 4-E to differentiate between the two readings or topics by recording similarities and differences.

7. Lead a discussion on one of the following topics:
   - Are the two more alike or more different?
   - What is the most important difference? What are the causes and effects of this difference?
   - What conclusions can you draw?

8. Move students toward independence in formulating criteria, describing items, and determining their similarities and differences.

Helping Struggling Readers

The following interventions can prove helpful in scaffolding this strategy for struggling readers and English language learners alike:

- Begin by identifying and addressing any vocabulary words or gaps in prior knowledge that may prove challenging.
- Read the text or texts aloud first before asking students to read independently. Read slowly, modeling expression that indicates when you are reading information relevant to the purposes of comparison.
- Use notemaking as a complementary tool for comparison. Notemaking tools such as Graphic Organizers (see Chapter 2), text glossing, and reader's vocabulary (e.g., a "+" to indicate a difference) can help students see critical relationships and make richer comparisons.
- For students who are having trouble analyzing the reading for similarities and differences, provide them with or show them how to create a two-column Description Organizer that will structure and focus their reading around similarities and differences. For example, using the Description Organizer below (Figure 4.7), students will have an easier time extracting key information from their reading.

	The Lion and the Mouse	*The Ungrateful Tiger*
Characters		
How the weaker animal helps the stronger animal		
Stronger animal's response		
Lesson of the fable		

Figure 4.7   Description Organizer

- Or, to further simplify the process, you might use a Comparison Matrix (see Figure 4.8 for an example) so that all students have to do is fill in + or − signs when analyzing topics in a reading or readings.

	Winter	Spring	Summer	Fall
Warm				
Hot				
Cold or cool				
Leaves fall				
Trees blossom				
Snow				
No school				

Figure 4.8   Comparison Matrix

- For those English language learners who are struggling with identifying similarities and differences in texts, consider using a visual strategy such as Find the Difference (Gibbons, 2002). In Find the Difference, two students are paired, and each is given an illustration. The two illustrations should have some common characteristics as well as some distinct characteristics (e.g., a picture of a bat and a picture of a bird). Students cannot show their picture to each other; instead, they must describe their own picture, ask questions about the other student's picture, and develop a list of the similarities and differences between the two.

ORGANIZER 4-C: TOP HAT ORGANIZER

Name: _____

Top Hat Organizer

Differences	Differences

Similarities

ORGANIZER 4-D: VENN DIAGRAM

Name: _____

Venn Diagram

Differences   Similarities   Differences

ORGANIZER 4-E: SIDE-BY-SIDE DIAGRAM

Name: _____

Side-by-Side Diagram			
Criteria for Comparison	**1.**	**2.**	**Both**

IMAGE MAKING

Overview

Making images in the mind is an essential skill for deep reading, yet it is often taken for granted. The ability to form quick, vivid mental pictures—to see a text unfolding in the mind—is one of the key elements that proficient readers possess but that struggling and average readers lack. This strategy models Image Making first for students, then breaks down the process into manageable steps so that students can practice and develop the skill with increasing confidence and competence.

The Strategy in Action

Teacher Jamie Gonzalez and a student, Marcie, sit facing each other. Marcie holds a book in her lap entitled *Outrageous Women of the Middle Ages* by Vicki Leon (1998). Jamie explains to students that today they will be exploring image making in reading. She asks Marcie to begin reading the biographical sketch called "Aud, the Deep-Minded" aloud and slowly.

At the end of the first page, Jamie stops Marcie and says, "Tall. Muscular. Armor. These are words of power, words of strength. When you were describing how Aud grew up, I could really see her decked out in armor and holding an axe. She seemed very powerful, like a woman athlete today."

Later on, Jamie stops Marcie again. "Converting to Christianity—I get a lot of images from that. When she converts to Christianity and becomes a wise woman I saw her and her people sitting around a fire. And Aud telling stories, and swaying while she talked. Aud the deep-minded—that's what I saw."

Near the end, Jamie stops Marcie yet again. "Being turned away by your own brother, that's very emotional. When you read about that, I felt so angry. She finally found her brother Helgi after 30 years—and he wouldn't take her in. I could feel my body getting tight and angry. I could see her throwing things around and storming out."

After they finish, the students break into pairs and take turns reading biographies of medieval women to each other and discussing the images that come to their minds. Later on, students work in their journals. Some draw pictures of the images they create. Others describe the images with words and speculate on the thoughts and feelings of the women they are studying. Still others use the Split Screen strategy (see pages 45–48) to record both words and pictures from their learning. Jamie discusses the journal entries with students to help them see how they are doing as image makers.

Why the Strategy Is Beneficial

Nothing could be less traditional than the classroom above, and, perhaps, nothing could be more essential. Books are not movies, and without moving pictures, sound effects, and music at their disposal, authors count on readers to supply the missing elements that make their words move, breathe, and give pleasure.

The failure of students to create images spontaneously goes a long way toward explaining gaps in students' reading comprehension. Wilhelm (2004) makes the case for visualization in the strongest terms imaginable: "Without visualization," he contends, "students cannot comprehend, and reading cannot be said to be reading" (p. 9). Proficient readers use their images "to draw conclusions, create unique interpretations of the text, recall details significant to the text, and recall a text after it has been read" (Miller, 2002, p. 91).

The reason behind visualization's power as a reading and learning strategy can be summed up in two words: *dual coding.* Dual coding (Paivio, 1990) tells us that storing information in two ways—through both language and images—improves students' abilities to recall and extend what they have learned. Sadoski and Wilson (2006) conducted a large-scale study on a dual-coding-based reading program in Pueblo School District 60, a heavily minority urban district in Colorado with a high concentration of Title I schools. Sadoski and Wilson tracked reading achievement levels in Grades 3–5 across 28 schools from 1998 to 2003. They found the dual coding program resulted in improved reading comprehension scores across the board, with Pueblo's students significantly outperforming students from comparable Colorado districts and Title I schools.

Although proficient readers create images automatically, most students must be trained to form images during reading (Pressley, 1977; Sadoski, 1985). Fortunately, teaching students to make images is a relatively simple and short procedure: both Pressley (1976) and Gambrell and Bales (1986) report that elementary students, including poor readers, can learn to form images rather easily. Image Making serves as an ideal method for developing this critical skill in students given that research has identified teacher modeling and Think Alouds (explaining what's happening in your mind as you create images) as ideal ways to teach visualization (Gambrell & Koskinen, 2002).

How to Use the Strategy

Incorporate Image Making into your classroom using the following steps:

1. Model the process by reading a selection and stopping periodically to describe the images you developed and how and why you developed them during the reading. (You may also involve students in modeling as readers and as tentative image makers.)

2. Have students form pairs to read texts (aloud or independently), form images, and discuss those images with their partners.

3. Expand students' image-making skills by having students:
   • Discuss their experiences and their images.

- Hold conferences on the relationship between reading and image making.
- Do journal work on image making in which students draw pictures, write descriptive paragraphs, describe their feelings, or use a word-image technique such as Split Screen.

Helping Struggling Readers

Gambrell and Koskinen (2002) suggest teachers should explain to students that there are no right or wrong images. Each person in the classroom will create a different picture in his or her head based on personal experiences and life history. This is particularly important to convey to English language learners, who bring diverse cultural backgrounds with them into the classroom. Remember, however, that background knowledge and experience are only part of the image-making process; students will also need to learn how to "read visually," so that the images they create promote a deeper understanding of the text.

In response, Nanci Bell (1991), teacher, researcher, and leading proponent of learning through visualization, makes some simple suggestions for helping struggling readers form images while reading, including:

1. Provide a purpose by explaining how and why image making is an important reading skill.

2. Have the student select a picture from a book and ask the student to describe it. Because you can't see the picture, you should ask questions about the picture, which the student should answer as descriptively as possible. This activity helps build the connection between words and images.

3. Use a progressive structure so that students start by imaging words and gradually move on to imaging paragraphs and extended passages.

4. Use questions to help students focus on big ideas and important information (e.g., What does this passage seem to be saying? What does this paragraph describe?), especially for longer and more complex passages where students may have trouble focusing and finding images.

MIND'S EYE

Overview

Similar to Image Making, Mind's Eye is a visualization strategy. What separates it from Image Making are its small group and conference structures, its use of nontextual image making to scaffold visualization skills, and its increased emphasis on teaching students how to find image-rich language in the text.

The Strategy in Action

For the last few days, Horace Witherspoon has been helping his second graders to practice forming images of everyday objects. "What does it look like? What colors, shapes, textures do you see? Does it have a smell? Does it make any sounds? How does it feel—is it soft or rough or smooth?" he asks students as they close their eyes and concentrate on things as simple as their books, their pets, and what they ate for breakfast.

Today, students are applying their image-making skills to reading as Horace teaches them how to find the visual words in a text. Today's reading comes from Jacob Lawrence's *Harriet and the Promised Land* (1993), a verse book about Harriet Tubman. Horace reads the first lines of the book aloud:

Harriet, Harriet,

Born a slave,

Work for your master

From your cradle

To your grave.

Harriet, clean;

Harriet, sweep.

Harriet, rock

The child to sleep.

Horace then goes back and shows students how he picks words to help him create an image. "It's important," Horace tells his students, "not to underline too many words—just the ones that can help you see the picture in the words. So, for these lines, the words *slave*, *clean*, *sleep*, and *rock* all help me make a picture in my head. In my picture, I see poor Harriet working all the time. She cleans and sweeps and takes care of the children. She has no time for herself. She just works so much that it hurts. She wants to do other things like play hide-and-seek, read, and have fun. But she's a slave, and she's only allowed to clean and sweep and take care of the children."

Horace repeats this process for the next few pages and then breaks students up into small groups to begin forming images of the text on their own by identifying a few key words and phrases. Students discuss their images with their groups, and then Horace conducts a whole-class discussion on reading using images.

Later in the week, after students have had time to practice, Horace meets with each image-making group and asks them questions about how they are doing at finding key words and developing images: "What do you see? Hear? Feel? What do you think the author will talk about next? How will that change your image? What key words did you underline?

How did you decide on those words?" Horace uses the information he learns from the conferences to determine which students need more practice and which students are ready to work independently.

Why the Strategy Is Beneficial

Mind's Eye is similar to Image Making: It teaches students how to form pictures in their minds to animate and deepen their reading, and it uses a Think Aloud procedure to model the use of the strategy. In addition, Mind's Eye draws from the same research base as Image Making. However, there are several key differences between the strategies:

- Mind's Eye begins with nontextual image making, giving students practice before they read. This nontextual approach helps students learn to create images using everyday objects and activities that involve all five senses and that require them to activate their prior learning.
- Mind's Eye places greater emphasis on the identification of key words and phrases than Image Making.
- Mind's Eye makes working in small groups and conferences an essential part of the process of assessing progress and addressing students' needs. According to Miller (2002), working collaboratively enhances the image-making process, as readers tend to adapt their own images after sharing their thoughts with others.

How to Use the Strategy

Incorporate the Mind's Eye strategy into your classroom using the following steps:

1. Ask students to practice thinking about and forming images of simple, well-known objects—a dog, an apple, a ringing bell, the sight and feel of a hamburger—anything that students know and can visualize. During these image-making sessions, use the following questions and prompts:
   - What do you see?
   - What do you hear?
   - How do you feel?

2. Have students practice this image making for brief periods of time over several days.

3. Show students how to pre-read a passage by identifying and underlining the key words necessary to create an image in the mind. Teach students to be economical in underlining words and to focus only on those words and phrases that contain the essential visual information.

4. Work with students individually and in small groups by asking them to read aloud and to discuss their methods for selecting words

and forming images. During these conferences and group-imaging sessions, use the prompts below in addition to those in step 1:

- What do you think will come next?
- How might your prediction change your image?
- What word did you use to create your image?
- How did you determine your key words?

5. Use conferences to assess student competencies. Encourage proficient image makers to work independently. Provide additional assistance to struggling students.

Helping Struggling Readers

Both struggling readers and English language learners will benefit from working with partners or in small groups before working on their own. Remind students that there are no right or wrong images—what is important is for them to share what they see in their minds when they hear the words.

To help students form images that promote deeper understanding, refer to Bell's (1991) suggestions for the Image Making strategy, on page 139.

DO YOU HEAR WHAT I HEAR?

Overview

As state and national standards place greater emphasis on literacy skills, teachers are faced with the prospect of developing a skill-based curriculum without cutting into content. Do You Hear What I Hear? (Strong & Silver, 1998) was designed specifically to address this challenge. The strategy sets the bar high, focusing on rigorous texts. Then, through listening, speaking, reading, and writing; through diagnostic coaching; and through regular and sustained commitment to student development, the strategy builds the skills needed to process and respond effectively to these rigorous texts.

The Strategy in Action

If you ask Victor Gramsci why his fourth graders did so well on the reading and writing portions of his state's tests, he'll give two reasons. First, he'll tell you about *Touchpebbles* (Zeiderman, 2003), a discussion-based reading program built on short but challenging texts from around the world. Second, Victor will talk about Rigorous Wednesdays. In Victor's class, every Wednesday is a Rigorous Wednesday. On each Rigorous Wednesday Victor conducts a Do You Hear What I Hear? lesson using a text from the *Touchpebbles* collection. Today, Victor is reading a Middle Eastern tale called "The Pillow" aloud to his students. "The Pillow" tells the story of a wise man who gives a greedy young man a special pillow that makes wishes come true. The young man quickly becomes a wealthy nobleman. Shortly after that, he is the victim of a plot for power and is sentenced to death. As he is about to be beheaded, the young man wakes up, happy to have his humble life back.

Victor reads "The Pillow" to students twice. During the first read-aloud, students simply listen. During the second read-aloud, students develop a set of notes that will help them retell "The Pillow" to another student.

Next, students pair up. Each student retells the story to the other student, who acts as a "retelling coach." Meanwhile, Victor circulates around the room, listening in on partnerships and providing coaching to partnerships that are having trouble. Victor is especially pleased by what he hears while listening in on Riley and Omar:

Riley: The part that I didn't really get was where all of a sudden, he went from being a rich guy to being about to get his head chopped off to being . . . uh . . .

Omar: To being what?

Riley: Whatever he is at the end. Um, a regular guy, I guess.

Omar: Right, a regular guy.

Riley: I still don't get how it all happened so fast.

Omar: Well, there's a part in there that tells us. Do you remember?

Riley: Uh . . . no. I don't think so.

Omar: Well what's he doing on the pillow?

Riley: Sleeping, I guess. Yeah, sleeping.

Omar: And then he . . .

Riley: OK, now I get it. He wakes up. He was dreaming. It was a pillow, and he was sleeping on it. The part about getting rich and getting his head chopped off was a dream.

Omar: Great! So now you can finish your retelling.

After both students in each pair have retold the story, each pair joins up with another pair. In teams of four, students use their copies of "The Pillow" to answer four questions. Today's questions are:

- What is the meaning of *crafty*? Use specific textual evidence in your answer. (vocabulary question)
- Why does the wise man give the young man the pillow? (theme/ motivation question)
- What does the young man mean when he says, "Now I know better how I should live well!"? (quotation question)
- What do you think the people who told this tale were trying to accomplish? (author's motivation question)

As students develop and discuss their responses, Victor walks around the room, again observing students at work and providing coaching as needed.

Once student groups have agreed on their responses to the four questions, Victor gives students their task, which is part of their month-long focus on persuasive writing: Write a letter to a friend that tells why "The Pillow" is important and that will persuade your friend to read it.

Do You Hear What I Hear? happens three Wednesdays each month. On the fourth Wednesday of the month, students select their best product for the month and meet in editor-response teams, where they read their selected piece and make revision notes using the group's feedback. As usual, Victor listens in on these revision sessions to help groups think through the process of providing thoughtful and constructive feedback. This process of selection, feedback collection, and revision helps students produce their best work. But that is only half the story. The same process helps Victor as well. With only one product to mark, Victor is able to dedicate more time to diagnosis and coaching.

Why the Strategy Is Beneficial

In our work in more than 300 schools across the United States, we have found that the classroom strategies that lead to the greatest gains in student performance on state tests tend to meet six essential criteria:

1. They must be easy to implement.

2. They must not require large amounts of planning or marking time.

3. They must allow teachers to work effectively with all students, including struggling students.

4. They must be aligned with state tests and develop the skills identified in state standards.

5. They must engage students in in-depth thinking as well as more routine forms of thought.

6. They must provide manageable opportunities for teachers to diagnose problems and provide coaching.

Do You Hear What I Hear? was designed in response to these findings. The strategy focuses on key standards-based skills (listening, retelling, notemaking, using evidence, writing in different genres) and, through repetition and built-in observation and coaching sessions, gives students the time and support they need to develop these skills. In addition, the strategy recognizes the evolutionary nature of deep thought. It begins with simple listening, then progresses through a series of ever-deepening thinking processes: notemaking, retelling, peer coaching, higher-order questions about meanings and themes, synthesis into a written product, and, last, revision. And perhaps best of all, the strategy is effective because it does not place planning or grading burdens on teachers. This, of course, is the point: Minimal planning and marking time translate into increased time for diagnosis and coaching—the building blocks of skill development.

How to Use the Strategy

1. Leave time to read a short, rigorous text to your students once each week for three weeks. Read each text twice: once for students to get the gist and once for them to take notes for retelling.

2. Instruct students to pair up and review their notes together. One student puts the notes aside, while the other coaches him or her to a complete retelling. Students then switch roles.

3. Shift from listening to reading by distributing a copy of the text and establishing two to four guiding questions. Guiding questions can focus on vocabulary (e.g., What is a polygon?), the meaning of quotations (e.g., What does Sojourner Truth mean when she says, "Ain't I a woman?"), characters' or authors' motivations (e.g., Why does Mother Bear pretend Little Bear is from outer space?), and main ideas/themes (e.g., How are birds and dinosaurs related according to this article?). Have students preview the questions, then read the text.

4. Team students up into small, collaborative groups to discuss answers and resolve differences. Observe and coach groups.

5. Establish a writing product based on the reading. The product should be short (one to one and a half pages) and can be in any of these formats: a retelling, a review or argument, a creative response (story, poem, play, etc.), or a personal response.

6. On the fourth week, have students review their three products, select their best, and work in editor-response groups to collect feedback and revision ideas from their peers.

7. Sit in on editor-response groups and provide coaching. Mark only the selected, revised piece.

Helping Struggling Readers

Do You Hear What I Hear? has numerous support structures built into its design that allow teachers to work effectively with the most challenged readers in their classrooms. Specifically, the strategy

- uses partnership and team structures throughout the process.
- "frontloads" comprehension by allowing students to listen (twice), make notes, retell with a coach, and preview questions about the text—all before they read it.
- happens regularly, creating an atmosphere of comfort and giving students the opportunity to practice and develop key literary skills over time.

- uses short texts, which greatly reduces the chance that students will "get lost" in the reading.
- scaffolds and supports the evolution of students' literary skills by moving them, step-by-step, through a series of increasingly sophisticated thinking processes.
- greatly increases the amount of time that the teacher can work directly with struggling learners.

For students who need extra help in retelling and notemaking, see the "Helping Struggling Readers" section of Read and Retell (pages 41 and 42) and the various notemaking tools described in Chapter 2 (pages 61 to 85).

5

A Question
Is a Quest

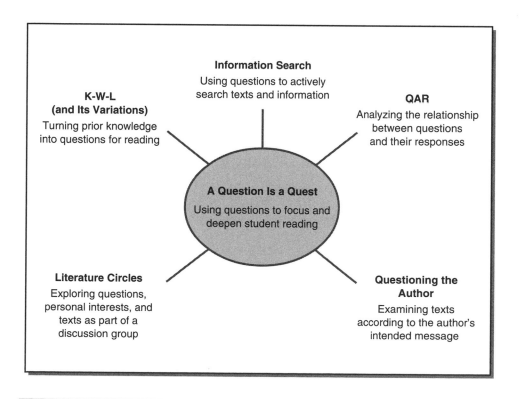

Information Search
Using questions to actively
search texts and information

**K-W-L
(and Its Variations)**
Turning prior knowledge
into questions for reading

QAR
Analyzing the relationship
between questions
and their responses

A Question Is a Quest
Using questions to focus and
deepen student reading

Literature Circles
Exploring questions,
personal interests, and
texts as part of a
discussion group

**Questioning the
Author**
Examining texts
according to the author's
intended message

Figure 5.1   Chapter Overview: Advance Organizer

> *"Try to learn to love the questions."*
>
> —Rainer Maria Rilke,
> twentieth-century German poet

WHERE QUESTIONS AND ANSWERS COME FROM

In the beginning, a person has an experience: A child reads a book; a woman ruffles the back of her dog's head every day after work. Then, something happens: The child becomes confused by the reading; the dog doesn't greet the woman for his customary pat. That's when a question blossoms: What is the author saying? Is there something wrong with Spot? But this is only the beginning. The questions we form lead us into a search for answers. The child may reread the confusing passage to see what caused the confusion. The woman may begin to speculate about her dog's health and call the vet. Along the way and as this process progresses, we begin to develop answers to our questions: The book is using ideas that are new to me; Spot is sick. As we begin to solidify our answers by restating them to ourselves or talking to other people or writing in our journals, something remarkable happens: There is a response. For the reading child, the next chapter of the book clarifies the new ideas. The vet tells the woman her dog has an ear infection and will be fine.

THE QUESTIONING CYCLE

What all this means is that questions are inherently incomplete. They live and thrive as part of a cycle (Figure 5.2) that includes

- Experiencing
- Questioning
- Answering
- Response

Cut any part or "gear" of the cycle off from the others and the "gears" do not make contact with one another. They are left spinning in space, alone, incomplete. The process breaks down. Teaching students that questions and answers are cyclical is essential if we want students to do more than simply answer questions. If we are to develop quality thinkers and quality readers, we must teach students how to formulate their own questions, develop their own strategies for seeking answers, seek the responses of others, and begin the cycle over again with a new set of questions.

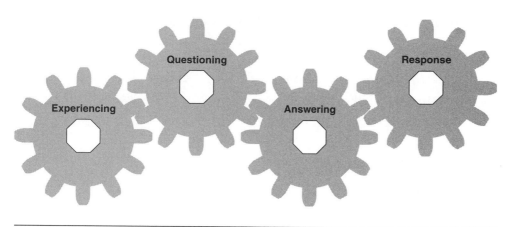

Figure 5.2   Parts or "Gears" of the Questioning Cycle

This view of questions differs sharply from traditional perspectives. In the more standard view, questions belonged to teachers and were asked after the reading experience was over. Students were not taught how to use their reading experiences to create questions before, during, and after reading. They were not guided in seeking answers or encouraged to use others' responses as spurs to seek further questions or deeper answers. Teachers asked the questions and students spooned up the answers.

In the new view, the teacher models the entire questioning cycle for the students. She helps students to find their own questions to guide and clarify the meanings of texts. She carefully models how to search for and construct answers. She provides and encourages students to give positive and constructive responses to other students' questions, and she teaches students to use these responses as tools to create further questions and deeper answers.

Teaching students how to ask and respond to questions is more than just good practice; it is a surefire way to get results in the classroom. Studies over the past two decades, including those by Wilen and Clegg (1986), Brualdi (1998), Cotton (2000), and Marzano, Pickering, and Pollock (2001), all show that good questioning practices are positively linked to higher student achievement. Meanwhile, the National Reading Panel concluded in 2000 that asking and answering questions during reading has a significant and positive impact on reading comprehension.

This chapter presents five strategies teachers can implement to help their students use questions, answers, and responses to promote deeper readings.

Know-Want-Learn (and its variations) and **Information Search** help students activate prior knowledge to create questions that guide them through a text or set of texts.

QAR shows students how to distinguish between four kinds of commonly asked questions and how to use these distinctions to craft quality responses.

Questioning the Author is a strategy designed to help students overcome common reading difficulties through a unique combination of questioning, modeling, and response.

Literature Circles work much like book clubs, giving students the opportunity to pursue their own questions and personal interests as part of a collaborative discussion group.

KNOW-WANT-LEARN (AND ITS VARIATIONS)

Overview

Know-Want-Learn (K-W-L) (Ogle, 1986) invites students into the questioning and reading processes. Students use their prior knowledge to form questions about the text(s) before reading. They then use those questions to guide their inquiry and to determine how their knowledge has changed as a result of the reading. In this section, we discuss the classic K-W-L strategy as well as several of the more recent variations on K-W-L that have emerged from classrooms and from the research community.

The Strategy in Action

Every year, Carla Mitchell conducts an integrated math unit with her second graders on money. She begins her unit by distributing to each student a sealed envelope containing a single coin. Students are encouraged to feel the envelope to identify all the things they know about what's inside and guess the envelope's contents. By doing this, Carla provokes student curiosity and gets them thinking about the topic of the unit. Carla provides students with a K-W-L organizer and asks them to open their envelopes. Carla next says to her students, "Now that you know it's definitely money inside the envelope, think about everything you know about money. Try to think about lots of different times you've had or used money. Also, think about what you notice when adults use money."

Carla gives students time to write their ideas in the first column (What I Know) of their K-W-L organizer (Figure 5.3) individually. Once students have completed their individual brainstorms, Carla engages the whole class in discussion and tallies the different ideas students have generated on a K-W-L poster (Figure 5.4) she has placed in the front of the room.

"You really know a lot about money," Carla tells the class. "What other things would you like to know about money?" Once again, Carla allows time for individual responses and uses a whole-class format to record questions and help all students process the idea being discussed.

Once Carla has recorded the class's questions in the second column (What I Want to Know) of the students' organizers (Figure 5.5) and on the poster (Figure 5.6), she provides various activities to help students find

Figure 5.3   Student's K-W-L Organizer
(First Column)

Source: Copyright © Thoughtful Education Press.
Reprinted with permission.

What We Know	What
1. People use money to buy things.	
2. Money is used in many places (stores, video games).	
3. When people do work, they are paid in money.	
4. People use symbols ($) and numbers to stand for money.	
5. Different countries use different money.	

Figure 5.4   Whole-Class K-W-L Poster
(First Column)

Source: Copyright © Thoughtful Education
Press. Reprinted with permission.

What I Know	What I Want to Know
I know you use money to buy things.	How do people in stores know how to give you change so fast?
When I do work, like chores, I get money.	
In Mexico, they use different money.	

Figure 5.5   Student's K-W-L Organizer
(Second Column)

Source: Copyright © Thoughtful Education Press.
Reprinted with permission.

What We Know	What We Want to Know
1. People use money to buy things.	1. How do people make change?
2. Money is used in many places (stores, video games).	2. Where does money come from?
3. When people do work, they are paid in money.	3. Why do different countries use different money?
4. People use symbols ($) and	

Figure 5.6   Whole-Class K-W-L Poster
(Second Column)

Source: Copyright © Thoughtful Education
Press. Reprinted with permission.

answers to their questions. For example, to help students understand how to make change, Carla first models and coaches students through the skill of making change. She then helps student groups set up "learning stores" in which students play roles as customers, cashiers, and notemakers. After each student has "bought" a number of items, made change for student "customers," and observed the change-making process and made notes, Carla pulls students together into groups. These groups examine and discuss their notes and identify patterns they noticed in the "learning stores." Carla has each group create a chart (see Figure 5.7) displaying the patterns they noticed about making change.

Patterns for Making Change

1. When you buy something, you always get back less money than you started with.

2. There is sometimes more than one way to make the same change.

3. Four quarters make a dollar.

4. Two dimes and a nickel make a quarter.

5. Two nickels make a dime.

6. Five pennies make a nickel.

Figure 5.7   Student-Created Chart

Source: Copyright © Thoughtful Education Press. Reprinted with permission.

To help students find answers to some of their other questions, Carla provides a range of learning opportunities in her unit (for example, a talk from a coin collector, books and articles about money in different cultures and civilizations). Throughout the unit, students add their discoveries to the third and final column of their K-W-L organizer. Carla conducts a final survey of the class's learning and records responses on the class poster. After all responses have been recorded, Carla reviews the big ideas in the unit and asks students to reflect on their learning and the K-W-L process in their reflection journals.

* * * *

Fourth-grade teacher Esteban Carr is using K-W-L in a more focused and more traditional way. He is using it in conjunction with a specific reading. Esteban has found that K-W-L can be made an even more powerful reading tool by making a slight modification to the organizer, which looks like Figure 5.8.

Before Reading		During Reading	After Reading	
What I Know	What I Think I Know	Big Ideas From Reading	What I Learned	What I Still Want to Learn

Figure 5.8   Modified K-W-L Organizer

By dividing reading into before, during, and after phases, Esteban enables students to see that the reading process is layered and progressive.

Esteban is using K-W-L and his adapted organizer to help students make sense of a reading in *Ranger Rick* that describes the delicate balance of predator-prey relationships in ecosystems across the globe. Before reading the selection, students develop two lists. In the first list, they generate as many hunting animals or predators as they can. In the second, they list all the prey animals they know. Then, in the first column of the K-W-L organizer, students use their lists to determine all they know about predator-prey relationships. Esteban reminds students that they do not need to be certain about their information. If they think they know something about predator-prey relationships, but aren't sure about it, they should record their thoughts in the "What I Think I Know" column.

Esteban then asks students what they'd like to know about these relationships. Esteban models this questioning process by asking students to think about the kinds of questions a biologist or ecologist might ask while reading the article (for example, What happens in an ecosystem when there are not enough prey animals to feed the predators?). Esteban and the students decide on three questions they think are the most interesting:

1. What happens if an ecosystem doesn't have enough predators?

2. What happens if an ecosystem doesn't have enough prey animals?

3. Is hunting cruel?

Esteban divides the class into groups, each of which focuses its attention on one of the three questions above. Students read the article individually and take notes in the center column of the organizer (Big Ideas From Reading) that correspond to the question guiding their search. Student groups then convene to discuss their findings and create a list of the most important ideas. Throughout the reading phase, Esteban circulates around the room to make sure students are gathering appropriate information and working together productively.

Why the Strategy Is Beneficial

Research on reading has shown consistently that proficient readers know how to tap into what they know and use that knowledge to make sense of the readings they encounter (Pressley, 2006). Several years ago, in looking at the role of prior knowledge in building students' reading skills, Ogle (1986) developed K-W-L, which has since become one of the most popular and recognizable strategies in classrooms across the country.

In K-W-L, after the teacher introduces a topic, students use a "fact-storming" technique (groups of three to five students generate as many facts as they can) to generate whatever they know about the topic. This process helps students access their prior knowledge, and it helps them use that background knowledge to make sense of the forthcoming reading.

After their fact-finding, students generate a list of what they would like to know about the topic, usually in the form of questions. These questions provide a purpose for reading actively, as students search the text for information relevant to their questions. Finally, students record what they have learned as a result of reading. Questions that go unanswered can become the basis for research projects.

Since the development of K-W-L, many teachers and researchers have made modifications to its basic structure. Several of these variations are outlined below. To implement one of the variations on K-W-L, use Organizers 5-B to 5-E.

Variations on K-W-L

One variation of the K-W-L technique is to organize the information the way Esteban Carr did, into Before Reading ("What I Know" and "What I Think I Know"); During Reading ("Big Ideas From Reading"); and After Reading ("What I Learned" and "What I Still Want to Learn"). This organizer helps students see the evolution of their learning more clearly and allows students to identify what they still want to know about their topic, thereby setting the stage for independent or group research projects (see Organizer 5-B).

To deepen students' reflection and post-reading thinking, Laverick (2002) developed Before-During-After (B-D-A). B-D-A asks students to list everything they know about the topic before reading, find new information during reading, and write a brief summary of the reading along with three questions they still have after reading. Finally, students develop a one-sentence main idea statement that captures the essence of the reading (see Organizer 5-C, B-D-A).

Sampson (2002) suggests a variation aimed at helping students learn to evaluate the reliability and validity of information while conducting research. In light of the proliferation of "sources" that students can access via the Internet, Sampson changes the "What We Know" column to "What We Think We Know" so that "faulty" information such as "toads give people warts" don't become pseudo-facts (see Organizer 5-D, Confirming Sources). Before moving on to what students want to know, students locate at least two sources (one of which must be a print source published within the last five years) that confirm the "facts" they have placed in the "What We Think We Know" column. Students then record their questions about the text or topic in the "What We Want to Know" column and begin the process of reading to locate information for the "What We Learned" column. The last step is to note the sources that support "What We Learned."

Science teachers Crowther and Cannon (2004) gave K-W-L a "makeover" designed to integrate language arts and literacy instruction into content-area teaching. Called Think-How-Conclude (T-H-C), the strategy provides a framework to guide students through the kind of inquiry-based expository reading and learning experiences they encounter in science classrooms. The strategy asks students to:

- List what they *think* they know about the topic.
- Develop ideas on *how* they can determine whether their thoughts are correct. (Teacher and students work together to select the most appropriate methods.)
- Draw *conclusions*.

When piloting T-H-C in a first-grade classroom, the authors found students wrote an average of three sentences when the first column was changed to "Think," as opposed to an average of one sentence when the column was titled "Know" (see Organizer 5-E, T-H-C).

How to Use the Strategy

Use Organizer 5-A, "K-W-L," on page 158. To use one of the Variations, use Organizers 5-B to 5-E, "Five Column K-W-L," "B-D-A," "Confirming Sources," or "T-H-C," on pages 159–162.

Incorporate the K-W-L strategy in your classroom using the following steps:

1. Introduce a topic to be studied or text to be read.

2. Distribute Organizer 5-A, "K-W-L," and explain what the initials stand for.

3. To activate students' prior knowledge, have them use the first column of the organizer, "What I Know," to create individual lists of what they already know about the topic.

4. Have students meet in groups of three to five and use the "fact-storming" technique to generate more ideas, share their findings, and add to their personal lists.

5. Conduct a whole-class discussion to further allow students to expand their lists. (This background knowledge will help students make sense of the forthcoming reading.)

6. Ask students to formulate a list of questions about what they want to know using the second column of the organizer ("What I Want to Know"). Encourage students to think openly and flexibly in generating this question "wish list," which will become the basis for determining what students think is important to know. The questions also provide students with a purpose for reading and a guide for their information search.

7. Have students read the text to verify their knowledge and to find answers to their questions, which they add to the third column ("What We Learned") on the organizer. (Questions not answered by the text may become the basis for independent research, group inquiries, or other kinds of research projects.)

8. Conduct a discussion in which students reflect on what they have learned as a result of this process.

Helping Struggling Readers

Student difficulties with K-W-L tend to fall into three categories:

1. Difficulties in accessing what is already known.
2. Difficulties in generating questions about the topic.
3. Difficulties in actively reading the text to find relevant information.

The first difficulty is often encountered by teachers who hear statements such as this: "I don't know anything about crocodiles!" To help these readers, teachers can use simple, even obvious questions to activate prior knowledge. For instance, in response to the student who thinks he knows nothing about crocodiles, you might use questions such as these:

"Are crocodiles as big as elephants?"

"No."

"Are they bigger than cats?"

"Yes."

"You do know something about their size then. Now, are crocodiles like any other animals you know of?"

"They're a lot like alligators."

"Good. That's something else you know. Do you know anything about where they live?"

"In the water."

"In the ocean?"

"No, in swamps, I think."

"Good. You know a lot more than you think about crocodiles."

English language learners face particular challenges accessing what information they already know because they may lack both the vocabulary and the relevant background knowledge that would give meaning to the text (Brisk & Harrington, 2000). With these students, it may be appropriate to incorporate visuals (e.g., a photo of a crocodile) so that they can correctly identify it in their native language and integrate the new vocabulary and facts they are learning into their existing schema.

For students who have difficulty generating questions about a topic, it is a matter of helping them realize they have questions to ask. Sometimes students believe they already know a lot about a topic, and their overconfidence can, in fact, become a detriment to curiosity and an inquiring attitude. For example, you might find the student who claims she already knows that reptiles lay eggs. By encouraging the student to look deeper into her knowledge base with probing questions such as How many eggs do they lay? or Yes, they lay eggs, but is there a reason they lay eggs instead of giving live birth like mammals? you help students realize that they always have questions. They just need to look for them.

Struggling readers may also have difficulty extracting information that verifies their knowledge and answers their questions. A variety of techniques can help students overcome this problem:

Modeling: For the struggling reader and the confident reader alike, modeling the K-W-L process, especially the active reading phase, is essential if you expect students to use the strategy on their own. Show them how you read a text. List steps on the board and coach students through them. Use Think Alouds (using a sample text, describe what's happening in your mind as you read) and directed practice to help them internalize the skill. Coach students through their learning.

Read Aloud: After students have determined what they know and what they want to know, have them listen to the text as you read it aloud. Encourage them to develop images or draw pictures of the reading in their mind. Then, have them read it on their own.

Collaborative Reading: Tap into the power of group learning by allowing students to work together. Each student in the group may be held responsible for finding one key piece of information rather than several. Or, use a strategy such as Peer Reading (page 32) or Collaborative Summarizing (pages 35–36) to help students read actively.

Multiple Inputs: Encourage students to use more than one text to gather information. If students want to read more, by all means, allow them to do it.

Post-it™ Notes: Instead of marking up a text, students can place Post-it notes in front of key ideas in the reading so that they can look back and locate essential information.

Name: _____

Three-Column K-W-L

What I Know	What I **Want** to Know	What We Learned

Adapted from Ogle, D. (1986).

Name: _____

Five-Column K-W-L

Before Reading		During Reading	After Reading	
What I Know	What I Think I Know	Big Ideas From Reading	What I Learned	What I Still Need to Learn

ORGANIZER 5-C: B-D-A

Name: _____

B-D-A

Before Reading (What you already know)	During Reading (New information)	After Reading (Summary and three questions)
		Brief Summary
		3 Questions
Main-Idea Sentence for the Reading:		

Adapted from Laverick, C. (2002).

ORGANIZER 5-D: CONFORMING SOURCES

Name: _____

Confirming Sources

Think We Know	Sources	Want to Know	Learned	Sources

Place a check mark (✔) next to any information that you can confirm.

Adapted from Sampson, M. B. (2002).

ORGANIZER 5-E: T-H-C

Name: _____

T-H-C

Think We Know	How We Can Find Out	Conclusions

(Text continued from page 157)

INFORMATION SEARCH

Overview

Information Search builds on the K-W-L strategy but enhances it by incorporating concept mapping, by situating the learning experience inside a collaborative structure, and by expanding students' opportunities to reflect and elaborate on how their thinking has evolved through reading. The strategy teaches students a systematic approach to activating prior knowledge, verifying that knowledge, and integrating it with new information they uncover during reading.

The Strategy in Action

Enda Anbey is preparing her students for a study of the American Revolution. On the chalkboard, she displays the beginnings of a concept map with the main subtopics to be addressed by the chapter, but she has translated these subtopics into questions (Figure 5.9).

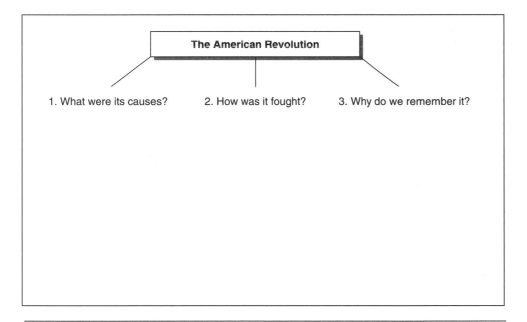

Figure 5.9   Starting a Concept Map

Enda then breaks the class into groups, which will each focus on one of the three questions by brainstorming about it. Enda tells students that in brainstorming, not only should they rely on what they know about the question, but they should also include what they think they know, what they believe, and how they feel about the question. Student groups create lists of their brainstorms, and Enda asks each group to share its ideas with the class. As students share their ideas, Enda records them on the board. Then Enda works with students to assess the information, placing a question mark next to whatever information students are unsure about or disagree over. The class's work looks like Figure 5.10.

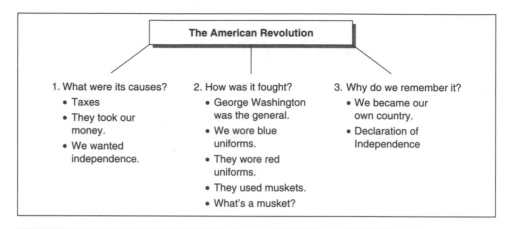

Figure 5.10 Brainstorming

Students use this organizer to structure their reading by verifying information and by focusing on the areas of uncertainty to find answers. As they read, students use a set of reader's punctuation, which Enda has modeled with them:

- An exclamation point (!) identifies new information.
- A lightning bolt (⚡) identifies information that disagrees with information on the organizer.
- An asterisk (*) identifies information that agrees with information on the organizer.

After reading, students work together to build visual organizers that blend old, new, and corrected information. Some students create more elaborate webs, but Charlotte and Murphy, for example, create a comparison organizer (see Figure 5.11) that compares and contrasts American and British positions relevant to each of the three questions.

	Colonists	British
Cause	Taxes Independence	Wanted to keep America as a colony Tobacco
War	Fought from trenches George Washington—General Benedict Arnold—traitor Saratoga, Trenton—major victories	Fought in lines Lord Cornwallis General Burgoyne
Importance	We gained independence	Book didn't say We think it's important because they lost a big colony
Both		
Used muskets—an old-fashioned rifle "Pride was at stake" Was an important event for both England and America Lost a lot of soldiers		

Figure 5.11 Charlotte and Murphy's Comparison Organizer

Why the Strategy Is Beneficial

Information Search is built on the framework of K-W-L. Although K-W-L provides a solid foundation for developing students' informational reading skills, its basic structure can be strengthened to help students become deeper readers. In response, Silver and Strong (1994) developed a variation on K-W-L known as Information Search to spur greater student engagement in the reading and learning process. Information Search maximizes the benefits of prior knowledge, active reading, elaboration, and deep reflection by making four important alterations to K-W-L:

1. In K-W-L, the simple naming of a topic as a way to activate prior knowledge is sometimes not enough to stimulate students' memories. With Information Search, students are given the topic and its important subtopics rather than just the topic. This provides a richer stimulus for activating prior knowledge and encourages students to delve deeper into their memory banks to access that knowledge. In addition, providing students with some of the key information (for example, a partially completed graphic organizer) leads to increased comprehension (Katayama & Robinson, 2000).

2. Students use more than their knowledge base to get a handle on the reading. Information Search allows students to use their tentative knowledge and their feelings about the topic and subtopics as pre-reading tools. By putting feelings and ideas on the table alongside facts, the strategy invites more students into the process and leads to richer and more varied forms of discussion.

3. In K-W-L, the questions students generate are sometimes too open and may not be answered by the reading. This may render the reading irrelevant to students' concerns, which can inhibit active reading. In Information Search, students mark the text for specific information using a set of meaningful symbols (!—new information, ✗—information that disagrees with information on the organizer, *—information that agrees with information on the organizer). This element ensures that students' reading is both active and directed toward relevant information.

4. K-W-L may not allow students to process the text in sufficient depth to elaborate on how their understanding has been changed or expanded by active reading. This potential weakness conflicts with research that shows elaborating on emerging comprehension is essential to building deep and permanent understanding (Reder, 1980). Using Information Search, once students have processed the text, they must work together to construct a new organizer showing old, new, and corrected information. In this way, not only must students determine what they have learned, as they do in K-W-L, but they must also elaborate on this information by synthesizing their pre-reading, reading, and post-reading activity into a complete picture of their understanding.

How to Use the Strategy

Use Organizers 5-F and 5-G, "What We Know, Think We Know, Feel (Before Reading)" and "What We Now Know as a Result of Our Reading and Discussion."
Incorporate the Information Search strategy in your classroom using the following steps:

1. Select an appropriate reading.

2. Survey the reading and identify the important subtopics.

3. Have students generate what they know, think they know, and feel about each subtopic using Organizer 5-F, "What We Know, Think We Know, Feel (Before Reading)." (To refine and maximize input, this process is often done individually, in small groups, and then with the whole class.)

4. Help students use the subtopics and the results of their brainstorming to identify questions for research.

5. Provide the reading for students to conduct their research. Show them how to use reader's punctuation to actively search for information:

   ! New information

   ∦ Information that disagrees with information on the organizer.

   * Information that agrees with information on the organizer.

6. Have students create a new concept map with the revised information using Organizer 5-G, "What We Now Know as a Result of Our Reading and Discussion."

Helping Struggling Readers

As with K-W-L, students may encounter difficulties in brainstorming about what they already know, in generating questions for reading, and in the actual reading of the text. English language learners in particular may struggle with activating their prior knowledge, because their cultural context and experience base are often different from other students'. In helping these students develop proficiency in using Information Search, you can use the same techniques as those described in the "Helping Struggling Readers" section of K-W-L (pages 156–157):

- Use simple, obvious questions that help students tap into their knowledge base to generate what they already know.
- Use probing questions to help students find the questions they have.
- Use various techniques, such as modeling, read alouds, collaborative reading, and multiple inputs to help students engage in active, in-depth reading.

ORGANIZER 5-F: WHAT WE KNOW, THINK WE KNOW, FEEL (BEFORE READING)

Name: _____

What We Know, Think We Know, Feel (Before Reading)

Subtopic/Question A	Subtopic/Question B

Topic

Subtopic/Question C	Subtopic/Question D

ORGANIZER 5-G: WHAT WE NOW KNOW AS A RESULT OF OUR READING AND DISCUSSION

Name: _____

What We Now Know as a Result of Our Reading and Discussion

Subtopic/Question A	Subtopic/Question B

Topic

Subtopic/Question C	Subtopic/Question D

QAR: QUESTION-ANSWER-RELATIONSHIP

Overview

There is no doubt that effective questions deepen comprehension. But questioning takes on a whole new level when students know how to look deeply into the question-and-response process—when they can recognize different types of questions and know how to go about developing quality responses. Question-Answer-Relationship is a strategy that provides students with a structure to analyze questions about the texts they read and determine what they need to do to construct a quality response.

The Strategy in Action

Alfie Maine's fourth graders are learning about Jackie Robinson. Today, the class is going to read an interview with Sharon Robinson, Jackie's daughter, which Alfie found in the biographies section of the *Time for Kids* Web site. In the interview, Sharon discusses her father's life and legacy.

Before reading, Alfie holds a group review session in which students practice asking and answering each of the four types of question-answer-relationships (QARs): "right there" QARs, which are answered by finding and restating information from the reading; "think and search" QARs, which are answered by pulling together several pieces of information from the reading; "author and me" QARs, which are answered by combining textual information with personal knowledge; and "on my own" QARs, which are not addressed by the text and are answered by tapping into personal knowledge and experience without reference to the text. During the group review session, Alfie walks around the room to make sure students understand the four types of QARs.

Alfie then pulls the class back together, has students read the interview, and begins asking students questions. Before students answer the question, they must identify the QAR.

Alfie: Jeff, according to Sharon Robinson, how did her father's career change baseball for African Americans?

Jeff: Oh, I remember where that part is. Right here. So then the question is a "right there" question because the answer is right in one place. Because of Jackie Robinson, other African Americans were allowed to play baseball and other professional sports too.

Alfie: Great, Jeff. You're right, that was a "right there" question. Here's another question. This one's for Heather. Heather, what was baseball like for African American players before Jackie Robinson broke into the Major Leagues?

Heather: Um, OK. Let me look a little bit. OK, that's a "think and search" question. The answer's not just in one place. To get an answer I need to kind of put different parts of the reading together.

Alfie: Excellent! So what's the answer?

Heather: Well, before Jackie Robinson, there were no African Americans in the Major Leagues. They weren't allowed to play because of segregation. And, um, African Americans played in their own leagues, the Negro Leagues. But they wanted to play in the Major Leagues and weren't allowed.

Alfie: That's a great summary, Heather. Did everyone see how Heather collected information from different parts of the interview to put her answer together? Some information, like the part about segregation, was at the beginning. But the part about the Negro Leagues was in the middle. Heather put it all together wonderfully for us. Now, Sam, I want you to imagine playing baseball under the circumstances that Jackie Robinson did. What would that have felt like for Jackie?

Sam: Well, she says that people insulted him and that some people even threatened to kill him. But she really doesn't talk about how Jackie felt. So I guess it's an "author and me" question, right?

Alfie: Why do you think that?

Sam: Because some of the information I need is here, um, like where it tells me about how people threatened to kill Jackie. But to talk about how Jackie felt, I have to kind of guess or imagine that part on my own.

Alfie: That's a great way of putting it Sam. Part of the answer to an "author and me" question is found in the reading, but not all of the answer. The rest comes from what you know or what you have experienced in your life. So, Sam, how do you think it felt for Jackie?

Sam: Well, it must've been really, really hard. He must've been really scared, you know, like wondering if people were going to come after him all the time. Like from the stands. That's scary. I couldn't do that. I'd stop playing if someone said they were going to kill me.

Alfie: Good answer, Sam. It must have been terrifying. Does anyone else want to add to Sam's answer?

Diaz: I'll bet Jackie felt really good when he showed everyone how good he was. Like he was stronger than them and they couldn't get to him.

Alfie: That's an interesting idea, Diaz. I hadn't thought about that before, but I'll bet you're absolutely right. Now, can anyone think of anyone else we've learned about who faced a very difficult situation and overcame it like Jackie did? Tiara?

Tiara: I know Sharon Robinson doesn't talk about that, so that makes it an "on my own question." The answer comes from . . .

After asking a few more questions, Alfie lets students ask one another questions about the interview.

Why the Strategy Is Beneficial

The QAR strategy (Raphael, 1982, 1984, 1986) was developed to help students analyze and answer the questions asked of them. It relies on the work of Pearson and Johnson (1978), who describe three basic types of responses to questions based on reading:

- Text-explicit responses come directly from the text. To generate a text-explicit response, the student determines what missing piece of information a question is asking him or her to find, and then finds it in the text.
- Text-implicit responses are constructed by the reader through a process of synthesizing information from the text. The student may need to piece together multiple bits of information to generate the answers.
- Script-implicit responses are generated outside the text, out of the reader's experience and personal knowledge base. These questions require the readers to take one of two actions to develop an effective answer: call on what they know and have experienced, or integrate their background knowledge with information the author has presented in the text.

Essential to the QAR strategy is training students to identify the way different questions call for different types of responses—and where they need to go to locate the information. To make the strategy more student-friendly, Pike and Mumper (2004) suggest explaining to students that the needed information is in one of two places: in the book or in their heads. Information that is in the book is either "right there" (text explicit), or requires the student to "think and search" (text implicit). Script-implicit questions ask students to access the information stored in their minds and require either an "on my own" response or an "author and me" response.

Research on QAR's effectiveness has shown that students who use QAR are better able to generate quality answers to questions about their reading (Raphael & McKinney, 1983; Raphael & Pearson, 1982; Raphael, Wonnacut, & Pearson, 1983). QAR training and instruction has also been found to enhance comprehension in content areas not typically associated with reading instruction, including mathematics (McIntosh & Draper, 1995).

How to Use the Strategy

Use Organizer 5-H, "QAR: Question-Answer-Relationship," on page 173.
Incorporate the QAR strategy in your classroom using the following steps:

1. Explain and model the four types of QARs.

2. Create a variety of QAR questions keyed to a specific reading. To help students internalize the questions and the QAR process, you may want to write questions in the "Question" column of Organizer

5-H, "QAR: Question-Answer-Relationship." Distribute the organizer to students.

3. Have students read the passage and use the text to identify the types of QARs and then to answer the questions, using the appropriate spaces in Organizer 5-H.

4. Ask students to reflect on the process of answering each type of QAR.

5. Gradually move students toward independence by having them read passages and generate their own QARs.

Helping Struggling Readers

The primary difficulty associated with QAR is that some students have trouble seeing the relationship between questions and the answers they ask readers to generate. Raphael (1982) offers four suggestions for helping students develop the analytical skills needed to make the connection between questions and their answers:

- Make sure that students, especially in the early phases, but also in the later phases, get immediate feedback so that their misconceptions do not solidify.
- Use a progressive reading structure so that students practice with short and simple texts and gradually move to longer and more complex ones.
- Make the question-answer-relationships as explicit as possible at the beginning and use a majority of right-there questions so that the students become more confident in their abilities.
- Allow students to work in groups as they learn to identify question-answer-relationships and construct responses. Over time, students will develop the skills needed to work independently.

Teachers should note that the timing of questioning has been shown to affect comprehension among struggling readers. Although questioning during reading is crucial to deep reading, van den Broek, Tzeng, Risden, Trabasso, and Basche (2001) found that the comprehension of less proficient fourth-grade readers can be compromised by too much during-reading questioning. As struggling readers work to comprehend the text, the introduction of questions can stretch their attention and reduce, rather than increase, their focus. So, when working with struggling readers during the early stages of QAR, it is a good idea to save questions until after a first reading. Then you can introduce the questions during a rereading and conduct a regular QAR lesson. This way, students gain comfort and confidence with the content of the reading before they need to attend to the questions.

ORGANIZER 5-H: QAR: QUESTION-ANSWER-RELATIONSHIP

Name: _____

QAR: Question-Answer-Relationship

Directions: _____

Question	Answer	Type of QAR			
		Right There	Think and Search	Author and Me	On My Own

Adapted from Raphael, T. E. (1986).

QUESTIONING THE AUTHOR (QTA)

Overview

As students progress as readers, they must learn to analyze and evaluate information and ideas they come across in their readings. Questioning the Author (QtA) helps students move away from passive acceptance of textual information. Instead, students are encouraged to "dialogue" with the author and wrestle with content through an active questioning process.

The Strategy in Action

George Billows has started a unit on ancient civilizations and is about to have his students read a passage about the importance of rivers in the formation of a civilization. He hands out copies of the reading to each of his students and asks them to follow along as he reads aloud.

George: Today we're going to try something a little different. Instead of reading this passage on your own, we're going to read it aloud together. As we read, I want you to think about what the author of this passage is trying to tell us. I'm going to be stopping during the reading to ask some questions, okay? Here we go.

George then begins the reading, stopping after certain sentences to spark discussion and to help students construct the meaning of the text by focusing on what the author is trying to say.

George: So what is the author trying to tell us here?

David: He says that when they plow the ground the soil gets looser and the rain washes it away.

George: David says that plowed soil gets washed away by the rain. Is the author clear about this? Does he say why this happens? Tanisha?

Tanisha: It says that plowing vertically makes the soil get washed away.

George: Tanisha has hit on a key word here, "vertically." Does anyone know what that means? Karen?

Karen: I think it means going up, you know, like a flagpole.

George: That's right. It means in an up and down direction. Now, where is the author trying to hint that people plow up and down? Try looking back a couple of sentences. What does the author mention? Joshua?

Joshua: He says that the mountains are a good place to defend against enemies because they're hard to climb but that they're not good for farming because the soil gets washed away.

George: So what Joshua is saying is that although the mountains are a great natural defense against enemies, trying to grow food on them is rather difficult. How does this connect to what the author has already told us?

Tanisha: I guess when they plowed up and down the mountain the rain would come and wash the soil away.

Lea: And so they couldn't grow crops.

George: Excellent thinking, Tanisha and Lea. So then what would make it easier to plow the soil and grow crops? Chris?

Chris: If the ground was flat then the soil couldn't wash away anywhere.

George: And does the author suggest where the ground is flat enough so that plowed soil won't wash away with the rain?

Chris: A river valley?

George: Exactly. Now the author of this passage could have just said that in a river valley the land is flat and that this keeps the soil in one place when it rains, but authors don't always write so directly. And even when they do write that clearly, sometimes they assume that readers will question what they mean and piece together what they are trying to say as we just did. Let's read on and find out just how important farming was to ancient civilizations.

George continues to read and question his students until they have finished the passage. After reading, the class holds a discussion on the author's main points in the passage, and students who are confused clarify their understanding by asking questions.

Why the Strategy Is Beneficial

Questioning the Author (Beck, McKeown, Hamilton, & Kucan, 1997; Beck, McKeown, Worthy, Sandora, & Kucan, 1996; McKeown, Beck, & Sandora, 1996) grew out of a body of research conducted in the 1980s and early 1990s that indicated that too many students—particularly young readers—were dealing with text only on a superficial level, thus leading to inadequate comprehension (Beck & McKeown, 2001). In many cases, the problem lay with the text rather than the reader. Beck et al. (1997), for example, found that many school texts are full of unclear references, are saturated with concepts, fail to establish a context for the content, or weakly link related information. In response, Beck et al. (1997) tried several interventions, such as revising texts for coherence and developing "voiced" versions of text to enhance student engagement during reading. However, they found these did not help students achieve the level of comprehension they desired. Faced with these disappointing results along with the understanding that students will encounter difficult and poorly written texts throughout their academic careers, they turned their focus to helping students deal more creatively with these challenging texts. Specifically, the researchers looked for ways to "set up the reading situation as a kind of dialogue with a text's author" (Beck & McKeown, 2001, p. 229).

The strategy they developed is QtA. Questioning the Author relies on four basic assumptions:

- Authors are human beings. They can be wrong. They can write poorly or unclearly.
- Reading is an active and segmented process. During their reading, readers wrestle with words and ideas by reading relatively short segments of text, questioning, constructing meaning, and then moving on to another relatively short portion of text.
- Wrestling with ideas requires talking as well as thinking. Collaboration, interaction, and idea "piggy-backing" are all part of constructing meaning and, therefore, are all part of the QtA process.
- The teacher, like the student, is also engaged in constructing meaning and must help students build understanding. To do this, the teacher uses queries, which differ from questions in that they:
    o Focus on helping students wrestle with ideas rather than assessing comprehension after reading.
    o Spur student interaction and discussion about the author's meaning rather than individual responses and teacher-to-student interaction.
    o Are used during the reading process rather than after it.

For nonfiction texts, Beck (1997) and her colleagues suggest teachers use initiating queries such as What is the author trying to say here? to get the author's ideas out in the open. Teachers should then use follow-up queries such as How does that compare with what the author said before? to focus thinking and group discussion. For narrative texts, the authors suggest using queries that focus primarily on characters and their motivations (How do things look for Frances right now? and Considering what the author's already told us about Willy Wonka, what do you think Willy's up to in this section?) and on how the author crafts the plot (How has the author resolved the problem of Tops Giraffe's sore throat? and How does the author let us know that the world around John Henry is changing?). Once the reading is complete, students reflect on the meaning of the text and on the QtA process so that they can see how the ideas of authorship and questioning are intimately related to reading. Over time, students can use these ideas to become independent and critical interrogators of the texts they read.

A 1999 study by Sandora, Beck, and McKeown on using QtA with complex literature found that students who participated in QtA discussions scored higher on recall items and open-ended responses. More specifically, students wrote and elaborated in greater depth and included more of the story's elements in their responses.

How to Use the Strategy

Questioning the Author is a useful strategy for both nonfiction and fiction reading; however, teachers must take into account the different characteristics of expository and narrative texts when using the strategy. Beck et al. (1997) contend there are three major areas of difference that affect the way the strategy is implemented: (1) Authorship—expository writers will tend to write like content experts, while narrative authors focus more on the craft of writing and the possibilities of language; (2) Purpose—expository texts convey information while narratives explore literary themes; and (3) Structure—nonfiction texts are often marked by heading and subheadings, whereas narratives have a more subtle and open structure.

Incorporate the strategy into your classroom using the following steps:

1. Begin by explaining that authors are not always clear and that sometimes what the author means is difficult to understand.

2. Direct students to begin reading a selected text. At key points in the reading, open a discussion with initiating queries such as, What is the author trying to tell us here? or What is the author's intended message?

3. To enable students to delve more deeply into a text's meaning, ask follow-up queries, such as What does the author mean by that? How does this connect or compare with what the author said before? Does the author explain why this happens?

4. When working with fiction, incorporate narrative queries into the process. Narrative queries help students think about characters and their motivations: "What's the outlook for this character now?" and "Considering what the author has already told us about this character, what do you think she's trying to do in this chapter?" To get students focused on the design of the plot, ask, "How has the author let us know that things are different now?" and "How has the author resolved this for us?"

5. Have students discuss and reflect on the meaning of the text and on the QtA process.

Helping Struggling Readers

Struggling readers, as well as more competent readers, may have difficulty comprehending the new idea that texts themselves may be unclear. This issue can be examined quite deeply through this simple activity that gives students the opportunity to work in small groups to build their confidence using the strategy:

1. Have students gather in groups of two or three, and instruct each member of the group to write a short piece a summary, an essay, a reaction. Alternatively, you can provide the necessary readings to students.

2. Direct students to exchange their writing within their groups. Each group member should try to summarize what the other person is trying to say in his or her piece.

3. After students have generated ideas, ask them to share their ideas with the class as you record them.

4. Then, ask the original student authors whether they agree or disagree with the ideas of their peers. When disagreements come up in the discussion, you can introduce the idea that, sometimes, authors and readers see things differently. Be sure to explain to students that this disagreement is natural and productive.

5. Other methods for helping students work through unclear passages include:
   - Using visualization strategies such as Mind's Eye and Image Making (pages 137–142), as well as Main Idea (page 5) and Graphic Organizers (page 16) to help students get a better grip on the reading.
   - Teaching students to stop regularly and write or draw a picture that explains what they believe the author is trying to say.
   - Reminding students that every author is trying to answer a question or a set of questions and that part of reading is asking oneself, What question is the author trying to answer?

LITERATURE CIRCLES

Overview

Although research groups like the National Reading Panel have helped many educators better understand which reading skills demand the greatest attention in the classroom, they have paid far less attention to how to motivate young readers. More than one critic has argued passionately that the current nationwide emphasis on a narrow range of reading skills may go a long way toward reducing rich classroom conversation and, in some students, snuff out the love of literature altogether. Few strategies respond to the challenge of motivating readers and instilling in them a love of reading as directly, as simply, or as effectively as Literature Circles. A Literature Circle is much like a good book club: Students bring their thoughts and questions about a text to a discussion group, where they share and explore ideas collaboratively.

The Strategy in Action

Fifth-grade teacher Lori Neeman explains how she uses Literature Circles:

"We start with a 'Welcome to Literature Circles' Day. The fifth-grade teachers have worked out this 'fishbowl' approach where we visit one another's classes over the course of the day and, in groups of four, we run a

Literature Circle for the different fifth-grade classes. Students watch, listen, and ask questions. But we all agree that it's important for students to see what a juicy discussion looks and sounds like. Students always comment that it looks like we're having a lot of fun in the Literature Circle, and, of course, we are. So should they—that's one of the most important lessons of all.

"I find it's easiest to run the first round of Literature Circles in my classroom with all the students reading the same book. Students are just getting used to the idea and process of Literature Circles, and I like the focus that a common book brings as we process the Literature Circles experience as a whole class. I also use this first round of Literature Circles to run mini-lessons on 'Literature Circle subskills,' such as active listening, using the text to support ideas, notemaking, and developing concise summaries. Then, during the group discussions as I move in and out of different Literature Circles, I'll do some coaching on these subskills.

"Another supplement I like to use is a 'Rules of the Road' poster (Figure 5.12). I post it in the front of the room, walk students through it, and have students copy these guidelines in their Literature Circle logs. The poster really works well. Students refer to it all the time. For example, during a recent Literature Circle session, one group of students used the 'The Rules of the Road' to turn an interesting digression into a catalyst for rich discussion. When one student was talking exclusively about the movie version of *The Lion, the Witch, and the Wardrobe,* the group referred to the poster to see how the movie might help them to understand the book. From there, the group launched into a spontaneous compare and contrast session, and even began to explore ideas about why the filmmakers might have chosen to make certain changes.

Literature Circles: Rules of the Road

Come to the Literature Circle prepared.

Be respectful of others' opinions—agree to disagree.

Give everyone a chance to talk.

Defend your opinions using the book.

If you feel the group gets off track, stop and ask:
    "How might this help us understand the book?"

Have fun!

Figure 5.12   Lori's Literature Circle Poster

"A lot of teachers really like the idea of having students in the Literature Circle play specific roles, like a 'Vocabulary Vulture,' who looks for interesting and important words during independent reading and then brings his or her ideas on the significance of these words to the discussion group. There are lots of roles students can take: a Summarizer, a Scene Setter, a Quotation Finder, etc. I'll use student-specific roles in the early stages to help students get a flavor of the different ways they can interact with texts. But I like to move away from roles pretty quickly because I find that they can sometimes get in the way of rich, exploratory conversation. Some students approach reading and discussion exclusively through the lens of their role and forget about everything else. So, after a few sessions of Literature Circles in which students try out different roles, I'll introduce a Question Menu (Figure 5.13). Question Menus give students choice and freedom to explore the text in ways that work for them. They also serve as a kind of 'reader's toolkit,' a bank of ways to think about any text. And over time, even the most rigid students start trying out different approaches from the menu.

Summarizing Questions	Personal Questions
• Who are the main characters? • What are their traits? • What problems do the characters face? • What actions do they take? • Where is the story taking place? • What is happening in the story?	• How can you relate your own experiences to the reading? • Which character do you like best? Why? • What feelings do you have as you read a particular passage? Why do you think the reading makes you feel this way?
Interpreting Questions	**Imagination Questions**
• What is the significance of a particular quotation? • What word stood out for you? • Why do these words seem important? • Why does a character do or say ____? • What evidence can you find for your position?	• What do you predict will happen next? Why? • What images stood out for you? • What do you imagine a particular character is thinking?

Figure 5.13   Question Menu

"Groups of four students meet during second period every Monday, Wednesday, and Friday for 35 minutes. We use the last 10 minutes of the period to process the experience as a class. In the beginning, I'll lead the reflection by drawing attention to specific things I saw happening in different groups. I'll say something like, 'Matt, Krystal, Emily, and Sasha developed a really interesting way to keep track of the action in the story. Can you guys tell everyone about the organizer you came up with?' After a few of these reflection sessions, students begin to take charge of the discussion themselves, exchanging ideas for solving problems that occur during Literature Circles. To synthesize the Literature Circle experience and to assess students' understanding, I like to end the unit with a Task Rotation (Figure 5.14), which asks students to think about the text in four different ways or 'styles' [for more information on Task Rotation and the four styles of reading, see Chapter 7].

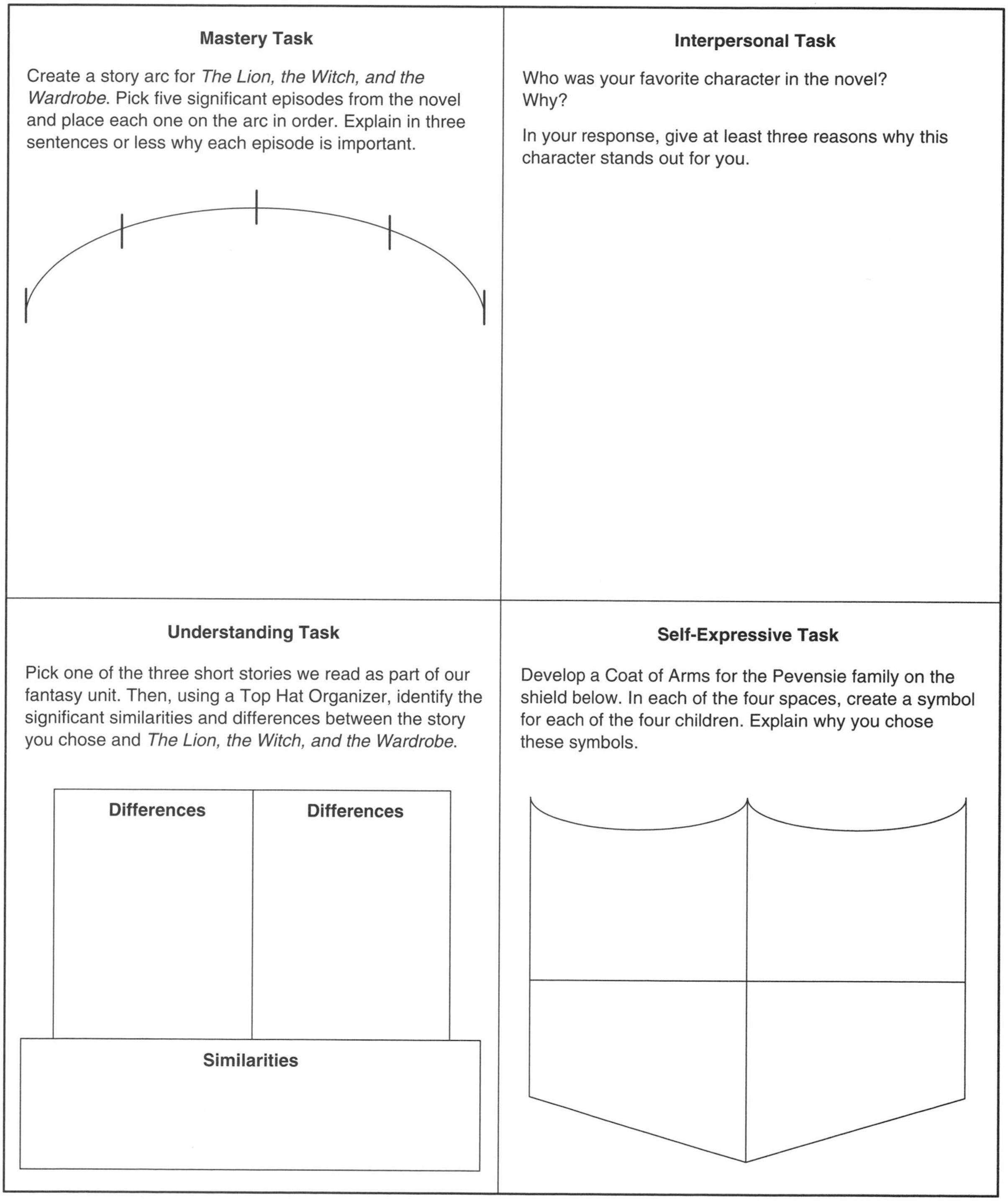

Mastery Task

Create a story arc for *The Lion, the Witch, and the Wardrobe*. Pick five significant episodes from the novel and place each one on the arc in order. Explain in three sentences or less why each episode is important.

Interpersonal Task

Who was your favorite character in the novel? Why?

In your response, give at least three reasons why this character stands out for you.

Understanding Task

Pick one of the three short stories we read as part of our fantasy unit. Then, using a Top Hat Organizer, identify the significant similarities and differences between the story you chose and *The Lion, the Witch, and the Wardrobe*.

Differences	Differences
Similarities	

Self-Expressive Task

Develop a Coat of Arms for the Pevensie family on the shield below. In each of the four spaces, create a symbol for each of the four children. Explain why you chose these symbols.

Figure 5.14   Task Rotation for *The Lion, the Witch, and the Wardrobe*

"After this first round designed around a common text, I let students choose the book they want to read. When we start our unit on growing up, for example, I'll do a quick book talk on five different books: *Sarah, Plain and Tall,* by Patricia MacLachan (1985), *Sounder,* by William H. Armstrong (1969), *Tales of a Fourth Grade Nothing,* by Judy Blume (1972/2003), *Holes,* by Louis Sachar (1998), and *The Giver,* by Lois Lowry (1993). Students then take 15 minutes to walk around the room, look at the cover of each book, read the back cover, and skim whatever passages they want. Students rank their preferences, and by the next day we're off!"

Why the Strategy Is Beneficial

Freedom. Fun. Flexibility. Choice. How often do these words pop up in current descriptions of traditional reading programs? Not often enough, and that's a shame because freedom, fun, flexibility, and choice are all natural motivators. Literature Circles help teachers create a classroom environment in which students develop their own questions about texts, pursue those questions through independent reading, and talk about them in an open, nonhierarchical forum. By giving students the chance to play with ideas a few times each week on their own terms without fear of judgment, Literature Circles put the pleasure back into reading and back into reading instruction.

As critical as pleasure is to the development of lifelong readers, we can be sure, based on the national demand for results-based practices, that Literature Circles would not have taken off as they have without a solid research base behind them. Here's a sampling of some of the findings on Literature Circles:

- Despite the common fear of off-task discussion, research shows that student discussion groups remain focused naturally. For example, a study of fourth-grade student discussion groups conducted by Klinger, Vaughn, and Schumm (1998) found that off-task conversation accounted for only 2 percent of discussion time.
- Literature Circles lead to significant gains in academic achievement. Although dozens of studies support this claim, one of the most dramatic comes from the Center for City Schools in Chicago. When Literature Circles were implemented in a group of low-performing schools in Chicago, students' reading and writing scores began improving. By the end of three years, those schools' students were outperforming students in other Chicago schools by wide margins. For example, reading scores for third graders were 14 percent higher than the citywide average and 10 percent higher among eighth graders. In writing, students outperformed the city average by 25 percent in third grade and 27 percent in eighth grade (Daniels, 2002).
- Literature Circles lead to a wide range of educational and social benefits for our most challenged students, including children living in poverty (Hanning, 1998), inner-city children (Pardo, 1992), and English language learners (Heydon, 2003).
- In 1996, the International Reading Association and the National Council of Teachers of English recognized Literature Circles as a "best practice" for both reading and writing instruction.

How to Use the Strategy

Of all the strategies and techniques outlined in this book, Literature Circles is one of the most flexible, resisting a sequenced list of implementation steps. Not only do Literature Circles look different in every classroom, they can also look quite different in the same classroom on Wednesday than they did on Monday or will on Friday. This is natural, given that Literature Circles encourage students to choose the books that interest them and make their own decisions about how to run their reading groups. Literature Circles suffer dramatically when they fall under the teacher's steadfast control or follow a rigid sequence of activities.

So how can teachers get successful Literature Circles up and running in their classrooms? Here are five ground rules (adapted from Daniels, 2002):

1. *Begin by telling students what Literature Circles are, why they are important, and the different kinds of roles they can play in a Literature Circle.* Also, remind students that one of the goals of a Literature Circle is to *have fun.*

2. *Model good Literature Circle discussions for students.* Literature Circles have a rhythm, a feel, and an openness that distinguish them from many other reading strategies. Students certainly need to see and hear what rich discussions about literature look and sound like, but they may also need "permission" to learn and work with minimal structure. That's why modeling is so important—it demonstrates how Literature Circles work and orients students to the classroom culture that allows Literature Circles to flourish. Good modeling can take several forms, including setting up a "fishbowl" in which a group of teachers conduct a Literature Circle while students watch and listen, modeling with older students, and even showing a video recording of Literature Circles from other classes or from last year's class and discussing it with students.

3. *Experiment with variations.* It is no exaggeration to say that there are dozens of ways to run Literature Circles. For example, you can:
   - Have students do their independent reading at home (or as sustained silent reading in class).
   - Have members of the Literature circles perform specific roles such as Vocabulary Vulture, Phrase/Quotation Finder, Scene Setter (tracks and describes setting), Summarizer, Illustrator, or Researcher (finds background information).
   - Have individual members of the circle conduct a text rendering of a section they liked. During a text rendering, a student reads the section aloud, identifies phrases and words that stood out, explains their significance, explains why he or she liked the section, then reads the section again. Students discuss and compare their renderings.
   - Provide students with a Question Menu (see Figure 5.13).

- Have students use the Literature Circle or a series of Literature Circles to explore a rich essential question, such as What does it mean to be a good friend?
- Synthesize the Literature Circle experience by asking students or groups to complete a writing task or culminating project.

4. *Talk about what happened and what students learned.* Ask students to pay attention to what goes well during the circle and where the process seems to bog down. After each circle, allow students to reflect on and discuss their findings and to trade ideas for improving the process. To deepen reflection about the content of the discussion, try a reflection tool like 3–2–1 (Silver, Strong, & Perini, 2001). Ask students to write about and then discuss:
   - Three things that really interested them (facts and details).
   - Two things they'd like to know more about (questions and predictions).
   - One big idea from the discussion (themes and concepts).

5. *Develop skills during the process.* In *Literature Circles: Voice and Choice in Book Clubs and Reading Groups,* Daniels (2002) explains how when he and his team first developed Literature Circles, they spent a lot of time up front highlighting "book club subskills" for students. But Daniels and his team have since found that plunging into Literature Circles works better. Ask students to notice and discuss what works or doesn't work in their circles, and then use this feedback to frame ongoing mini-lessons.

Helping Struggling Readers

The research is clear: Don't change the structure or intent of Literature Circles by trying out homogeneous or ability-based grouping. Literature Circles already come with a strong legacy of increasing the morale and comprehension of struggling readers. Let students make their choices on the basis of their interests and let natural conversation emerge.

Literature Circles are a wonderful way to help English language learners develop comfort and confidence with both the new language and the new classroom culture. In her work on using Literature Circles to build literacy skills, Rachel Heydon (2003) explains why Literature Circles are so effective for English language learners:

- *Literature Circles* give students the chance to hear the language and observe the practices of their native-language peers.
- *Literature Circles* permit English language learners to increase their level of involvement gradually.
- *Literature Circles* allow time for preparation, which reduces the number of "unknowns."
- *Literature Circles* give English language learners the opportunity to choose how they want to express themselves verbally, through writing, or through nonverbal representation.

- *Literature Circles* scaffold understanding by "starting where students are," connecting background knowledge, native language skills, and personal experiences to the new language and then allowing English language learners to move to new materials as they feel ready.

Heydon goes on to provide a set of practical suggestions for getting the most out of Literature Circles when working with English language learners. Among her suggestions are the following:

- Use modeling and Think-Alouds to clarify the process. Provide plenty of feedback as students try to approximate your models.
- Allow English language learners to work in less verbal roles such as "Illustrator" before they move into roles with greater verbal demands.
- Provide simple prompts that help English language learners make connections to the text, such as This reminds me of a time when I . . . or This reminds me of another book I read . . .
- Make English language learners "experts" by choosing culturally relevant texts on which they can provide unique insight.
- Help English language learners to build a bridge between their native language using vocabulary tools such as personal word lists (which can be bilingual), vocabulary notebooks, and classroom Word Walls.
- Keep bilingual dictionaries on hand.
- Provide picture books to facilitate comprehension.

6

Write to Read

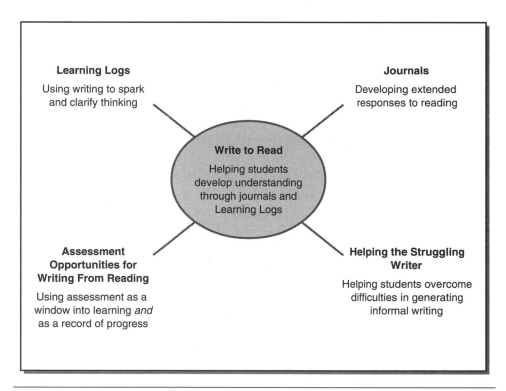

Figure 6.1   Chapter Overview: Advance Organizer

> *"Language permits us to see. Without the word we are all blind."*
>
> —Carlos Fuentes,
> twentieth-century Mexican writer

People write for many reasons: to retell what they are reading and make sure they understand it; to note what's important and what's not; to express themselves and their ideas; and practice using new words; to connect what they're reading to their own knowledge and experience; to go beyond the information given to form predictions and images; and to raise questions for themselves and the author. We ask students to write before, during, and after reading in order to develop all the skills discussed in the previous chapters.

James Boyd White, the great scholar of law and literature, once declared, "Reading is an engagement of the mind that changes the mind" (1984, p. *x*). We might say the same thing about writing. Writing is a primary tool for thinking—for improving, deepening, and changing our thoughts about what we read and what we learn. Third-grade teacher Beatrice Singh-Arnone (2006) explains how this process works in the classroom:

> One of the great powers of writing is that it slows down the thinking process. When students have to stop and think about what they are learning, what their minds are doing as they learn, and how they can put their own ideas about that learning into words, they not only clarify their thinking; they also get their tentative ideas out in the open where they can fuel new and surprising insights. (p. 3)

Therefore, a good rule of thumb for all teachers of reading is the old Latin proverb: "Never a day without a line."

However, there are two other—and potentially deeper—reasons for not letting a day go by without asking students to think and write about their reading. Here's the first reason: proficient reading depends on writing. As *Reason to Write* author Douglas Reeves (2002) tells us, "students will not become proficient readers unless they begin writing about what they have read" (p. 4). Writing about reading, in other words, not only deepens students' thinking but makes students better, more competent readers.

Now to the second reason for infusing writing into reading instruction: that little thing called state testing. Just 10 to 15 years ago, most testing left writing out of the learning equation. Students responded to multiple-choice questions. Now constructed-response or open-ended questions that require everything from one-paragraph answers to extended multiparagraph responses are the norm. This means that if we expect students to succeed on these tests, they will need practice—lots of practice—in learning how to use writing to develop, organize, and elaborate on their ideas.

Yet despite the many good reasons for asking students to write regularly about their reading, many students see maintaining journals as a mindless and meaningless chore. Many teachers express frustration at the low quality of student writing in journals. Why does this happen? And what's more, how can we change this dynamic?

This chapter focuses on increasing student engagement in the kinds of informal writing processes that go hand-in-hand with skilled reading. We can think of writing about reading—and present it to our students—as a skill reminiscent of the questioning skills we explored in the previous chapter. Writing, like questioning, tends to:

- Emerge from experience
- Improve with modeling and guided practice
- Flourish when responded to in a positive and thoughtful manner and when used to provoke both more reading and more writing

Of course, writing from reading needs to be carefully introduced and cultivated in the classroom. In this chapter, we present a set of tools and techniques to help students gain expertise in the kind of writing that will help them become better readers.

We begin our journey into writing about reading with Learning Logs and journals. Learning Logs and journals are two of the most practical and versatile writing tools that teachers have at their disposal, yet the two are frequently confused with one another. Although both tools use informal writing to slow down the thinking process and deepen comprehension, there are significant differences between Learning Logs and journals. Figure 6.2 outlines the key similarities and differences between these two informal writing tools.

Learning Logs	Journals

• Often part of a Kindling process:
  – Think about the question
  – Write for two minutes
  – Share with a partner
  – Discuss with the class
  – Apply or refine
	• Not part of a Kindling process; Teachers often provide samples of good journal entries and prompts or writing frames that journal writers use to "get the fire burning."

• Students "get their thoughts down"—create notes toward a response.	• Students develop personal responses and practice different kinds of writing.
• Focus on the development of thinking via writing.	• Increased focus on writing fluency, expressiveness, and "voice."
• Entries tend to be short—no more than one or two paragraphs.	• Entries tend to be longer, more essaylike in nature, and contain deeper elaboration.
• Support constructed-response forms of writing for state tests.	• Support more extended forms of writing on state tests.

Similarities
• Both emphasize informal writing.
• Both offer teachers great flexibility in incorporating writing about reading into the classroom.
• Both take place in a special composition book or section of a student's notebook.

Figure 6.2   Learning Logs Versus Journals—Similarities and Differences

After the sections on Learning Logs and journals, you'll find these sections:

Helping the Struggling Writer, which offers practical help for specific difficulties students experience in writing from reading.

Assessment Opportunities for Writing From Reading, which shows teachers two ways to think about and evaluate students' writing: as a "window" into the student's mind and as a "ladder" that leads to progress over time.

LEARNING LOGS (AND KINDLING)

Overview

A Learning Log is an active response journal that allows teachers to infuse writing into the daily instructional routine. Learning Logs teach students how to use writing to build up thinking—how to turn first thoughts into more nuanced and more thoughtful responses. For this reason, Learning Logs serve as an ideal way to prepare young learners for the type of short-answer, constructed-response items that are so prevalent on today's tests.

Typically, Learning Logs are used in conjunction with an instructional technique known as Kindling, which is also discussed in this section.

The Strategy in Action

Joanne Aliazar uses Kindling to introduce her students to their Learning Logs.

Joanne: The books you have in front of you are very important. They are your Learning Logs. You are going to use your Learning Log all year long—to explore ideas, ask questions, and think about how your learning affects your life. It will become a record of you—of how you think and what you like and don't like. I want to begin today's lesson by showing you how Learning Logs work. And I'm going to start with a strange question: Does anyone know what kindling is?

Jack: Isn't that like tree branches?

Joanne: Yes, that's right. Does anyone know more about kindling?

Hayley: They're little branches.

Joanne: That's also correct. Does anyone know what kindling is used for?

Ellen: In the winter, my father lights fires in our basement. I help him. He carries in the big logs, and I carry in the kindling branches.

Joanne: And what do you and your father do with the kindling?

Ellen: We put it at the bottom of the fire to make the big logs catch on fire.

Joanne: That's exactly right. Kindling is what you use to start a fire. A good fire begins with small, dry branches that catch fire quickly and that help to ignite a larger flame. What we're going to learn today is how to kindle your thinking, how to turn little ideas into big and powerful ones. Think back for a minute about what you learned yesterday during our computer lab and in our reading from our computer lab manuals. Now, think about this: Only 30 years ago, very few people owned or knew how to use a personal computer. Why do you think computers have become so important so quickly? Spend a minute or two thinking about this question. [Joanne pauses for two minutes while students write.] Next, I want you to pair up with a partner and share your ideas with each other. Together, note which ideas are similar and which are different. Then, as a team, generate one new idea about why computers became so popular. [Joanne pauses for three minutes while students work.] So, what ideas did you come up with? [Joanne surveys student responses.]

Chuck: Computers help people because you can use them for doing research. They have whole encyclopedias for free online. They help you get ideas and information for writing. And you use the word processor for typing reports.

Jon: The Internet lets people talk to each other and find lots of information. There's e-mail and instant messenger.

Ashley: We found out that computers aren't as expensive as they used to be. So we bought one.

Caryn: They're fun. You can play games on them.

Athena: You can download music, too. And videos.

Maria: We have a program that helps me with my math homework.

Boris: My father uses a money program to help him keep track of our money.

Krystof: My brother just bought a new baseball bat on our computer.

[During this student response period, Joanne keeps track of student answers on the board by building a web (Figure 6.3).]

Joanne: All your ideas are great. We now know that some of the reasons computers became so popular so quickly are that they're fun, they're helpful, they're good for research and writing, they're not so expensive to buy, and because the Internet lets you get information, buy things, and talk to people. Now, I want you to use the class's ideas to think some more about computers. Turn

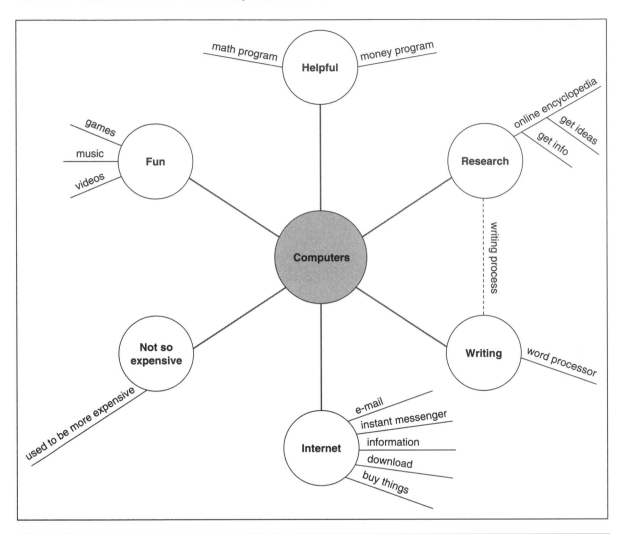

Figure 6.3   Organizing Ideas With a Web

to page 5 in your computer lab manual and read the section titled "Welcome to the Computer Age." Then, meet with your partner to discuss the reading. Note which things in the reading are similar to the ideas we came up with and which are different. When you are finished, write a brief entry in your Learning Log that explains three ways the world has changed because of computers. Use the ideas from our discussion and those from the reading to help you create this entry.

* * * *

Tin Nguyen, a second-grade teacher, also uses Kindling. To make his Kindling lessons especially focused, he uses a set of icons he has placed on flashcards to cue his students to engage in productive learning behaviors. These icons, which Tin models with students at the beginning of the year, appear in Figure 6.4.

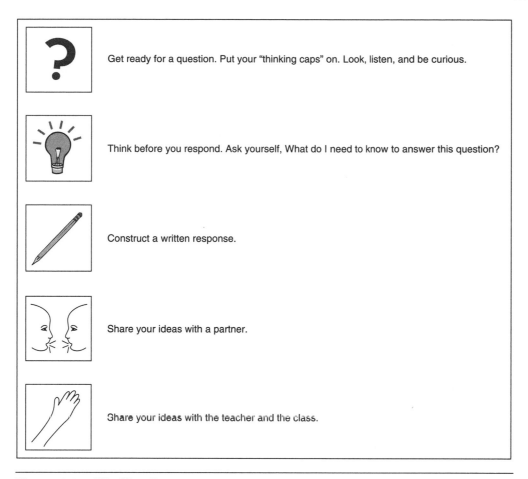

Figure 6.4   Kindling Icons

Source: Copyright © Thoughtful Education Press. Reprinted with permission.

Why the Strategy Is Beneficial

The Learning Log is simply the physical writing space—the notebook, composition book, or binder section—where each student "writes to learn." What makes the Learning Log work in the classroom is the process known as Kindling.

At the literal level, kindling is a technique for starting a fire. A good fire begins with small pieces of dry wood that catch fire quickly and help to ignite a larger flame. The same is true for kindling a question; with the correct technique, we can ignite student thinking, reading, and writing.

Kindling is a questioning technique used to create anticipation and promote involvement in new learning. It is used to enhance classroom participation, ensure class discussion, and deepen the connections between reading, thinking, and writing. The strategy achieves these goals because:

- It provides students with significant time to construct a quality response before they answer the question, thereby making covert thinking overt and eliminating impulsive answering.

- It asks students to process information and create a quality response in four separate ways. First, students think about the question on their own. Then, they write their answers in their Learning Logs. Next, they discuss and refine their answers with a partner. Finally, students share and discuss their ideas with the whole class and the teacher.
- It builds security for students who are tentative about participating. Kindling ensures that all students think about the question, because every learner is required to generate a response on paper. The strategy also includes a sharing process, which allows students to test their ideas in small groups before sharing with the whole class.

Kindling is a flexible strategy that can support a host of instructional purposes. Kindling can be used after a reading to help students reflect and to check for understanding. It can be used at any time during a lesson to make learning more active and to promote deeper thinking about the reading or topic. Kindling can also be used before a reading, as a "hook" to help students connect prior learning and experience to the text they are about to read. Here, for example, are some Kindling hooks:

- Think for a moment about what you know about communities and about what people do in communities. After you generate your initial ideas, share them with a neighbor. Note which ideas are the same and which are different. Now, the reading we're about to tackle is all about communities. Can you find any similarities between your ideas and the reading?
- Imagine you came back to the U.S.A. 500 years from now and discovered it was no longer a great power. What do you suppose caused this change? Write down some ideas, then share them with a neighbor. Together, generate one new idea together. Now, as we read about the fall of Rome, I want you to see if you can find any similarities to your ideas about our country.
- Here are two long-division problems. What differences do you notice between the two? Jot down your thoughts and ideas. Meet with a neighbor and compare your ideas. Then, explain how you would solve each problem. Now, let's see what our textbook has to say about how problems with remainders are different from the kinds of problems we've already learned about.
- Think about a time when you were really scared. Jot some of your thoughts and associations down on paper. Now, share your ideas with a neighbor. Great! Now let's see how your time of fear compares with Harriet Tubman's.

How to Use the Strategy

Incorporate Learning Logs and Kindling into your classroom using the following steps:

1. Pose an open-ended question for students to consider on their own. Depending on your purposes, the question can come before, during, or after the reading.

2. Have students pause and think about what they need to know to answer the question.

3. Ask students to "jot down," write, or even sketch their responses in their Learning Logs.

4. After students have recorded their ideas, ask them to share their written thoughts with either a neighbor or a small group. The students can synthesize ideas, critique each other's responses, determine the similarities and differences in their responses, or generate additional ideas.

5. Survey student responses to determine how many students have similar ideas, and record the ideas on the board so that they can be examined and explored further.

6. Ask students to apply what they have learned through writing and Kindling. For example, students may use their new understanding to help them
   - Read a text more actively and purposefully.
   - Create a new Learning Log entry that synthesizes their learning.
   - Develop a more formal piece of writing.

JOURNALS

Overview

As with Learning Logs, journals ask students to stop, think, and write. But while Learning Logs emphasize getting thoughts *toward a response* down on paper, journals say: "Respond." Journals allow for deeper reflection and greater elaboration than Learning Logs. They also tend to be more personal, fostering a deeper attachment to the writing process, much as a diary does. Last but not least, the emphasis that journals place on elaboration helps students build the writing fluency they need to respond well to extended writing items on state tests.

Journal entries can focus on students' free and open responses to what they read, or responses can be centered on prompts, questions, or writing frames. For example, Figure 6.5 is a menu of 40 writing frames ideal for "getting the fire started." These frames are based on 11 distinct types of thinking and can be developed over the course of the year to develop students' capacities as writers and thinkers.

C	**Compare and Contrast**	*To determine differences or similarities on the basis of certain criteria:* • List similarities and differences. • Compare and contrast the following . . . • What are the significant similarities or differences between _____ and _____? • Which two are most similar or most different? • What can you conclude based on the similarities/differences?
R	**Relate Personally**	*To describe one's emotional state or feeling or how one would apply what was learned to some part of his or her own life:* • What are your feelings about _____? • How would you feel if _____ happened to you? • What would you do if _____ happened to you? • What are some feelings you had when that happened? • Can you think of a time when _____?
E	**Evaluate**	*To appraise the value or worth of a thing or idea or to make a quantitative or qualitative judgment concerning specific criteria:* • Which alternative would you choose and why? • What are the advantages or disadvantages of _____? • Given the following choices, justify or substantiate your selection.
A	**Associate**	*To relate objects/thoughts as they come to mind:* • Is this a free, controlled, or linked association? • What words/ideas come to mind when I say _____? • What do you think of when you listen to _____? • What do you think of when you see _____?
T	**Trace/ Sequence**	*To arrange information in a logical order according to chronology, quantity, quality, or location:* • Trace the development of _____. • Sequence the events leading up to _____. • What do you do first when you _____?
E	**Enumerate**	*To list in concise form or to name one after another:* • List the causes of the _____. • List the facts regarding _____. • List the steps involved in _____.

I	**Identify & Describe**	*To identify the properties of particular items, happenings, or concepts:* • What did you see, hear, note? • Describe the facts. • What did you observe? • Describe the characteristics or properties of the object.
D	**Define**	*To give the meaning of a word of concept:* • Define the following concept: _____ . • Define what is meant by _____ . • Define the word from the context clues.
E	**Explore & Predict**	*To generate alternatives and assumptions concerning cause and effect:* • How many ways can you _____? • What would happen if _____? • Suppose _____ happened? What would be the consequences?
A	**Argue a Position**	*To explain good reasons for a particular position; to present facts to support your position:* • Where do you stand on this issue? • Justify your position. • Explain your argument. • What are your reasons for taking this position?
S	**Summarize**	*To state briefly or in conclusive form the substance of what has been observed, heard, or explained:* • Summarize what you have read. • Think of a title for the story. • Draw a picture that summarizes what you learned. • The point of view of the lecture was _____.

Figure 6.5 CREATE IDEAS Writing Frames

Source: Adapted from Silver, H. F., Strong, R. W., and Perini, M. (2001) *Tools for Promoting Active, In-Depth Learning.* Trenton, NJ: Thoughtful Education Press. (p. 75).

The Strategy in Action

The following examples introduce four teachers and the types of journals they use successfully in their classrooms:

- Response Journals, in which students react to what they have read.
- Dialogue Journals, where students record key statements from the reading and respond with their own thoughts and questions.
- Proficient Reader's Journals, where students focus their journal writing around the skills of expert readers.
- Menu-Based Journals, in which students practice working in different types or genres of writing through a menu of writing frames.

Response Journals

Michele Chang
Fourth-Grade Teacher
"We do many kinds of writing in our classroom, but Response Journals play a regular and important role in everything we do. Three times a week, I ask my students to write a response or a reaction to something we've read. I'm looking for their thoughts and feelings as they occur to them. I want their connections, not mine. In the beginning, the work with Response Journals is very hard. I see an awful lot of 'I liked it' and 'It was nice.' But by keeping my own journal and sharing it with the kids and bringing in excerpts from scientists' and artists' and authors' journals, I see the kids' writing really improve. They get deeper. What I really like about David's entry (Figure 6.6) is the way he saw the plight of the farmers and ranchers. The author didn't mention that at all. That all comes from David!"

Dialogue Journals

Jerry Longman
Third-Grade Teacher
"We've been using Dialogue Journals for three years now. I simply ask the students as they read, or afterward, to write some quotes from what they're reading on the left side of the page and to write their thoughts and ideas on the right. I tell the kids I want them to catch themselves thinking. It's like playing tag with your mind. By the end of the year, most of the projects my students do come directly out of these Dialogue Journals. But I don't use them all of the time. I'll work with them for a month or so, then put them away. Then I'll bring them back a month or two later. That way they don't become routine. What I like about Terri's entry (Figure 6.7) is all these questions. That's a real pattern with Terri. Always questions, and good questions too. Look how she asks questions about how the author gets information for these books. That's something I like to see."

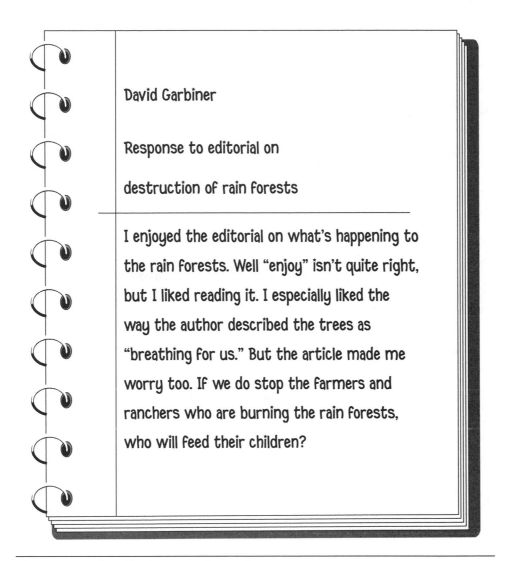

David Garbiner

Response to editorial on

destruction of rain forests

I enjoyed the editorial on what's happening to the rain forests. Well "enjoy" isn't quite right, but I liked reading it. I especially liked the way the author described the trees as "breathing for us." But the article made me worry too. If we do stop the farmers and ranchers who are burning the rain forests, who will feed their children?

Figure 6.6   David's Response Journal

Source: Copyright © Thoughtful Education Press. Reprinted with permission.

Proficient Reader's Journals

Janet Barrilogna
Fourth-Grade Teacher

"I guess one of the most important experiences of my career was reading *Mosaic of Thought* by Ellin Keene and Susan Zimmermann (1997). Up until then I'd been using a sort of modified whole-language approach. What that book did was show me how to organize my curriculum. I divide my year into eight units—two for each of the four proficient reader skills Keene and Zimmermann discuss metacognition, questioning, synthesizing, and imagery. Half of these units are in literature, and half are nonfiction. Anyway, I start a unit by modeling the skill during mini-lessons. Then, during readers' workshops, students use their journals to work with

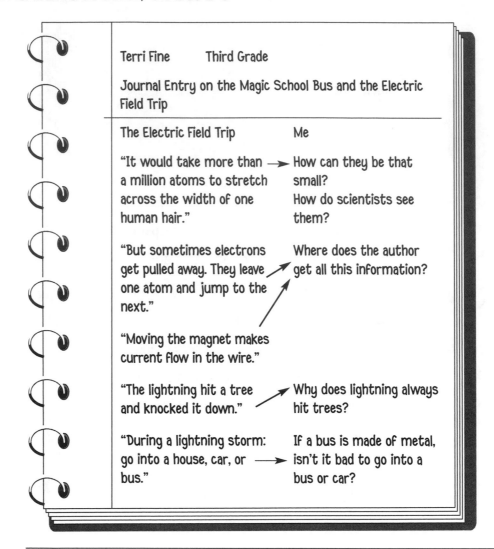

Figure 6.7   Terri's Dialogue Journal

Source: Copyright © Thoughtful Education Press. Reprinted with permission.

that skill on books they've chosen for themselves. Mark's entry (Figure 6.8) comes from one of our units on imagery. Just look at that language!"

Menu Approach

Barrett Paxson
Fifth-Grade Teacher
"I love using the CREATE IDEAS writing frames menu (see Figure 6.5) to get students practicing and writing different kinds of pieces. But it took me a while to learn how to use it well. At first, I just gave the kids the menu, and asked them to read, pick a question, and answer it. Well, by the end of the first month I could see the results weren't what I was expecting. A lot of the kids' responses were vague and didn't answer the question. And they seemed to be gravitating to the questions they felt were easiest. I saw an awful lot of drawings, not enough writing. So I backed up and started over. I'd select a kind of writing—just one, say, summarizing—for

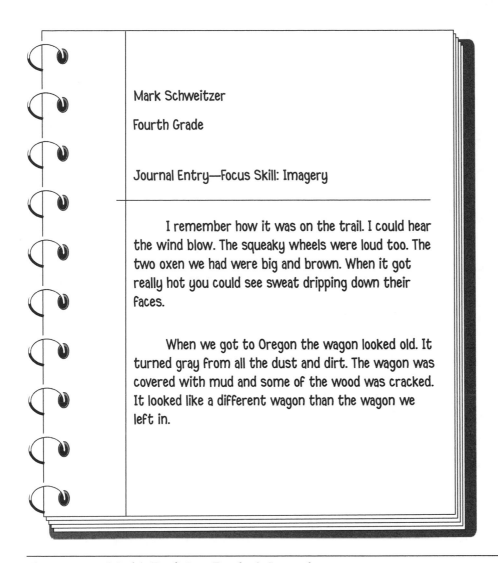

Mark Schweitzer

Fourth Grade

Journal Entry—Focus Skill: Imagery

I remember how it was on the trail. I could hear the wind blow. The squeaky wheels were loud too. The two oxen we had were big and brown. When it got really hot you could see sweat dripping down their faces.

When we got to Oregon the wagon looked old. It turned gray from all the dust and dirt. The wagon was covered with mud and some of the wood was cracked. It looked like a different wagon than the wagon we left in.

Figure 6.8   Mark's Proficient Reader's Journal

Source: Copyright © Thoughtful Education Press. Reprinted with permission.

a week or two. I'd model how to do it, ask the kids to focus on it, and read strong examples during sharing time. I built in a revision cycle too. I showed the kids how to select their best work in summarizing and rework it to make it better. Not right away, but eventually I saw real improvement. It's hard, but you know what? Teaching reading and writing *is* rocket science. Just as hard, just as rewarding. Anyway, for this particular week, we were working on building arguments. I chose Miles's example (Figure 6.9) because I liked how he stated his position up front and then used evidence from the reading to support it."

Why the Strategy Is Beneficial

What do Pablo Picasso, Charles Darwin, and Louisa May Alcott all have in common? How about the great Mexican artist Frida Kahlo, Major League slugger Carlos Delgado, and Renaissance Man par excellence Leonardo da Vinci—what's their connection? The answer is journals. The

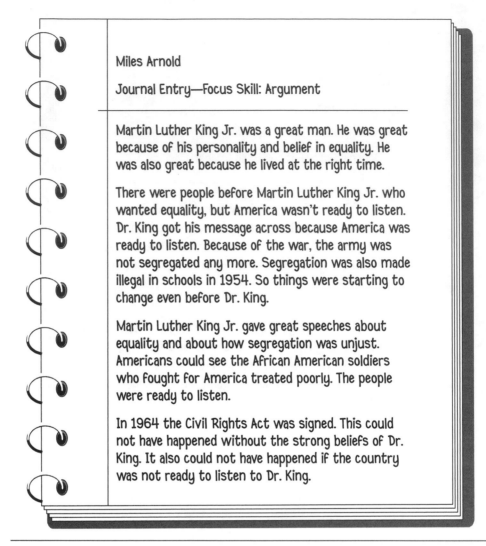

Miles Arnold

Journal Entry—Focus Skill: Argument

Martin Luther King Jr. was a great man. He was great because of his personality and belief in equality. He was also great because he lived at the right time.

There were people before Martin Luther King Jr. who wanted equality, but America wasn't ready to listen. Dr. King got his message across because America was ready to listen. Because of the war, the army was not segregated any more. Segregation was also made illegal in schools in 1954. So things were starting to change even before Dr. King.

Martin Luther King Jr. gave great speeches about equality and about how segregation was unjust. Americans could see the African American soldiers who fought for America treated poorly. The people were ready to listen.

In 1964 the Civil Rights Act was signed. This could not have happened without the strong beliefs of Dr. King. It also could not have happened if the country was not ready to listen to Dr. King.

Figure 6.9   Student's Journal Entry Based on CREATE IDEAS Menu

Source: Copyright © Thoughtful Education Press. Reprinted with permission.

truth is, experts in all the disciplines use journals to help them solve problems, refine their craft, and communicate their thoughts and feelings as they work and learn.

The value and benefits of journals as tools for learning are rather obvious. So, too, are their value and benefits in reading instruction—as tools for helping students become proficient readers. After all, we already know that the more students write about reading, the better they become as both writers and readers. What makes journals so powerful and practical for teachers and students alike is their versatility. There are as many uses for journals as there are for writing. For example, journals can be used to help students:

- Develop personal reactions and responses to their reading (as in Michele Chang's Response Journals).

- Keep track of the big ideas in reading as well as their minds' reaction to the reading (as with Jerry Longman's Dialogue Journals).
- Practice particular skills after a teacher's mini-lesson or modeling session (as Janet Barrilogna does with her Proficient Reader's Journals).
- Develop their ability to write using different techniques and genres (as Barrett Paxson does by using a Menu Approach).
- Forge personal connections to the content or reading.
- Clarify thoughts and expose confusions (e.g., what do you still find confusing?).
- Express opinions, emotions, feelings, frustrations, joys, etc.
- Ask Why? or What if?
- Imagine new ideas and possibilities (e.g., If I ruled the world . . .).
- Take a position and defend it.
- Prepare for discussions, tests, and quizzes.
- Periodically summarize their learning.
- Increase their reflective and metacognitive capacities.
- Practice integrating new vocabulary into their writing.
- Develop their fluency and "voice" as writers.

How to Use the Strategy

How can we make sure that journals are the powerful learning tools we know they can be? Our work with thousands of teachers across the country has taught us that there are five key ways to make journals come to life in the classroom:

1. *Modeling:* The best way to help students learn how to engage in thoughtful journal writing is to keep one yourself. Write about your experiences as a teacher, reader, parent, cook, golfer. Show students model entries from your journal. Talk about how you go about the process of keeping a journal. Think aloud to show them your thinking process in creating an entry.

2. *Criteria:* Students should regularly select a journal entry as the basis for more formal written work. In making a selection and working to expand and revise it, students need to be able to evaluate their own work according to clear criteria (e.g., Is it organized in a way that makes sense to the reader? Does it use the vocabulary we have learned about this topic?). Criteria can be provided to students or developed with students through modeling and analyzing samples.

3. *Feedback:* Far more important than grading is feedback. Give students a grade, and that's the end of the process; there is little reason or encouragement to expand, refine, or explore further. But give them constructive, criteria-based suggestions on how they might improve, or provoke them to deepen their thinking through questions, and a different dynamic emerges—one that's in keeping with the cyclical nature of the writing process. For this reason, students

should receive at least one or two personal responses to their writing every other week. To make this manageable, you might have students label every fifth page "Feedback."

4. *Blending choice and assigned entries:* Good classroom journal writing does not begin with statements such as: "Write about whatever you want." Instead, you should strive to develop a structure that encourages *controlled freedom.* Controlled freedom means that the student is not constrained by overly specific assignments (e.g., What are the steps in long division?) but that the freedom students have to explore ideas is tied to essential learning and themes. By blending personal reactions with provocative, open-ended journal assignments (e.g., Why do you think people claim that the Harry Potter novels will never go out of style?) with choice-based question menus (see Figure 6.5, above) that provide students with options about how best to respond, you can create a perfect balance between freedom and focus.

5. *Samples.* Experts in all the disciplines use journals. Bring in samples of journal writing from masters like Thomas Edison, Anne Frank, and Louisa May Alcott. Allow students to discover and discuss what makes for great journal writing.

HELPING THE STRUGGLING WRITER

In applying information to their reading lives, struggling writers face one large problem: elaboration. They are frequently unable to generate enough ideas to produce interesting and thoughtful entries. This dilemma results from one of three factors or a combination of these factors:

- **Memory:** Struggling readers simply may not remember a text well enough to write about it.
- **Connection to Prior Knowledge:** Struggling readers may remember and be able to retell a text, but the information in the text is isolated—disconnected from other knowledge and experience. This makes it extremely difficult to write meaningfully about text content. English language learners face further complications, as the bulk of their background knowledge is often situated in a different cultural and linguistic perspective.
- **Text Structure:** Given that struggling readers rarely read very much on their own, they tend to be unfamiliar with text structure. When asked to write about reading, therefore, they have a great deal of difficulty planning what to write because they cannot readily imagine what elements make up a thoughtful response to a writing prompt, let alone generate an open response of their own. Some of the suggestions below may help alleviate these problems.

Memory of the Text

Because struggling readers frequently don't remember a text well enough to write about it, asking them to look back at the text and retell it or helping them to create a set of notes on the text may provide a sufficient platform on which they can build a more thoughtful response.

Connection to Prior Knowledge and Experience

Notice the problem is not that the student lacks the knowledge or experience. If that were the case, the only solution would be for the teacher to provide the relevant knowledge by telling the student what he needs to know or by providing background readings. The problem here is that the knowledge in the text has been separated, locked in a mental compartment away from the student's own knowledge and experience. Rebuilding the connection can be accomplished in a number of ways:

- *Use the Mind's Eye Strategy* (pages 139–142). Ask the student to read over the passage and identify five or six key words and phrases. Then, ask the student to close her eyes and create images connected to those words and phrases. Finally, help the student use these images to create a response.
- *Conduct a Think Aloud.* Ask the student to read the passage aloud and stop whenever a thought occurs to her. Keep a running record of the student's thoughts as she reads. Then, help her use these thoughts as a platform to build a response.
- *Use Concept Maps* (pages 72–75). Provide the student with a list of five to six key vocabulary elements from the reading. Ask the student to place the words or phrases in circles and draw lines outward from each. At the end of each line, ask the student to record something she learned from the text that relates to the idea in each circle. Now, ask the student to add two or three more lines to each circle and help her to generate ideas, experiences, thoughts, or feelings related to each.

Understanding of Text Structure

This difficulty is not with the structure of the text the student has read but the structure of the text she wants to produce. In this case, the student may face one of two problems. If the informal writing is an open response, the student's own thoughts may be too confused to permit her to get started. On the other hand, if the informal writing expected of her is a response to a question or prompt ("Compare animals in a desert community with animals that live in your neighborhood"), the lack of understanding of text structure may make it very difficult for her to generate an answer. In both cases, the problem is primarily organizational. Because teachers often encourage spontaneous writing in journals and Learning Logs, they frequently take a hands-off policy when students write informally, but this approach misses the extreme difficulties some struggling readers face in being spontaneous. Their organizational disabilities, in effect, block their ability to be spontaneous in a meaningful way. In response to this situation, a teacher can:

- Provide a generalization a student can use to get her writing started (e.g., "I think desert animals lead a much harder life than the animals in my neighborhood").
- Provide students with an appropriate graphic organizer to group and reshape their thoughts (pages 16–31).
- Use the Inductive Learning strategy (pages 123–128). Ask the student to generate a list of things she might want to say. Then, help her group and label them by common characteristics.

Another factor that struggling writers—and especially English language learners—face in their writing lives is the problem of vocabulary. They may not know enough words, the right words, or the academic vocabulary associated with the content to communicate what is in their minds. Here, vocabulary-immersion strategies such as Word Walls (page 97) go a long way toward helping students find and use the right words for their writing. Chapter 3 offers many other suggestions for building vocabulary words directly into unit design and reading instruction, including a specific section on how to help struggling readers and English language learners acquire and use new words (pages 107–111).

A more intensive and focused approach to accommodating the wide range of skills and instructional needs in the classroom comes from King-Sears (2005) and her work with reading and writing Learning Centers. Drawing from the research of Vaughn, Gersten, and Chard (2000) on the best use of instructional time when working with learning-disabled students, King-Sears explains the philosophy behind Learning Centers:

Large-group instruction as the *primary* method of demonstrating new skills and strategies—whether in a special or general education setting—is not the most efficient way to differentiate. Teachers need to conduct small-group instruction. In order to provide small-group instruction, part of the class needs to be engaged in alternative practice tasks so that teachers' attention can be with the small group. (pp. 401–402)

For example, to develop a "Read, Then Write" Learning Center, the teacher would

- Break up instructional time into segments (e.g., if instructional time totals 60 minutes, the session might be broken up into four 15-minute segments).
- Reserve some of the segments for large-group instruction and some for small-group instruction.
- While working directly with a selected small group, have the other small groups "read, then write" at a Learning Center.
- Design Learning Centers so that all students are working on the same kind of writing (e.g., summaries, personal reactions, imagery) but at appropriate levels. For example, teachers can differentiate Learning Centers by:
  - The difficulty of the reading on which the writing will be based.
  - Students' interests (one reading on sports, one on music, one on animals, etc.).
  - The level of guidance for the writing task (some Learning Centers might include writing prompts, Concept Maps that outline the big ideas of the reading, etc., while other centers provide less or no support).
- Ensure that students are working productively at Learning Centers through modeling and by setting up behavioral guidelines, personal checklists, or learning contracts.

ASSESSMENT OPPORTUNITIES FOR WRITING FROM READING

In thinking about how to assess writing from reading, a clear distinction needs to be made: Do we want our assessments to be more like a window or more like a ruler?

A common misconception about assessment concerns its purpose. Many people assume that the only purpose of assessment is evaluation of student progress. In this view we observe students, confer with them, and examine their work in order to measure their progress on a scale of achievement. But this rulerlike vision of assessment is only half the story. We can also use assessment to gain insights into students' interests, concerns, preoccupations, and styles of thinking. Assessment should serve as a window into how students work and think, as well as a ruler for measuring their progress.

Assessment as a Window

Perhaps no strategies we have studied provide better windows into student thinking than those associated with informal writing. For example, in Figure 6.10, one student writes:

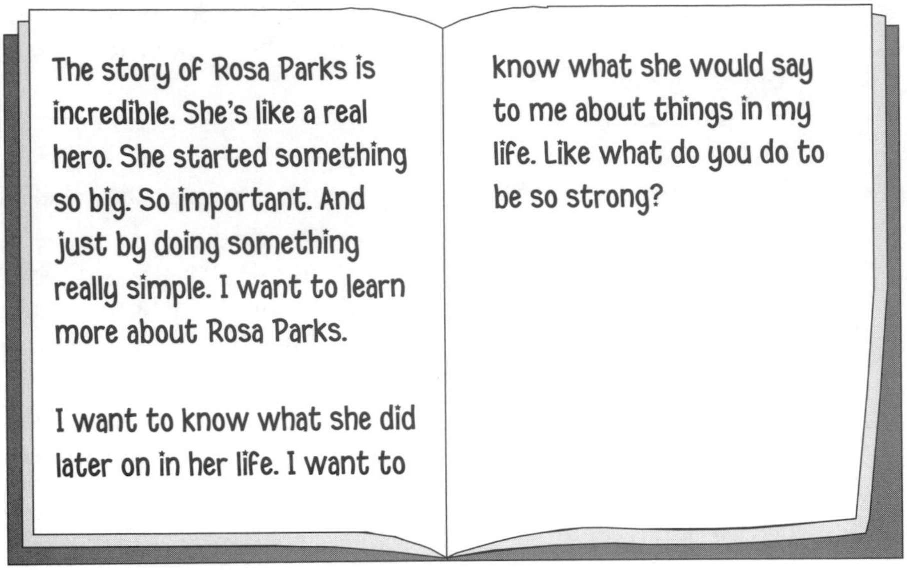

> The story of Rosa Parks is incredible. She's like a real hero. She started something so big. So important. And just by doing something really simple. I want to learn more about Rosa Parks.
>
> I want to know what she did later on in her life. I want to know what she would say to me about things in my life. Like what do you do to be so strong?

Figure 6.10 Sample Entry One

Source: Copyright © Thoughtful Education Press. Reprinted with permission.

Another student declares (Figure 6.11):

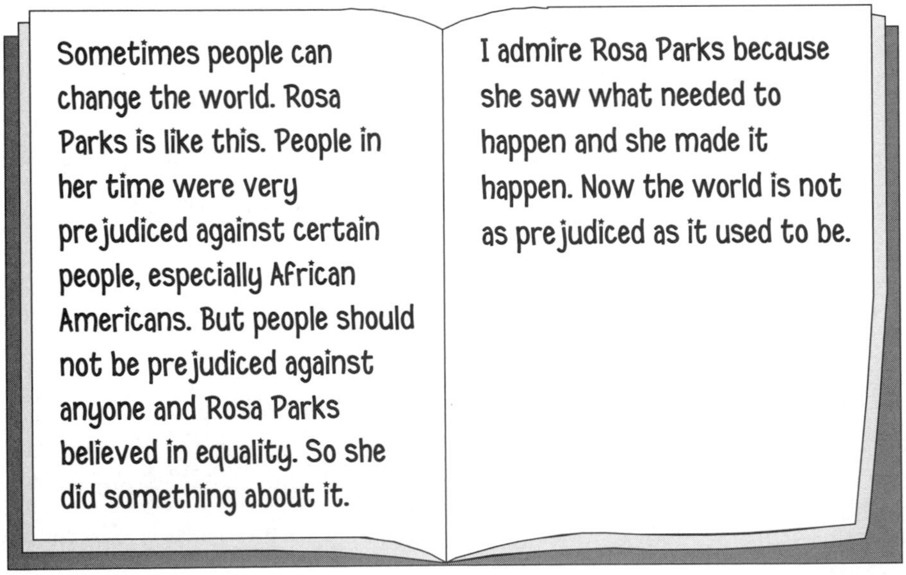

> Sometimes people can change the world. Rosa Parks is like this. People in her time were very prejudiced against certain people, especially African Americans. But people should not be prejudiced against anyone and Rosa Parks believed in equality. So she did something about it.
>
> I admire Rosa Parks because she saw what needed to happen and she made it happen. Now the world is not as prejudiced as it used to be.

Figure 6.11 Sample Entry Two

Source: Copyright © Thoughtful Education Press. Reprinted with permission.

In these examples, we can see much more than how well students are doing. We can see their interests, their concerns, and their personal styles of reading and thinking. Teachers need to keep records not only of students' progress but also of the other aspects they learn about students through observation. One way to address this issue is to keep a running record of what you learn about students' reading and learning. Look, for instance, at the following Weekly Reading Record (Figure 6.12) kept by the teacher of the two students whose work we have just read.

Weekly Reading Record				
	Reading	**Interests**	**Thinking**	**Next Steps**
Morris	Biography of Rosa Parks.	Seems very engaged in our biography study. Possible connection to hero study last month.	Imaginative. Likes to ask "What if?" Interested in relationship between himself and Rosa Parks.	Writes sparsely—big ideas, not so many details. Reads for a little while then dreams. Try visual organizers to focus.
Wende	Biography of Rosa Parks.	Interested in history and idea of change.	Organized and likes to argue. Likes to find causes and effects. Likes Rosa Parks because she takes action.	Give her *Nettie's Trip South*. Ask which is better history: biography or historical fiction.

Figure 6.12   Students' Reading Experiences Recorded and Teacher's Next Step Devised

Assessment as a Ruler

Looked at from a more rulerlike, evaluative perspective, informal writing—whether in journals or Learning Logs—resembles a portfolio. In both cases we have a collection of pieces arranged over time. This directs our attention not at the single piece but at student progress across an array of pieces. This change in orientation—looking at many pieces rather than just one—changes the nature of the question we ask about student work. In looking at students' informal writing this way, we ask ourselves:

- Is the student making progress in her ability to generate thoughtful responses that go beyond the information given? (Insight)
- In which kinds of writing (e.g., process entries, comparisons, personal responses, reviews, or critiques) is the student making the most progress? Which kinds of writing is she avoiding or completing in only a minimal way? (Flexibility)
- Overall, is the student's ability to build on her ideas (to use examples and evidence and to consider other points of view) increasing? (Development)

- Where is the student around richness of language and variety of sentence structure now, as opposed to last month? (Vocabulary and language)
- How about writing conventions? What conventions still elude her? (Conventions)
- On the whole, what is the level of organization that marks this student's writing? Is her spontaneous writing more organized and easier to follow than it was in September? (Organization)

Viewed in this light, a teacher might keep a different sort of running record (Figure 6.13) of her understanding of her students' reading as revealed in their informal writing.

Weekly Reading Record					
Morris—November					
Insight	**Organization**	**Development**	**Flexibility**	**Conventions**	**Language**
1 2 ③ 4	1 ② 3 4	1 ② 3 4	1 2 ③ 4	1 2 ③ 4	1 2 3 ④
Good ideas. Need more of them.	Doesn't write much—hard to tell.	Here's where we need work.	Fine.	Great with familiar word spellings. Now get him to look up the unfamiliar.	Wonderful. Introduce him to dialogue.

Figure 6.13 Reading Record Showing Student's Progress and Where Student Needs Help

7

Reading Styles

The Key to Reading Success

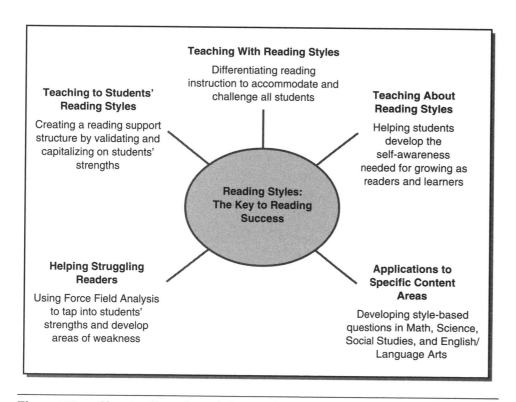

Figure 7.1   Chapter Overview: Advance Organizer

> *"What counts, in the long run, is not what you read; it is what you sift through your own mind; it is the ideas and impressions that are aroused in you by your reading."*
>
> —Eleanor Roosevelt

What are you like as a reader? Do you have preferences, routines, or personal "reading rituals" that define your approach to reading? Is where you read important? Does the level of background noise matter to you? Are there times of the day that tend to be most productive for you to read?

Even more important, *how* do you read? Are you more likely to search for specific information or make a movie of the text in your head? Do you more often find yourself arguing with the author and her ideas, or personalizing them by connecting them to experiences from your own life?

The truth is far too many reading programs pretend these questions—and the issues they raise for students and teachers—simply don't exist. Here's a list of skills that all readers need, they tell us. It's not that they're wrong. In fact, a central idea of this book has been that all students can and must develop the skills of proficient readers. It's just that there's more to the story than skills. We can't roll the credits without acknowledging the deeply *personal* side to reading as well. We can't forget that all readers have interests, preferences, and ways of thinking and talking about texts that they bring to the reading experience. Although in this age of standards and state testing it can be easy to forget just how personal the act of reading is, a wide body of research shows that failing to take student differences into account leads to lower, not higher, levels of academic achievement.

To get a better understanding of the kinds of differences we're talking about, let's listen to two fifth-grade students, Trumann and Wilma. In Figure 7.2, Trumann and Wilma share their experiences as readers.

Trumann	Wilma
We just finished a unit on fantasy stories, and I couldn't wait for it to be finished. I'm not into all that make-believe stuff with wizards and magic potions and all that. I like books that teach me how to do things. I have this one book on how to make your own Web site which is pretty cool. But my favorite book is the *Sports Almanac*. It's got stats, averages, records, all the best players in one book. Nobody in my class knows how many touchdowns Joe Namath threw in his career or the longest home run of all time, but I do!	*The Little Prince* was my favorite book ever. There were so many cool parts in it. I would imagine myself in the book, like it was me bouncing around and visiting different planets and talking to the flowers. I guess most of my favorite books are kind of like that. They let you use your imagination. They let you just go there and forget about everything else for a while. It's almost like going to the movies, except the movie is inside your head.

Figure 7.2   Two Fifth-Grade Readers

At a quick glance, we can see that there are profound differences between Wilma and Trumann as readers. Each is attracted to different kinds of texts—Trumann to instructional and information texts, Wilma to fantasy. Even more significantly, Trumann and Wilma process textual information differently. Trumann focuses on facts, details, and practical skills, while his distaste for fantasy may suggest difficulty with imaginative reading. Wilma, on the other hand, processes readings directly through her imagination by trying to "see" the cinematic quality of the characters, settings, and ideas she encounters. Last, each student has very different purposes for reading: Trumann wants to turn his reading into knowledge he can master or skills he can apply, whereas Wilma savors the images she has created in her head. We call these differences *reading styles*.

FROM LEARNING STYLES TO READING STYLES

Before we can discuss reading styles, we must start with a more basic and more well-known concept: learning styles. Our learning style model is based on the groundbreaking work of Carl Jung (1923), who discovered that the way people take in information and make decisions about the importance of that information develops into personality types. It is also based on the work of Briggs and Myers (1962/1998), who elaborated on Jung's work to develop a comprehensive model of human differences made famous by their Myers-Briggs Type Indicator®. In synthesizing this work with our 35 years of experience in helping schools differentiate learning, we have identified four primary learning styles. Each style represents a pattern of cognition—a set of sensitivities (What draws the student's attention?), inclinations for certain kinds of behaviors (What does the student enjoy doing?), and abilities (What competencies does the student exhibit?). Figure 7.3 provides a broad outline of these four primary learning styles by listing the sensitivities, inclinations, and abilities associated with each style.

Learning Style	Sensitivity to	Inclination for	Ability to
MASTERY	acts details physical actions steps	remembering describing manipulating ordering	organize report build plan and carry out projects
UNDERSTANDING	gaps/flaws questions patterns ideas	analyzing testing/proving examining connecting	argue research develop theories explain
SELF-EXPRESSIVE	hunches images possibilities inspiration	predicting/speculating imagining generating ideas developing insights	develop original solutions think metaphorically articulate ideas express and create
INTERPERSONAL	feelings people gut reactions experiences	supporting personalizing expressing emotions learning from experience	build trust and rapport empathize respond teach

Figure 7.3   The Four Learning Styles

Source: Adapted from Silver, H. F., Strong, R. W., and Perini, M. (2000). *So Each May Learn: Integrating Learning Styles and Multiple Intelligences.* ASCD. Copyright © 2000, by Thoughtful Education Press. Reprinted with permission.

What does all this have to do with reading? A lot. The patterns of attention, preferred behaviors, and natural abilities that a reader brings to a text have a huge impact on how that student reads. Students of differing styles interact differently with texts and select different strategies for finding their way through them. By applying the insights of learning styles to our own research on reading, we get four distinct *reading styles*. The four reading styles are shown in Figure 7.4.

Mastery Readers . . .	**Interpersonal Readers . . .**
Read because they want to learn practical information.	*Read because* they want to understand themselves and other people.
Like texts that are clear, to the point, and have useful applications.	*Like texts that* focus on feelings, relationships, and human stories.
Like reading questions that ask them to recall information.	*Like reading questions* that ask them how they feel or what they would do in a given situation.
Experience difficulty when texts become too poetic and fantasy oriented.	*Experience difficulty* when texts become too abstract or complicated.
Understanding Readers . . .	**Self-Expressive Readers . . .**
Read because they want to be challenged to think.	*Read because* they want to use their imagination.
Like texts that contain provocative ideas and controversial issues.	*Like texts* that are poetic, fantasy-oriented, and stylistically creative.
Like reading questions that ask them to explain, prove, or take a position.	*Like reading questions that* ask them to speculate, imagine, and ask "What if?"
Experience difficulty when texts focus too strong on feelings.	*Experience difficulty* when texts are loaded with details.

Figure 7.4   Four Styles of Readers

Of course, no one has just one style. Reading styles are not fixed categories that make one person a Mastery reader, and another an Interpersonal reader. Throughout our lives and in various situations, we use all four styles to solve the problems posed by various texts. But it is also true that most of us develop familiarity and strength in one or two styles, and we tend to be weaker in one or two other styles. This means that reading styles are the key to motivating students and helping them experience the joys of success. The trick is to help students capitalize on their strengths by accommodating their dominant styles while encouraging them to stretch and expand their capacities in their weaker styles.

WHY ARE READING STYLES IMPORTANT?

Because of our reading styles, different texts prove more difficult than others for us. Appreciating the humor and imagery in Shel Silverstein's poems requires a different kind of thinking than reviewing the steps in long division from a math textbook. Reading both texts in the same way will likely lead to a severely diminished understanding of at least one, whether it's *A Light in the Attic* or *Level 4 Mathematics*. Similarly, the processes involved in working to identify with the plight of Native Americans during the settlement of the American colonies will not be of much use when it comes to analyzing the causes behind volcanic eruptions. The different thinking processes involved in appreciating poetry, learning skills, identifying with content, and developing explanations enlist different reading styles, meaning that some types of reading will be more or less challenging for us, depending on our styles.

Making matters more complex, most texts operate on multiple levels at the same time. Students cannot simply read one text for its literal and factual information, another for its imagery, a third for its emotional relevance, and a fourth with an eye toward its logic. Take, for example, a fairly typical elementary school reading, say a *National Geographic Kids* article discussing the problems that African elephants face as a species. Some portions of the text will be laden with facts (e.g., the estimated number of elephants in existence, where they are concentrated, what's being done to help them); other parts of the text may need to be pieced together or inferred (e.g., the complex cause-effect relationships involved in elephant endangerment); other portions of the article might focus on imagery or on speculative thinking (e.g., what might happen ecologically if the elephant is driven to extinction); while still others might derive their power by appealing to the personal and emotional aspects of their content (e.g., urging readers to help elephants survive by eliciting sympathy for their plight).

We can see, by examining new state testing systems, the growing awareness of the different demands that different texts make on the readers and that all texts need to be understood in multiple lights. In New York state, for example, the four overarching reading standards require that students be able to read for information (Mastery), for critical analysis and evaluation (Understanding), for literary response and expression (Self-Expressive), and for social interaction (Interpersonal).

We can also see, in the four reading styles and in the different kinds of reading that states such as New York are emphasizing, a map for differentiating reading instruction. Unlike differentiation models that overwhelm teachers by highlighting all the ways students can be different, a style-based approach makes the important work of differentiating reading instruction manageable. In this chapter, we explore three ways of using style to differentiate reading instruction:

- *Teaching to students' styles,* or creating a support structure for struggling readers that validates and capitalizes on their strengths as readers.
- *Teaching with styles* by differentiating instruction and assessment so that all students are both accommodated by working in their strong styles and challenged to grow by developing their weaker styles.
- *Teaching about style,* or helping students to understand their own reading strengths and weaknesses so that they can achieve the balance needed to become A+ readers.

After the strategies for teaching to, with, and about style, we provide a set of style-based question stems and starters in each content area, and we demonstrate a strategy called Force Field Analysis, designed specifically to work one on one with struggling readers.

TEACHING TO STUDENTS' READING STYLES

Teaching *to* students' styles means using reading styles as a support structure so that students have the opportunity to learn via their natural strengths. Students who are weak in one or two styles may be missing out on essential learning because reading instruction so regularly focuses on their weak styles rather than their preferred ones. Think about it: If a student is a predominantly Self-Expressive reader who loves to focus on imagery, "What if?" questions, and creative projects, how likely is it that he or she will be thwarted by reading instruction that focuses only on textbook reading and end-of-the-chapter questions? Or, on the flip side, how well would a Mastery reader, who seeks direction and clarity in reading instruction, do in an environment where unstructured project work is the rule? The fact is, all styles should be validated in the classroom if we expect students to be engaged and productive. The payoff is that once students sense their styles are valued, they become willing to develop areas of weakness and, more generally, to stretch and grow as learners. The proof of this can be found in a number of research studies (Carbo, 1992; Dunn, Griggs, & Beasley, 1995; Hanson, Dewing, Silver, & Strong, 1991; Lovelace, 2005) demonstrating significant improvements in performance and motivation when teachers pay attention to students' styles.

The organizers shown in Figures 7.5 through 7.8 provide easy-to-remember guidelines for working with all four styles of readers, as well as examples of how to meet those guidelines in reading instruction.

TEACHING WITH READING STYLES

Teaching *to* students' styles means helping them overcome reading difficulties by delivering instruction and providing coaching that match the student's style as a reader. Teaching *with* reading styles is a broader approach that accommodates all students' styles while also challenging them to work in the styles that need development. Because the ultimate goal of style-centered instruction is to help students achieve balance and flexibility by developing their capacities in all four styles, we might think of the techniques in this section as instruction and assessment management systems: They make it easier for teachers to work with the entire class in all four styles.

(Text continues on page 220)

MASTERY READERS	
Start with clear expectations.	1. State the purpose of the reading and explain the importance of its content. 2. Demonstrate and model the skills needed to conduct the reading.
Tell students what they need to know and how to do it step by step.	1. Establish what students already know about the content and help them tap into their prior knowledge. 2. Teach students how to break larger texts into more manageable segments. 3. When showing students how to apply a reading strategy, teach one step at a time and allow time for practice and coaching. 4. Encourage students to determine difficult vocabulary and look up these terms before and during the reading. 5. Move students from "getting the gist" to forming broader interpretations.
Establish opportunities for concrete experiences and for exercise and practice.	1. Model and teach active notemaking strategies such as Split Screen, Cornell Notes, and Window Notes. 2. If possible, fold in hands-on materials and active processing activities. 3. Teach students how to create and use graphic organizers. 4. Provide for directed, guided, and independent practice in key reading skills.
Provide speedy feedback on student performance complete the word	1. Regularly check for understanding. 2. Teach students how to look for gaps in their understanding. 3. Provide regular feedback aimed at helping students improve specific skills.
Separate practice from performance.	1. Provide opportunities for students to apply content and skills to concrete projects and activities.

Figure 7.5 Guidelines for Working With Mastery Readers

UNDERSTANDING READERS	
Provide questions that puzzle and data that teases.	1. Use questions that spur curiosity and require students to take a position. 2. Use "Yes, but why?" questions to encourage students to probe more deeply. 3. Explore the idea that reading is a form of problem solving.
Respond to student queries and provide reasons why.	1. Establish purpose and reason for reading. 2. Allow students to generate their own questions before, during, and after reading. 3. Encourage students to generate not only what they know before a reading but also what they think they know and want to know.
Open opportunities for critical thinking, problem solving, research projects, and debate.	1. Use critical thinking strategies such as Compare and Contrast, Inductive Learning, and Do You Hear What I Hear? to guide reading. 2. Structure units around inquiries, themes, and problems. 3. Allow students to conduct independent research around their interests.
Build in opportunities for explanation and proof using objective data and evidence.	1. Conduct discussions or Socratic seminars in which students develop positions using a text or set of texts. 2. Probe student explanations for reasons and evidence. Seek alternative explanations and points of view. 3. Use thesis essays (or I-Think essays in younger grades), debates, persuasive essays, editorials, and the like to assess learning.
Evaluate content and process.	1. Encourage students to reflect upon the content and their own learning processes. 2. Help students convert their reflections into self-directed learning plans.

Figure 7.6   Guidelines for Working With Understanding Readers

SELF-EXPRESSIVE READERS	
Inspire students to use their imaginations and explore ideas.	1. Focus reading instruction around imaginative texts and let students apply what they learn. 2. Provide opportunities for journal writing. 3. Encourage students to make pre-reading predictions. 4. Allow students to explore content through metaphors and "What if?" questions. 5. Encourage the use of Image Making as a tool for making inferences. 6. Use Literature Circles.
Model creative work so that students can examine models and establish criteria for assessment.	1. Allow students to examine high-quality work and to generate assessment cirteria for their own work. 2. Teach students to pay attention to techniques so they can apply "authors' tricks" to their own written work. 3. Model creative reading processes like making predictions, visualizing, deep processing, and developing metaphors.
Allow students choice in demonstrating what they know and understand.	1. Provide alternative activities, media, and learning opportunities for students to deepen their understanding and explore ideas not addressed directly by the text. 2. Use culminating assessment tasks that challenge both academic understanding and creative capacities. 3. Assess understanding through Task Rotation.
Give feedback, coach, and provide audiences for sharing work.	1. Provide opportunities to share ideas, interpretations, and work and to obtain feedback from an audience. 2. Use a "coach, mini-lesson, revise for improved quality" teaching structure. 3. Organize cooperative learning groups around students' shared interests.
Evaluate and assess performance according to established criteria.	1. Provide or develop with students assessment rubrics that indicate what superior work looks like. 2. Encourage students to practice self-assessment. 3. Set up "quality circles" and peer feedback groups.

Figure 7.7 Guidelines for Working With Self-Expressive Readers

INTERPERSONAL READERS	
Try to personalize the content.	1. Look for ways to activate students' prior knowledge about the reading. 2. Use personal hooks; connect students' life experiences to the reading. 3. Fold in group discussion, peer work, and direct interaction with students. 4. Provide time for journal writing.
Reinforce learning through support and positive feedback throughout the process.	1. Make sure the environment is comfortable. 2. Encourage expression of personal feelings during the reading process. 3. Provide praise and constructive feedback regularly. 4. Organize cooperative reading groups around students' shared interests. 5. Provide modeling, coaching, and direct instruction.
Use the world outside the classroom to make current, real-world connections to content.	1. Find and discuss real-world examples connected with the unit or reading. 2. Apply reading to current student concerns. 3. Fold in interviews, field trips, letter writing, and community work whenever possible.
Select activities that build upon personal experiences and cooperative structures.	1. Allow students to explore ethical and moral dilemmas and social issues related to content. 2. Use cooperative learning and peer practice activities. 3. Encourage discussions. 4. Try role playing as a learning strategy in which students act out the ideas and issues in their reading. 5. Use Literature Circles.
Take time to help establish personal goals, encourage reflection, and praise performance.	1. Remind students that reading is a personal journey. 2. Emphasize the role of reflection in helping students become better readers. 3. Hold conferences in which you help students develop personal learning plans.

Figure 7.8 Guidelines for Working With Interpersonal Readers

Comprehension Menus

As we have seen, most texts operate on more than one level and make multiple demands on readers. Comprehension Menus give students a framework for managing this textual layering by helping them develop their abilities to think about texts in all four reading styles. To develop a Comprehension Menu, a teacher asks students to respond to at least four different questions, one in each style. To simplify the process of designing

Comprehension Menus, we have included a Question Menu (Figure 7.9), which outlines the kinds of thinking associated with each style and provides a set of stems or question starters for creating your own questions in style.

Figure 7.10 shows a Comprehension Menu developed by a second-grade teacher for a reading on traditional Japanese meals.

Mastery Questions ask students to. . .

Recall facts:

- Who? What? Where? When? How?

Describe and retell:

- Can you describe how it works?
- Can you retell or summarize what happened?

Sequence and rank:

- What are the steps?
- What are the two most important ideas?

Interpersonal Questions ask students to. . .

Empathize and describe feelings:

- How would you feel if _____ happened to you? How do you think _____ felt?
- What decision would you make?
- Can you reflect on your own thoughts and feelings?
- Can you reflect on your own learning and the process?

Value and appreciate:

- Why is _____ important to you?
- What's the value of _____?
- Can you connect this to your own life?

Explore human-interest problems:

- How would you advise or console _____?
- How would you help each side come to an agreement?

Understanding Questions ask students to. . .

Make connections:

- What are the similarities and differences?
- What are the causes and effects?
- How are the parts connected?

Interpret, infer, and prove:

- Why? Can you explain it?
- What evidence supports your position?

Explore underlying meanings:

- What are the hidden assumptions?
- What conclusions can you draw?
- What does the author mean by_____?
- Can you define a concept or idea?

Self-Expressive Questions ask students to. . .

Explain metaphorically or symbolically:

- How is _____ like _____?
- Develop a metaphor for _____.

Develop images, hypotheses, and predictions:

- What would happen if _____?
- Can you imagine _____? What would it look/be like?
- Can you form a hypothesis or prediction?

Develop original products:

- Create a poem, icon, skit, or sculpture to represent _____.

Figure 7.9 Comprehension Menu Questions

Source: Adapted from Silver, H. F., Strong, R. W., and Perini, M. (2001). *Tools for Promoting Active, In-Depth Learning.* Trenton, NJ: Thoughtful Education Press (p. 128).

Mastery	**Interpersonal**
List four different foods that are part of a traditional Japanese meal. 1. 2. 3. 4.	The thing I found most interesting about Japanese meals was: _____ _____ _____ I thought this was interesting because: _____ _____ _____ _____
Understanding	**Self-Expressive**
How is the traditional Japanese dinner different from a typical dinner in your home? How are both dinners similar? Use the Top Hat Organizer to identify two similarities and two differences: | Japanese Dinner	My Dinner
	| Similarities	What two rules do many Japanese diners follow when they eat? List the rules. Then for each rule, make a sketch or a symbol that will help you to remember it when we have our Japanese meal next week.

Figure 7.10 Comprehension Menu—Japanese Meals

Task Rotation

A Task Rotation (Silver et al., 1996) also uses four-style questioning to help students develop a comprehensive understanding of the texts they read. The key difference between a Comprehension Menu and a Task Rotation lies in the scope of the responses students are asked to generate. Whereas Comprehension Menus tend to require brief responses and are usually applied to a single reading, Task Rotations go deeper, often uniting a range of texts across a unit with more project-driven work. The separate tasks in a Task Rotation may be distributed throughout a unit. For instance, over the course of a unit on the Seminole Indians, students might be asked to:

- Create a table showing how the Seminoles responded to each of the four seasons in terms of both clothing and food sources. (Mastery)
- Pick a specific Seminole cultural or religious practice and explain its significance. (Understanding)
- Create a comic strip, short story, or diorama depicting an episode or aspect from Seminole life. (Self-Expressive)
- Develop a series of journal entries exploring the parallels between their own lives and the lives of young Seminoles. (Interpersonal)

Alternatively, tasks may be given all at once as a culminating assessment. The teacher may assign all four tasks, allow students to choose the tasks they wish to complete, or combine choice and assignment. Figure 7.11 shows one such culminating assessment that allows students to choose two tasks they wish to complete. The Task Rotation was designed by a sixth-grade teacher for a unit on Lois Lowry's novel, *The Giver* (1993).

Mastery	Interpersonal
Make a list of the ten rights that you think every human should have. Then pick the five rights from your list that you believe to be the most important. Describe each right, and tell why it should be protected at all costs.	Imagine that you are Jonas and that you've been given the choice of staying in the safe community or leaving for the unknown. Write a diary entry from Jonas's point of view that talks about what you are feeling as you try to make your decision.
Understanding	**Self-Expressive**
Write a brief thesis essay that supports or refutes this statement: *Jonas made the right choice by escaping to Elsewhere.* Use evidence from the text to support your position.	Write a brief extra chapter to the novel that tells about the Giver's life in the community after Jonas escaped, or about Jonas's new life in Elsewhere. Try to follow the author's style of using strong sensory imagery to describe settings and events.

Figure 7.11   *The Giver* Task Rotation—Culminating Assessment

Task Rotations are not restricted to units; they can also be used to facilitate deep, multifaceted explorations of a single text. This approach is most common for texts that raise issues central to the discipline or that the teacher believes bear thorough examination. Figure 7.12 shows a Task Rotation based on an article on the depletion of the world's rain forests.

Mastery	Interpersonal
Draw a diagram showing two different rain forest habitats (*ecosystems*) that the author describes. Label your diagram.	The article describes how thousands of trees are cut down every year in the world's few remaining rain forests. What is your reaction to this situation? Describe what you felt as you read about the depletion of the world's rain forests.
Understanding	**Self-Expressive**
In the article, the author presents several reasons why we all need to save the rain forest. Choose the reason that you found to be most important and use evidence from the text to support your choice.	Imagine a world with no rain forests. What would it look like? Who or what could live there? What would life be like?

Figure 7.12   Rain Forest Task Rotation

Teaching Around the Wheel

The third approach to teaching with styles is called Teaching Around the Wheel (Silver & Hanson, 1998). Focused on instruction more than assessment, Teaching Around the Wheel means planning a series of learning opportunities in all four styles. By linking lesson planning to styles in this way, the teacher ensures that the learning and reading needs of all students are met. At the same time, the learning experience is enriched by styles: All students are challenged to master literal and factual information (Mastery), use critical thinking and interpretive skills (Understanding), explore and apply learning (Self-Expressive), and connect learning to their own lives and personal experiences (Interpersonal).

Figure 7.13 shows a series of learning opportunities that a fourth-grade teacher designed around the core concept of character using the main characters from George Selden's novel *A Cricket in Times Square* (1960). Notice how the teacher kept track of the styles each instructional episode enlisted (M = Mastery, U = Understanding, S = Self-Expressive, I = Interpersonal).

Instructional Activity	Style
Colorful Impressions In your journal, record your first impressions of Mario, Tucker, Chester, and Harry. Select a color to represent your first impression of each character and explain your choice of color.	M ✓ U ____ S ____ I ✓
Character Matrix Make a character matrix to collect information about each of the characters. Collect information about the physical characterisitcs and specific actions of Mario, Tucker, Chester, and Harry.	M ✓ U ____ S ____ I ____
Speculations Based on your observations, speculate about what is going on inside each character—what his feelings are and the motivations for his behavior.	M ____ U ✓ S ✓ I ✓
Predictions Based on your speculations, predict what the interactions between Chester and Tucker will be like as their relationship moves forward. How will they react to each other and treat each other? Will they be encouraging? Competitive? Admiring? Be prepared to defend your ideas about their personalities and interactions in group discussion.	M ____ U ✓ S ✓ I ✓
Rank Order Ladder Of the four characters, which one is most like you? Which one is least like you? Rank the characters in descending order from most like you to least like you. Give two reasons for each ranking.	M ____ U ✓ S ____ I ✓

Figure 7.13 Teaching Around the Wheel

TEACHING ABOUT READING STYLES

If we think of teaching *to* reading styles and teaching *with* reading styles as ways to support student learning and manage style-based instruction respectively, then teaching *about* reading styles can be characterized as *helping students to understand and improve themselves as readers.* Research on the power of metacognition (Baker & Brown, 1984)—of teaching students how to pay attention to their own thinking processes—shows that when students understand their own strengths and weaknesses as learners (self-knowledge), they have an easier time determining what skills and strategies they will need to apply to particular texts or to perform specific tasks (task knowledge). Development of self-knowledge and task knowledge, in turn, leads to self-regulation—an ability possessed by all proficient readers that enables them to monitor their own comprehension and shift reading strategies when difficulties arise.

One of the simplest and most powerful tools for helping students learn about themselves as readers and as learners is good old-fashioned observation. What kinds of reading tasks are students drawn to? How do they go about completing those tasks? What kinds of questions do they like? Which give them a hard time? The power of observation can be increased significantly when combined with another old-fashioned tool: conversation. How deep you can go in these conversations depends on what grade you are teaching. In the beginning of the year, especially in the early grades, we look to set the frame for a yearlong conversation about learning and reading. For example, question and discussion sessions about why we come to school and what it means to learn are safe and powerful ways to set that framework. As students develop comfort with this kind of discussion, move them toward a deeper investigation of reading by posing questions such as:

- Why do we read?
- What does it mean to read?
- What do we know about reading?
- How can a book be a teacher?

You can deepen reflection and increase the insights students develop about themselves by asking them to turn their thoughts about reading into a reading autobiography. A reading autobiography can be as brief as two paragraphs. It should answer questions like these:

- What was your favorite book? Why was it your favorite?
- What do you find hard as a reader?
- Who was your favorite reading teacher? Why? What made this teacher special? What tricks or skills did you learn from this teacher?
- What kind of help or attention do you like?
- What kind of reading questions do you like to answer?

By keeping track of the patterns that emerge in the discussions, the idea of differences—of styles—will emerge naturally. Students can revisit their autobiographies periodically to update and revise them. Meanwhile, the conversation about reading styles will be in full swing.

Another way to build self-learning into reading instruction is to use an assessment instrument, such as the *Learning Style Inventory for Students (LSIS)* (Silver, Strong, & Perini, 2004). Currently the most valid and reliable student learning style instrument available, the *LSIS* provides a wealth of information about how each student learns. A friendly letter explaining the student's profile is provided directly to the student, while the teacher receives an in-depth report that explains

- What *motivates* the student.
- What kinds of *assessments* and *activities* excite him or her.
- What kind of *content* draws the student's attention.
- How the student *processes* information.
- Which *teaching techniques* address the student's needs.
- The student's ideal *learning climate*.
- How the student defines his or her own strengths and weaknesses (*self-concept*).

A sample set of items from the *LSIS* is shown in Figure 7.14.

---

2. I'm good at

① ② ③ ④ A. Finishing what I start
① ② ③ ④ B. Explaining ideas
① ② ③ ④ C. Working with others
① ② ③ ④ D. Creating things

4. I like questions that ask me to

① ② ③ ④ A. Explain why things happen
① ② ③ ④ B. Express my personal opinions
① ② ③ ④ C. Think of new and different ideas
① ② ③ ④ D. Choose the correct answer

5. I like to learn about

① ② ③ ④ A. Things I can do and use
① ② ③ ④ B. Important ideas and why things happen
① ② ③ ④ C. Myself and other people
① ② ③ ④ D. How people and ideas can change the world

6. I prefer a teacher who

① ② ③ ④ A. Challenges me to think
① ② ③ ④ B. Encourages me to be creative
① ② ③ ④ C. Tells me exactly what to do and how to do it
① ② ③ ④ D. Cares about me as an individual

7. The best kind of classroom for me is one where

① ② ③ ④ A. I can choose what I want to learn
① ② ③ ④ B. The teacher takes time to get to know me
① ② ③ ④ C. I am given challenging problems to solve
① ② ③ ④ D. I can practice what I have to do

19. In a classroom discussion, I'm good at

① ② ③ ④ A. Listening to what other people say and feel
① ② ③ ④ B. Using my imagination to say something interesting
① ② ③ ④ C. Using evidence to argue a point
① ② ③ ④ D. Stating my position clearly

21. If I had a challenging assignment, I would

① ② ③ ④ A. Research everything I needed to know
① ② ③ ④ B. Talk to other people to see how they'd do it
① ② ③ ④ C. Try to find a different way to do it
① ② ③ ④ D. Make a list of what I had to do and check things off as I finished them

36. I care most about

① ② ③ ④ A. How things work
① ② ③ ④ B. Pursuing my dreams
① ② ③ ④ C. Understanding why
① ② ③ ④ D. People's feelings

Figure 7.14 Sample *LSIS* Items

Source: Adapted from Silver, H. F., Strong, R. W., & Perini, M.J. (2004). *The Learning Style Inventory for Students.* Ho-Ho-Kus, NJ: Thoughtful Education Press.

By assessing students' styles with the *LSIS,* both teacher and student get a comprehensive portrait of each student's preferences, strengths, and weaknesses as a learner. In this way, the instrument facilitates the personal reflections, conferences, and coaching sessions that lead to self-regulated learning and reading. Because a letter to the student is included, the *LSIS* makes it easier to invite critical allies—the parents—into the process of helping students become better learners, deeper thinkers, and more proficient readers.

For younger students, friendlier and less formal assessments, such as the *Learning Style Inventory for Elementary Students* (Silver, Strong, & Perini, 2003), are ideal. The *Learning Style Inventory for Elementary Students (LSIE)* contains a series of fun and interactive activities, a simple checklist to help students think about their own preferences, and four characters that help students make a deep and personal connection to different styles. Figure 7.15 shows these four style-based characters from the *LSIE.* Notice that the style terms Mastery, Understanding, etc. have been changed to friendlier terms, Step-by-Step learner, Curious learner, Creative learner, and Social learner.

Figure 7.15 The Style Characters From the *LSIE*

Source: Copyright © Thoughtful Education Press. Reprinted with permission.

APPLICATIONS TO SPECIFIC CONTENT AREAS

Developing Style-Based Questions in the Content Areas

Earlier in this chapter, we provided a menu of question stems and starters (see Figure 7.9) to help teachers create style-based questions. That menu was a general one, applicable to all content areas. In Figures 7.16–7.19, you will find a set of menus geared to social studies, math, science, and English, respectively. Although these menus are by no means comprehensive, they demonstrate how the specific content and types of texts found in each discipline lend themselves to examination through the lens of style.

SOCIAL STUDIES	
Mastery Questions	**Interpersonal Questions**
• Can you retell a story or sequence of events? • Can you make a chart or map to display what you a learning?	• Can you describe your feelings about historical characters or events? • Can you create a diary that shows how people in another culture or time thought or felt?
Understanding Questions	**Self-Expressive Questions**
• Can you define a concept or restate a position? • Can you explain the causes and effects of a decision?	• Can you predict what will happen next? • Can you speculate on what might have happened?

Figure 7.16 Social Studies Questions in Style

Source: Adapted from Strong, R. W., & Silver, H. F. (1996). *An Introduction to Thoughtful Curriculum and Assessment.* Trenton, NJ: Thoughtful Education Press.

MATHEMATICS	
Mastery Questions	**Interpersonal Questions**
• Can you list the steps in a mathematical procedure? • Can you find an error and explain why it happened?	• Can you describe your thoughts and reactions to what you are learning? (When am I EVER gonna use this stuff?) • Can you tell how a mathematical concept affects your life?
Understanding Questions	**Self-Expressive Questions**
• Can you define a mathematical concept in your own words? • Can you explain how you solved a problem? • Can you describe a pattern?	• Can you make up a problem on your own?

Figure 7.17 Mathematics Questions in Style

Source: Adapted from Strong, R. W., & Silver, H. F. (1996). *An Introduction to Thoughtful Curriculum and Assessment.* Trenton, NJ: Thoughtful Education Press.

SCIENCE	
Mastery Questions • Can you retrace a sequence in a process or experiment?	**Interpersonal Questions** • Can you describe the implications of a scientific idea on your own life?
Understanding Questions • Can you explain a scientific concept in your own words?	**Self-Expressive Questions** • Can you imagine a world in which a scientific concept does not apply?

Figure 7.18 Science Questions in Style

Source: Adapted from Strong, R. W., & Silver, H. F. (1996). *An Introduction to Thoughtful Curriculum and Assessment.* Trenton, NJ: Thoughtful Education Press.

ENGLISH/LANGUAGE ARTS	
Mastery Questions • Can you retell a story or summarize an opinion?	**Interpersonal Questions** • Can you describe your thoughts and reactions to pieces or characters?
Understanding Questions • Can you define a literary concept and give examples and counterexamples from your reading? • Can you explain a character's motivation?	**Self-Expressive Questions** • Can you rewrite a story or poem from another perspective?

Figure 7.19 English Questions in Style

Source: Adapted from Strong, R. W., & Silver, H. F. (1996). *An Introduction to Thoughtful Curriculum and Assessment.* Trenton, NJ: Thoughtful Education Press.

HELPING STRUGGLING READERS

Using Force Field Analysis to Help Struggling Readers

Reading styles, by capitalizing on students' strengths and minimizing weaknesses, provide an ideal framework for working productively with struggling readers. One of the most intensive and personal ways to help a struggling reader is to use a style-based process known as Force Field

Analysis. A Force Field Analysis entails plotting the positive and negative forces operating within a student's reading profile and using that information to develop a prescriptive plan.

Steps for conducting a Force Field Analysis follow, along with a teacher's analysis and plan for a struggling reader named Jason.

1. Identify a student who is experiencing reading difficulty in your class.

2. Briefly describe, in writing, what you know about the student as a reader. Include the student's specific difficulties as you've diagnosed them. Also include what you know about the broader picture, including interests, talents, learning behaviors, and personality.

> Jason's primary difficulty lies in staying rooted in the text. During our reading of *Holes*, he's been making lots of connections to his own experiences from summer camp, but he has a hard time moving those experiences back into the reading. Instead, he'll keep talking about the personal experience or bring up a new one. He likes to talk and participate, but when I ask him to provide support for his ideas, he'll say something like, "Because that's what happened to me when I was in summer camp."
>
> In content area reading, like science, the situation is similar. Staying grounded in the text is a real problem for Jason. Main-idea reading and any kind of reading task that requires Jason to find evidence proves very difficult. When the content doesn't allow Jason to make personal connections, Jason likes to draw on his considerable creativity. Whenever I use metaphorical activities, Jason comes up with some of the most original ideas in class. He's also a pretty good artist. When we had to design a book cover for our short story unit, Jason's was among the most creative and visually appealing.
>
> In general, it seems that Jason draws on his personal and creative strengths but too often at the expense of wrestling with what the text actually says. He gets an idea or makes a personal connection and goes with it.
>
> In class, Jason is well-liked. He likes working in groups, especially when he can tell stories about his own experiences and listen to other students' experiences. He's also passionate about skateboarding and is known in class for being very good at it.

3. Based on your description, identify what you believe to be the student's preferred style. Try to connect reading behaviors to the larger picture of the overall learning style.

I'm not sure if Jason is more of an Interpersonal or more of a Self-Expressive learner/reader. He has real strengths in both. On the Interpersonal side, there's his ability to make personal connections and his enjoyment of group work. On the Self-Expressive side, there's his creativity with metaphors and his artistic sense. I think he's fairly strong in both styles.

4. Compare your perceptions and observations with the results from the *Learning Style Inventory for Students* (or *Learning Style Inventory for Elementary Students*).

Results From Learning Style Inventory for Students

Most preferred: Interpersonal

Second: Self-Expressive

Third: Mastery

Least preferred: Understanding

These results make sense. My observations told me that Interpersonal and Self-Expressive were strong, and both are. Both his Mastery and Understanding scores are quite low, which points to his weaknesses in main-idea reading and in finding evidence in the text.

5. On the basis of your observations and the results from the *LSIS*, use a Force Field Analysis to analyze the positive and negative forces operating in the student's profile.

Forces Working For	Forces Working Against
Looks to personalize content	Has a hard time staying rooted in the text
Likes to participate	Is not very reflective
Good at working in groups	Often answers impulsively without consulting the text
Good at creative work	Has a hard time with main-idea reading
Has a strong artistic sense	Weak at finding/using evidence
Excellent skateboarder	

6. Establish goals and objectives based on your analysis.

> Goal: To help Jason use his natural strengths to develop two key reading skills that are currently weak.
> - Identifying main ideas/key details
> - Using evidence to support ideas

7. Develop a plan for potential activities and teaching strategies. The goal here is to tap into the student's strengths while developing areas of weakness.

Potential Activities for Jason

1. *Personal Interviews.* Work with Jason to assess strengths and weaknesses. Ask him what he believes good readers do when they read. Together, identify behaviors that will support Jason's learning.
   Taps into: Need to work with others
   Develops: Ability to reflect and minimize impulsivity

2. *Personalize Content.* Ask Jason, "What if you were an idea and wanted to become a main idea? How would you make yourself stand out?"
   Taps into: Desire to personalize content
   Develops: Reflection, ability to move beyond the personal, deeper grasp of concept

3. *Metaphor.* How is finding a main idea like a game of Connect-the-Dots?
   Taps into: Creative side
   Develops: Reflection, deeper grasp of process of finding main idea

4. *Split Screen Notemaking and Concept Maps.* Model how to use sketches, drawings, and Concept Maps to capture main ideas and details.
   Taps into: Need to work with others, creative side
   Develops: Ability to use visual strategies to capture textual information

5. *Work With an Understanding Learner.* Working with a student whose strengths address Jason's weaknesses, Jason will use a Main Idea organizer to find big ideas and critical details.
   Taps into: Need to work with others
   Develops: Ability to discriminate between main ideas and supporting details

6. *Making a Case.* To help Jason learn how to use evidence, ask him to provide evidence for or against statements related to his personal interests, such as: "Skateboarding is much easier than riding a bike." Reflect on the process, then move him to text-based evidence gathering.

    Taps into: Need for personal connection

    Develops: Ability to use evidence, build interpretations

7. *Collaborative Summarizing.* Students work in groups of four. Individually, they identify three to five big ideas. Then they negotiate their lists and reach agreement on three big ideas. Together, they write a summary.

    Taps into: Love of group work

    Develops: Ability to summarize and interpret beyond personal level

References

Adams, M. J. (1990). *Beginning to read: Thinking and learning about print.* Cambridge: MIT Press.

Afflerbach, P. P., & Johnston, P. H. (1986). What do expert readers do when the main idea is not explicit? In J. F. Baumann (Ed.), *Teaching main idea comprehension* (pp. 49–72). Newark, DE: International Reading Association.

Alvermann, D. (1986.) Graphic organizers: Cueing devices for comprehending and remembering main ideas. In J. F. Baumann (Ed.), *Teaching main idea comprehension* (pp. 210–226). Newark, DE: International Reading Association.

Armbruster, B. B., Lehr, F., & Osborn, J. (2003). Fluency instruction. In C. Ralph Adler (Ed.), *Put reading first: The research building blocks for reading instruction. Kindergarten through grade 3* (2nd ed., pp. 21–31.) Retrieved February 2007, from www.nifl.gov/partnershipforreading/publications/PFRbooklet.pdf

Armstrong, W. H. (1969). *Sounder.* New York: Harper & Row.

Baker, L., & Brown, A. L, (1984). Metacognitive skills and reading. In P. D. Pearson, R. Barr, M. L. Kamil, & P. Mosenthal (Eds.), *Handbook of reading research: Volume II* (pp. 353–394). White Plains, NY: Longman.

Baumann, J. F., & Serra, J. K. (1984). The frequency and placement of main ideas in children's social studies textbooks. *Journal of Reading Behavior, 16,* 27–40.

Beck, I. L., & McKeown, M. G. (2001). Inviting students into the pursuit of meaning. *Educational Psychology Review, 13*(3), 225–241.

Beck, I. L., McKeown, M. G., Hamilton, R. L., & Kucan, L. (1997). *Questioning the author: An approach for enhancing student engagement with text.* Newark, DE: International Reading Association.

Beck, I., McKeown, M., & Kucan, L. (2002). *Bringing words to life: Robust vocabulary instruction.* New York: Guilford Press.

Beck, I. L., McKeown, M. G., Worthy, J., Sandora, C., & Kucan, L. (1996). QtA: A yearlong classroom implementation to engage students with text. *Elementary School Journal, 96*(4), 385–414.

Bell, N. (1991). *Visualizing and verbalizing for language comprehension and thinking.* Paso Robles, CA: Academy of Reading Publications.

Benevento, E. (1998). *The drinking gourd: A curriculum resource guide.* Woodbridge, NJ: Silver, Strong, & Associates.

Blume, J. (2003). *Tales of a fourth grade nothing.* New York: Scholastic. (First published in 1972 by Dutton.)

Bowyer-Crane, C., & Snowling, M. J. (2005). Assessing children's inference generation: What do tests of reading comprehension measure? *British Journal of Educational Psychology, 75*(2), 189–201.

Briggs, K. C., & Myers, I. B. (1998/1943). *Myers-Briggs type indicator form M.* Palo Alto, CA: Consulting Psychologists Press.

Brisk, M., & Harrington, M. (2000). *Literacy and bilingualism: A handbook for ALL teachers.* Mahwah, NJ: Lawrence Erlbaum.

Brown, H., & Cambourne, B. (1987). *Read and retell.* Portsmouth, NH: Heinemann.

Brown, R., Pressley, M., Van Meter, P., & Schuder, T. (1996). A quasi-experimental validation of transactional strategies instruction with low-achieving second grade readers. *Journal of Educational Psychology, 88,* 18–37.

Brownlie, F., Close, S., & Wingren, L. (1990). *Tomorrow's classrooms today: Strategies for creating active readers, writers, and thinkers.* Markham, Ontario: Pembroke.

Brualdi, A. (1998). *Classroom questions: An ERIC/AE digest.* Washington, DC: ERIC Clearinghouse on Assessment and Evaluation.

Burleigh, R. (1997). *Hoops.* New York: Silver Whistle.

Burns, P. C., Roe, B. D., & Ross, E. P. (1998). *Teaching reading in today's elementary schools* (7th ed.). Boston: Houghton Mifflin.

Byars, B. (1977). *The Pinballs.* New York: Harper & Row.

Byrd, D., & Westfall, P. (2002). *Guided reading coaching tool.* Peterborough, NH: Crystal Springs Books.

Cain, K., & Oakhill, J. V. (1999). Inference-making ability and its relation to comprehension failure in young children. *Reading and Writing, 11,* 489–503.

Cain, K., Oakhill, J. V., Barnes, M., & Bryant, P. (2001). Comprehension skill, inference-making ability, and their relation to knowledge. *Memory and Cognition, 29*(6), 850–859.

Carbo, M. (1992). Giving unequal learners an equal chance: A reply to a biased critique of learning styles. *Remedial and Special Education, 13*(1), 19–29.

Carver, R. P. (2003). The highly lawful relationships between pseudo word decoding, work identification, spelling, listening, and reading. *Scientific Studies of Reading, 7*(2), 127–154.

Cataldo, M. G., & Oakhill, J. (2000). Why are poor comprehenders inefficient searchers? An investigation into the effects of text representation and spatial memory on the ability to locate information in text. *Journal of Educational Psychology, 92*(4), 791–799.

Cheung, A., & Slavin, R. E. (2005). *Effective reading programs for English language learners and other language minority students.* Baltimore, MD: Success for All Foundation.

Cotton, K. (2000). *The schooling practices that matter most.* Alexandria, VA: Association for Supervision and Curriculum Development.

Crowther, D. T., & Cannon, J. (2004). Strategy makeover: From "know," want," "learned" to "think," "how," "conclude," a popular reading strategy gets a science makeover. *Science and Children, 42*(1), 42–44.

Cunningham, J. W., & Moore, D. W. (1986). The confused world of main idea. In J. F. Baumann (Ed.), *Teaching main idea comprehension* (pp. 1–17). Newark, DE: International Reading Association.

Daniels, H. (2002). *Literature circles: Voice and choice in book clubs and reading groups.* Portland, ME: Stenhouse.

Derewianka, B. (1990). *Exploring how texts work.* Newtown, Australia: Primary English Teaching Association.

Dickinson, D., & Smith, M. (1994). Long-term effects of preschool teachers' book readings on low-income children's vocabulary and story comprehension. *Reading Research Quarterly, 29*(2), 104–122.

Doctorow, M., Wittrock, M. C., & Marks, C. (1978). Generative processes in reading comprehension. *Journal of Educational Psychology, 70,* 109–118.

Dunn, R., Griggs, S. A., & Beasley, M. (1995). A meta-analytic validation of the Dunn & Dunn model of learning style preferences. *Journal of Educational Research, 88*(6), 353–362.

Egan, M. (1999). Reflections on effective use of graphic organizers. *Journal of Adolescent and Adult Literacy, 42*(8), 641–645.

Fisher, B. (1995). Things take off: Note taking in the first grade. In P. Cordeiro (Ed.), *Endless possibilities: Generating curriculum in social studies and literacy* (pp. 21–32). Portsmouth, NH: Heinemann.

Gambrell, L., & Bales, R. (1986). Mental imagery and the comprehension-monitoring of fourth- and fifth-grade poor readers. *Reading Research Quarterly, 21*(4), 454–464.

Gambrell, L. B., & Koskinen, P. S. (2002). Imagery: A strategy for enhancing comprehension. In C. Block & M. Pressley (Eds.), *Comprehension instruction: Research-based best practices* (pp. 305–318). New York: Guilford Press.

Gardill, M. C., & Jitendra, A. K. (1999). Advanced story map instruction: Effects on the reading comprehension of students with learning disabilities. *Journal of Special Education, 33*(1), 2–17.

Gardner, J. (1975). *Dragon, dragon and other tales.* New York: Knopf.

Gersten, R., & Baker, S. (2000). What we know about effective instructional practices for English-language learners. *Exceptional Children, 66*(4), 454–470.

Gibbons, P. (2002). *Scaffolding language, scaffolding learning.* Portsmouth, NH: Heinemann.

Griffith, L., & Rasinski, T. (2004). A focus on fluency: How one teacher incorporated fluency with her reading curriculum. *Reading Teacher, 58*(2), 126–137.

Hanning, E. (1998). What we've learned: The reading connections book club after two years. *Journal of Children and Poverty, 4*(1), 25–37.

Hanson, J. R., Dewing, T., Silver, H. F., & Strong, R. W. (1991). Within our reach: Identifying and working more effectively with at-risk learners. *Students At-Risk.* (Workshop materials produced for the 1991 ASCD Conference, San Francisco, CA.) Alexandria, VA: Association for Supervision and Curriculum Development.

Heller, R. (1983). *The reasons for a flower.* Fort Worth, TX: Alice Craighead Books.

Herber, H. (1970). *Teaching reading in the content areas.* Englewood Cliffs, NJ: Prentice Hall.

Herrmann, B. A. (1992). Teaching and assessing strategic reasoning: Dealing with the dilemmas. *Reading Teacher, 45*(6), 428–433.

Heydon, R. (2003). A touch of . . . class! Literature circles as a differentiated instructional strategy for including ESL students in mainstream classrooms. *The Canadian Modern Language Review, 59*(3), 463–475.

Hyerle, D. (2000). *A field guide to using visual tools.* Alexandria, VA: Association for Curriculum and Supervision.

Jackson, J. (2005). *The water cycle.* Ho-Ho-Kus, NJ: Silver, Strong, & Associates.

Jacobs, H., H. (2006). *Active literacy across the curriculum: Strategies for reading, writing, speaking, and listening.* Larchmont, NY: Eye on Education.

Jacobs, H. H. "Active Literacy Workshop." November 30, 2006. San Diego, CA.

Jitendra, A., Chard, D., Hoppes, M. K., Renouf, K., & Gardill, M. C. (2001). An evaluation of main idea strategy instruction in four commercial reading programs: Implications for students with learning problems. *Reading and Writing Quarterly, 17*, 53–73.

Jitendra, A., Hoppes, M. K., & Xin, P. X. (2003). Enhancing main idea comprehension for students with learning problems: The role of a summarization strategy and self-monitoring instruction. *Journal of Special Education, 34*(3), 127–139.

Jones, B. F., Pierce, J., & Hunter, B. (1988–1989). Teaching students to construct graphic representation. *Educational Leadership, 46*(4), 20–25.

Jung, C. (1923). *Psychological types* (H. G. Baynes, Trans.). New York: Harcourt Brace & Company.

Katayama, A. D., & Robinson, D. H. (2000). Getting students "partially" involved in note-taking using graphic organizers. *Journal of Experimental Education, 68*(2), 119–134.

Keene, E. O., & Zimmermann, S. (1997). *Mosaic of thought: Teaching comprehension in a reader's workshop.* Portsmouth, NH: Heinemann.

King-Sears, M. (2005). Scheduling for reading and writing: Small-group instruction using learning center designs. *Reading and Writing Quarterly, 21*(4), 401–405.

Klingner, J. K., & Vaughn, S. (1996). Reciprocal teaching of reading comprehension strategies for students with learning disabilities who use English as a second language. *Elementary School Journal, 96,* 275–293.

Klingner, J., Vaughn, S., & Schumm, J. (1998). Collaborative strategic reading during social studies in heterogeneous fourth-grade classrooms. *Elementary School Journal, 99*(1), 3–22.

Kobayashi, K. (2006). Combined effects of note-taking/reviewing on learning and the enhancement through interventions: A meta-analytic review. *Educational Psychology, 26*(3), 459–477.

Kuldanek, K. (1998). *The effects of using a combination of story frames and retelling strategies with learning disabled students to build their comprehension.* Unpublished master's thesis, Kean University, Union, New Jersey.

Laverick, C. (2002). B-D-A strategy: Reinventing the wheel can be a good thing. *Journal of Adolescent and Adult Literacy, 48*(2), 144–147.

Lawrence, J. (1993). *Harriet and the promised land.* New York: Simon & Schuster Books for Young Readers.

Lehman, H. G. (1992). Graphic organizers benefit slow learners. *The Clearing House, 66*(1), 53–55.

Lehr, S. (1988). The child's developing sense of theme as a response to literature. *Reading Research Quarterly, 23*(3), 337–357.

Leon, V. (1998). *Outrageous women of the middle ages.* New York: John Wiley and Sons.

Lovelace, M. (2005). Meta-analysis of experimental research based on the Dunn & Dunn model. *Journal of Educational Research, 98*(3), 176.

Lowry, L. (1993). *The giver.* Boston: Houghton Mifflin.

MacLachlan, P. (1985). *Sarah, plain and tall.* New York: Harper & Row.

Mandler, J. M., & Johnson, N. S. (1977). Remembrance of things parsed: Story structure and recall. *Cognitive Psychology, 9,* 111–151.

Marent, T. (2006). *Rainforest.* New York: DK Publishing.

Marzano, R. (2004). *Building background knowledge for academic achievement: Research on what works in schools.* Alexandria, VA: Association for Supervision and Curriculum Development.

Marzano, R. J., Paynter, D. E., Kendall, J. S., Pickering, D., & Marzano, L. (1995). *Literacy plus resource book: An integrated approach to teaching reading, writing, vocabulary, and reasoning.* Columbus, OH: Zaner-Bloser.

Marzano, R., Pickering, D., & Pollock, J. (2001). *Classroom instruction that works: Research based strategies for increasing student achievement.* Alexandria, VA: Association for Supervision and Curriculum Development.

McGee, M., & Beck, I. (2006). *Winston the book wolf.* New York: Walker.

McIntosh, M., & Draper, R. (1995). Applying the question-answer relationship strategy in mathematics. *Journal of Adolescent and Adult Literacy, 39,* 120–131.

McKeown, M. G., Beck, I. L., & Sandora, C. A. (1996). Questioning the author: An approach to developing meaningful classroom discourse. In M. G. Graves, B. M. Taylor, & P. van den Broek (Eds.), *The first R: Every child's right to read* (pp. 97–119). New York: Teachers College Press.

McMaster, K., Fuchs, D., & Fuchs, L. (2006). Research on peer-assisted learning strategies: The promise and limitations of peer-mediated instruction. *Reading and Writing Quarterly, 22*(1), 5–25.

Miller, D. (2002). *Reading with meaning: Teaching comprehension in the primary grades.* Portland, ME: Stenhouse.

Miller, W. (1997). *Richard Wright and the library card.* New York: Lee & Low Books.

Monjo, F. N. (1993). *The drinking gourd: A story of the underground railroad.* New York: HarperCollins.

Moore, D. W., Bean, T. W., Birdyshaw, D., & Rycik, J. A. (1999). *Adolescent literacy: A position statement.* Newark, DE: Commission on Adolescent Literacy of the International Reading Association.

Moore, D. W., Cunningham, J. W., & Rudisill, N. J. (1983). Readers' conception of the main idea. In J. A. Niles & L. A. Harris (Eds.), *Searching for meaning in reading/language processing and instruction.* Thirty-second yearbook of the National Reading Conference (pp. 202–206). Chicago: National Reading Conference.

Morrow, L. M. (1983). Reading and retelling stories: Strategies for emergent readers. *The Reading Teacher, 38,* 870–875.

Muth, D. K. (1987). Structure strategies for comprehending expository text. *Reading Research and Instruction, 27*(1), 66–72.

Nagy, W. E., & Herman, P. A. (1987). Breadth and depth of vocabulary knowledge: Implications for acquisition and instruction. In M. McKeown & M. Curtis (Eds.), *The nature of vocabulary acquisition* (pp. 19–35). Hillsdale, NJ: Lawrence Erlbaum.

National Center for Educational Statistics. (2003). *National Assessment of Educational Progress (NAEP).* Washington, DC: U.S. Department of Education.

National Reading Panel. (2000). *Teaching children to read: An evidence-based assessment of the scientific research literature on reading and its implications for reading instruction. Reports of the subgroups.* Washington, DC: National Institute of Child Health and Human Development.

Oakhill, J. V. (1982). Constructive processes in skilled and less-skilled comprehenders' memory for sentences. *British Journal of Psychology, 73,* 13–20.

Oakhill, J. V. (1984). Inferential and memory skills in children's comprehension of stories. *British Journal of Educational Psychology, 54,* 31–39.

Ogle, D. (1986). K-W-L: A teaching model that develops active reading of the expository text. *The Reading Teacher, 39,* 564–570.

Paivio, A. (1990). *Mental representations: A dual coding approach.* New York: Oxford University Press.

Pardo, L. S. (1992). *Accommodating diversity in the elementary classroom: A look at literature-based instruction in an inner-city school.* Paper presented at the National Reading Conference, San Antonio, TX, December 1992.

Pauk, W. (1974). *How to study in college.* Boston: Houghton Mifflin.

Pearson, P. D., & Comperell, K. (1994). Comprehension of text structures. In R. B. Rudell, H. Singer, & M. R. Rudell (Eds.), *Theoretical models and processes of reading* (4th ed., pp. 448–468). Newark, DE: International Reading Association.

Pearson, P. D., & Johnson, D. D. (1978). *Teaching reading comprehension.* New York: Holt, Rinehart, & Winston.

Pike, K., & Mumper, J., (2004). *Making nonfiction and other informational texts come alive.* Boston: Pearson Education.

Pikulski, J. J., & Chard, D. J. (2005). Fluency: Bridge between decoding and reading comprehension. *Reading Teacher, 58*(6), 510–519.

Pressley, M. (1976). Mental imagery helps eight-year-olds remember what they read. *Journal of Educational Psychology, 68,* 355–359.

Pressley, M. (1977). Imagery and children's learning: Putting the picture in developmental perspective. *Review of Educational Research, 47,* 586–622.

Pressley, M. (2006). *Reading instruction that works: The case for balanced teaching.* New York: Guilford Press.

Pressley, M., & Afflerbach, P. (1995). *Verbal protocols of reading: The nature of constructively responsive reading.* Hillsdale, NJ: Lawrence Erlbaum.

Raphael, T. E. (1982). Question-answering strategies for children. *The Reading Teacher, 36,* 186–190.

Raphael, T. E. (1984). Teaching learners about sources of information for answering comprehension questions. *Journal of Reading, 28,* 303–311.

Raphael, T. E. (1986). Teaching question-answer relationships, revisited. *The Reading Teacher, 39,* 516–522.

Raphael, T. E., & McKinney, J. (1983). An examination of fifth- and eighth-grade students' question-answering behavior: An instructional study in metacognition. *Journal of Reading Behavior, 15,* 67–86.

Raphael, T. E., & Pearson, P. D. (1982). *The effect of metacognitive awareness training on children's question-answering behavior* (Tech. Rep. No. 238). Urbana: University of Illinois, Center for the Study of Reading.

Raphael, T. E., Wonnacott, C. A., & Pearson, P. D. (1983). *Increasing students' sensitivity to sources of information: An instructional study in question-answer relationships* (Tech. Rep. No. 284). Urbana: University of Illinois, Center for the Study of Reading.

Rasinski, T., Blachowicz, C., & Lems, K., (Eds.). (2006). *Fluency instruction: Research-based best practices.* New York: Guilford Press.

Reder, L. (1980). The role of elaboration in the comprehension and retention of prose: A critical review. *Review of Educational Research, 50*(1), 5–53.

Reeves, D. (2002). *Reason to write.* New York: Kaplan Publishing.

Ruta, K. W. (1992). Teaching text patterns to remedial readers. *Journal of Reading, 35,* 657–658.

Rylant, C. (1988). Stray. In *Every living thing.* New York: Simon & Schuster Children's Publishing.

Sachar, L. (1998). *Holes.* New York: Farrar, Straus, and Giroux.

Sadoski, M. (1985). The natural use of imagery in story comprehension and recall: Replication and extension. *Reading Research Quarterly, 19,* 110–123.

Sadoski, M., & Paivio, A. (2004). A dual coding theoretical model of reading. In R. B. Ruddell & N. J. Unrau (Eds.), *Theoretical models and processes of reading* (5th ed., pp. 1329–1362.) Newark, DE: International Reading Association.

Sadoski, M., & Willson, V. L. (2006). Effects of a theoretically based large-scale reading intervention in a multicultural urban school district. *American Education Research Journal, 43*(1), 137–154.

Sampson, M. B. (2002). Confirming a K-W-L: Considering the source. *Reading Teacher, 55*(6), 528–532.

Sandora, C., Beck, I., & McKeown, M. (1999). A comparison of two discussion strategies on students' comprehension and interpretation of complex literature. *Journal of Reading Psychology, 20,* 177–212.

Santa, C., Havens, L., & Maycumber, E. (1996). *Project CRISS: Creating independence through student-owned strategies.* Dubuque, IA: Kendall/Hunt.

Selden, G. (1960). *A cricket in Times Square.* New York: Dell.

Siegel, M.G. (1984). *Reading as signification.* Unpublished doctoral dissertation, Indiana University, Bloomington.

Silver, H. F., & Hanson, J. R. (1998). *Learning styles and strategies* (3rd ed.). Woodbridge, NJ: Thoughtful Education Press.

Silver, H. F., Hanson, J. R., Strong, R. W., & Schwartz, P. B. (1996). *Teaching styles and strategies* (3rd ed.). Trenton, NJ: Thoughtful Education Press.

Silver, H. F., & Strong, R. W. (1994). *Reading styles and strategies.* Trenton, NJ: Thoughtful Education Press.

Silver, H. F., Strong, R. W., & Perini, M. J. (2000). *So each may learn: Integrating learning styles and multiple intelligences.* Alexandria, VA: Association for Supervision and Curriculum Development.

Silver, H. F., Strong, R. W., & Perini, M. J. (2001). *Tools for promoting active, in-depth learning* (2nd ed.). Ho-Ho-Kus, NJ: Thoughtful Education Press.

Silver, H. F., Strong, R. W., & Perini, M. J. (2003). *The learning style inventory for elementary school students.* Ho-Ho-Kus, NJ: Thoughtful Education Press.

Silver, H. F., Strong, R. W., & Perini, M. J. (2004). *The learning style inventory for students.* Ho-Ho-Kus, NJ: Thoughtful Education Press.

Singh-Arnone, B. (2006). Lessons from my thoughtful classroom. *Lessons from the thoughtful classroom: Making students as important as standards* (the official newsletter of *Thoughtful Education Press*), *2,* 1–3.

Snow, C. E., Barnes, W., Chandler, J., Goodman, I., & Hemphill, L. (1992). *Unfulfilled expectations: Home and school influences on literacy.* Cambridge, MA: Harvard University Press.

Spander, L. (1998). The magic scissors. In W. Cooling & P. Dann (Eds.), *Read me a story, please: 50 readaloud stories chosen by Wendy Cooling*. London: Orion Children's Books.

Sparks, J. E. (1982). *Write for power*. Los Angeles: Communication Associates.

Strauss, B. (2005). *The big book of what, how, and why*. New York: Sterling.

Strong, R. W. (2005, January). From blasé to hooray. *Education Update, 47*(1), 2.

Strong, R. W., & Silver, H. F. (1996). *An introduction to thoughtful curriculum and assessment*. Trenton, NJ: Thoughtful Education Press.

Strong, R. W., & Silver, H. F. (1998). *Simple and deep: Factors affecting classroom implementation and student performance*. Unpublished research. Ho-Ho-Kus, NJ: Silver, Strong, & Associates.

Taba, H. (1971). *Hilda Taba teaching strategies program*. Miami: Institute for Staff Development.

Taylor, B. M., & Beach, R. W. (1984). The effects of text structure instruction on middle-grade students' comprehension and production of expository text. *Reading Research Quarterly, 19*, 134–146.

Thomas, E. (2003). *Styles and strategies for teaching middle school mathematics*. Ho-Ho-Kus, NJ: Thoughtful Education Press.

Thorndike, R. L. (1974). Reading as reasoning. *Reading Research Quarterly, 9*, 135–147.

Thoughtful Education Press. (2004). *Word works: Cracking vocabulary's CODE, teacher planning and implementation guide*. Ho-Ho-Kus, NJ: Author.

Tierney, R. J., & Cunningham, P. M. (1984). Research on teaching reading comprehension. In P. D. Pearson (Ed.), *Handbook of reading research*. New York: Longman.

Turner, R. M. (1991). *Georgia O'Keeffe: Portraits of women artists for children*. Boston: Little, Brown.

van den Broek, P., Lynch, J. S., Ievers-Landis, C. E., Naslund, J., & Verduin, K. (2003). The development of comprehension of main ideas in narratives: Evidence from the selection of titles. *Journal of Educational Psychology, 95*(4), 707–718.

van den Broek, P., Tzeng, Y., Risden, K., Trabasso, T., & Basche, P. (2001). Inferential questioning: Effects on comprehension of narrative texts as a function of grade and timing. *Journal of Educational Psychology, 93*(3), 521–529.

Van Dijk, T. A., & Kintsch, W. (1983). *Strategies of discourse comprehension*. New York: Academic Press.

Vaughn, S., Gersten, R., & Chard, D. J. (2000). The underlying message in LD intervention research: Findings from research syntheses. *Exceptional Children, 67*(1), 99–114.

Vaughn, S., & Linan-Thompson, S. (2004). *Research-based methods of reading instruction: Grades K–3*. Alexandria, VA: Association for Supervision and Curriculum Development.

White, J. B. (1984). *When words lose their meaning: Constitutions and reconstitutions of language, character, and community*. Chicago: University of Chicago Press.

Wiggins, G., & McTighe, J. (2005). *Understanding by design*. Alexandria, VA: Association for Curriculum and Supervision.

Wilen, W. W., & Clegg, A. A. Jr. (1986). Effective questions and questioning: A research review. *Theory and Research in Social Education, 14*(2), 153–161.

Wilhelm, J. (2004). *Reading IS seeing*. New York: Scholastic.

Williams, J. (2005). Instruction in reading comprehension for primary grade students: A focus on text structure. *The Journal of Special Education, 39*(1), 6–18.

Williams, J., Lauer, K., Hall, K., Lord, K., Gugga, S., Bak, S. J., Jacobs, P., & de Cani, J. (2002). Teaching elementary school students to identify story themes. *Journal of Educational Psychology, 94*(2), 235–248.

Zeiderman, H. (2003). *Touchpebbles: Volume A*. Annapolis, MD: Touchpebbles Discussion Project.

Index

CORWIN PRESS

The Corwin Press logo—a raven striding across an open book—represents the union of courage and learning. Corwin Press is committed to improving education for all learners by publishing books and other professional development resources for those serving the field of PreK–12 education. By providing practical, hands-on materials, Corwin Press continues to carry out the promise of its motto: **"Helping Educators Do Their Work Better."**